Yer Father's Yacht

Paddington basin

Mum   Dad
Grandad Fred Dyer   neighbours
        Uncle Bill
            Grandma Leah
            carrying Auntie Mary

ART.   LAURENCE
         RONNIE (7)   TED   1956

RONNIE

The Autobiography

St. Martin's Press ♒ New York

All photographs are from the author's private collection unless otherwise stated. *Section One*—Pattie Boyd: p. 8 (both); Getty Images: pp. 4, 5 (both), 6, 7; PTS Studios: p. 1 (bottom); Rex Features: p. 3 (both). *Section Two*—Getty Images: p. 2; Diana Lyn: p. 5 (top). *Section Three*—Brian Aris: p. 3 (top); Michael Collopy: p. 7 (top); L. Howard: p. 4 (center); Alistair Morrison: p. 4 (bottom); Duncan Paul Associates: p. 3 (bottom right); Ken Regan/Camera 5 Inc.: p. 5. *Section Four*—John Paul Brooke: p. 6 (center); Getty Images: pp. 3 (both), 7 (both); Healy Racing Photographers: p. 4 (bottom).

All artwork by Ronnie Wood.

www.stmartins.com

ISBN-13: 978-0-312-36652-0
ISBN-10: 0-312-36652-3

Also published in Great Britain by Macmillan, an imprint of Pan Macmillan Ltd

First U.S. Edition: October 2007

10 9 8 7 6 5 4 3 2 1

Dedicated to those loved and lost;
Mum, Dad, Ted and Art

Thanks to
Jack Macdonald and Jeffrey Robinson
who assisted me in writing this book.

Additional thanks to
Sally and Geraint Humphries,

and a special thank you to
Jo for her unrelenting support and love
and all my family.

Contents

Prologue

It was 1964. The Rolling Stones were playing the Richmond Jazz and Blues festival. The gut essence of the music was gripping, it has gripped me ever since. The Stones were my bait and I was hooked on the line.

The whole tent surrendered to the unstoppable, primal lure of the beat. The guys in the crowd all knew their music. Many of them were massive record collectors themselves. The quality of the women was unsurpassed; funky, sexual and tempting. I banged my leg hard on a tent post as I left but felt no pain. I was moved deep to the bone and knew I could perform with these boys.

2005: Peering through the balcony from my hotel room, down on to the millions waiting for our momentous Rio gig to start, I truly realized how far we'd come. The way the anticipation and sheer adrenaline built and built until we actually hit the killing floor on Copacabana Beach was immense. Walking across the custom-built connecting bridge, straight from hotel to stage, there was a pure exhilaration no drug could come close to matching. We wished each other good luck before our storming entrance on to the stage, and as Keith would say, 'the cage was opened'.

Prologue

Here I was – more than three decades after my first glimpse of the Stones rocking the blues festival, and I was asked to relate my life story. Daunting as it was, I would do this by drawing every house I have lived in these past sixty years. I'd draw and depict each place and introduce people, places and things that I have stumbled across and into by way of music and art. I'd like to lead you through these places, and point out these people.

Written in gypsy ink.

1

Yer Father's Yacht

My story begins where the drawing begins. My brothers and I were the first in my family to be born on dry land; my mother and father were born on barges in the Paddington Basin, West London. Both were water gypsies, as were my grandparents and theirs before them. My dad was Arthur, known as Archie, and his family's barge was the *Antelope*. My mum was Mercy Leah Elizabeth, always called Lizzie, and her family's barge was the *Orient*.

Out of the water and here I am. A tiny, warm council house. In bed listening to local sounds. An old couple argue as they walk past my window. The town is Yiewsley, the house Number 8 Whitethorn Avenue. Yiewsley was a place that was very quiet at night, because there weren't many cars, and after 10:30 p.m. everything was shut. On weekends, the parties at Number 8 lit up the night, but during the week, whilst I was snuggled up, the only noise was at eleven o'clock when Belle and her husband, George, walked home from the Red Cow. Belle was old and tall, George was short and older, and they'd walk down Whitethorn Avenue, fifty feet apart, arguing with each other at the top of their lungs.

She'd shout back to him, 'Don't you dare talk to me like that,' and I'd lie in bed thinking, there's Belle. A minute later, George would scream ahead to her, 'Shut your mouth, you old cow,' and I'd say to myself, there's George. You could set your watch by them.

3

My family loved to huddle round the radio after dinner listening to comedy. This kind of real life episode was like an extension of Jimmy Edwards' programme *Take It From Here* or Frankie Howerd, *The Goons* and *Life with the Lyons*.

Number 8 Whitethorn Avenue was the centre of the universe for the first fifteen years of my life and the first dry home for my parents. Our council house was two-up two-down, with a tiny storage room at the top of the stairs just large enough for a single bed. Everyone on the block referred to these as their box rooms. When I was little, my brothers Art and Ted shared a bedroom, my parents had their bedroom and I had the box room.

Everything I knew was on this housing estate in Yiewsley, in the shadow of Heathrow Airport, and everyone I knew lived within a stone's throw of Whitethorn Avenue. Most of my aunties, uncles and cousins also lived around there, I was surrounded by family. Dad was one of eleven children and Mum was one of eight. The brickworks were nearby, and most people living in the area had someone in the family working there. If not, they worked on the Grand Union Canal running right past Yiewsley (as my dad and grandads did). We all called it 'The Cut' because that's what the Irish labourers who had cut into the land to form the canal had called it.

Grandad Sylvester Wood was on the boats. He was a little man who dressed like a Chicago gangster dandy: trilby, waistcoat, watch on a chain and a carnation in his lapel. His tug was the *Fastnet*, and every day he pulled five or six barges of sand and ballast from Yiewsley to London for the building trade. One of his wives was my nan Phoebe – I say that because I've only recently learnt that he had several. My uncle Fred, who was one of my mother's brothers, told me that Sylvester liked to 'put it about a bit', and that he kept a second family further up the canal in Stratford-upon-Avon, and possibly a third in Manchester.

Happiness is having a large, caring, close-knit family in another city.

George Burns.

I only have vague memories of Sylvester and Phoebe, but I knew my grandad Fred Dyer and my nan Leah. She was the greatest little lady, right off the barges, and couldn't read or write. She died when I was young, but Grandad Fred lived to a ripe old age. He'd lost a leg late in life and reminded me of a pirate with his replacement wooden limb. I can still see him standing at the gate in front of Number 101 Yew Avenue, wearing his apron with cigars sticking out of one pocket and a bottle of rum sticking out of the other, greeting people as they passed by. I was a small child, in Fred's eyes small enough to be a girl, so the greeting he assigned for me was 'Hello, Ronda.'

My mum was one of the oldest of his seven daughters and grew up on the *Orient* tug, docked opposite St Mary's Hospital. She wore hand-me-downs, we all did. My mum had disfigured feet from her bad shoes and would walk miles back and forth to school alongside Nan Leah, and they pushed us little ones in a wheelbarrow. My mum was tiny, just like her mother, and stood five foot nothing. I remember someone once said to her, 'Stand up, Mrs Wood,' and she answered, 'I am.'

Eventually, both my grandads worked on the same boat, along with my dad. That's sort of how my folks met. One evening Nan Leah chaperoned Mum at the Nag's Head pub, just a few minutes from our house. Liz walked in while Archie was cavorting about and playing his harmonica. Dad told me that as soon as he spotted Mum, he thought to himself, 'That's mine.' He'd just won the pub raffle, which in those days was a hamper of food and booze, and immediately decided that the winnings should be hers. 'You've won the leg of pork' was his chat-up line.

My brother Arthur was born in 1937, and my brother Ted was born two years later. I arrived on 1 June 1947, a year noted for a remarkable amount of UFO sightings, post-war depression and the coldest winter on record. Hopefully my arrival helped to warm things up a little.

I was a hyperactive child and Mum worried that I'd run out the kitchen door and roll down the back steps, so she tethered me to the leg of the kitchen table. I was also small enough that she could stand me on the washboard and bathe me in the kitchen sink.

As I got older, I began to idolize my brothers and tried to copy whatever they did. Most of the time, because I was so small, all I did was get up their noses. Art and Ted would be doing their homework on the table and I would kneel on the chair with a pen and paper to imitate and distract them. Art and Ted used to collect birds' eggs, which as a three-year-old I had great fun smashing with a hammer. They'd complain to Mum, 'That little bloke you bought just smashed all of our eggs, why did you buy him?' One day I flushed all of their bronzed carp down the toilet. I told Mum that I'd set them free. They didn't like that, or understand that it was just my way of fighting back. After that they spent a lot of time trying to scare me to death. Frightening me at every chance they got was their bit of fun. I was so highly strung that I'd get nervous. I couldn't take being scared like that and developed a stutter. Didn't last long though.

Two girl cousins lived near by – Beryl and Rita. They were both four years older than me and spent a lot of time at our house. They also enjoyed scaring me. They'd pretend to be spiders or monsters and wake me up or chase me around the house while I ran for my life, screaming at the top of my lungs. Beryl was also always washing me. She had dolls and when she finished washing them and combing their hair, she experimented on me.

COUNTY COUNCIL OF MIDDLESEX EDUCATION COMMITTEE.
ST. MARTIN'S CHURCH OF ENGLAND SECONDARY SCHOOL,
WEST DRAYTON.

S C H O O L   R E P O R T.

Pupil's Name... Ronald Wood ....July............ 19 59...

Year.... 1st .... Form.... 1 8 .... Average age of Form.. 12 4/12 .. Position in Form.. 11..
No. on Roll '31'

GRADING: A. - VERY GOOD. B. - GOOD. C. - SATISFACTORY. D. - WEAK. E. - VERY WEAK.

SUBJECT.	GRADING.	FORM POSITION ON EXAM. RESULT.	REMARKS.
RELIGIOUS EDUCATION.	C	17	Shows interest. N.J.B.
ENGLISH COMPOSITION.	B+	6	
GRAMMAR.	A	3	Ronald has done a good year's
LITERATURE.	B+	7	work. A diligent pupil. C.N.B.?
READING & SPEECH.	B	15	
MATHEMATICS.	C	14	Works well. N.J.B.
SCIENCE.	B	3/11.	A good year's work. H. NI.
MUSIC (THEORY).	C	16	Satisfactory progress. O.M.C
HISTORY.	B-	25th	Neat but inattentive. Examination exposed serious lack of knowledge. Disappointing. A.P.B.
GEOGRAPHY.	B	14=	Satisfactory work. C.N.B.T
DOMESTIC SCIENCE(THEORY)			
Citizenship	C	18	Has done fairly well. O.M.C
PRACTICAL SUBJECTS (ASSESSED ON YEAR'S WORK)			
DOMESTIC SCIENCE.			
WOODWORK.	C		With more concentration he will improve. A.P.B.
ART & CRAFTS.	A	1	Very advanced in this subject. E.B
NEEDLEWORK.			

Conduct: Fair   Punctuality: Fairly good

Form Teacher's Remarks: I hope Ronald will be able to take Art and
English for the G.C.E. His work in the Art Room is outstanding.

Headmaster's Remarks: Ronald's work and achievement would be
even more pleasing if he took School a little more seriously.
His ability is being spoilt by this   L. F. Reasey.
tendency. He is thoroughly well mannered (Headmaster.)
and pleasant lad. I am pleased to see his ability at Art.

By the time I began school, we had an Old English sheepdog called Chum, who was big enough that I could ride on his back all the way to St Martin's, a few blocks away. Chum was very special because, unlike most dogs, Chum could tell the time. Every afternoon at 3:15 p.m. Chum would leave the house, walk down the high street and wait outside the school for me. Towards the end of his life, when Chum was really old, he'd stagger down to school to fetch me, but usually wound up lying in the middle of the road. Cars had to stop because Chum was waiting there for his passenger. Someone would have to come out of a shop to take Chum off the zebra crossing.

We had other dogs after Chum died. There was a black Labrador named Buster and a mongrel named Kim who had to be put down because he bit everyone in the neighbourhood. When I asked where Kim was, my dad told me he'd gone to live on a farm. I knew that wasn't true.

Art and Ted had some novel pets: two mice called Thunder and Lightning, and I had a few terrapins. There were always plenty of empty Guinness bottles around the house, so I made a camp for my little buddies down by the air shelter. One day Art and Ted decided my terrapins would like to take a walk, so they let them out of the Guinness-bottle fort and watched as my terrapins headed straight out the gate. Maybe it was payback for crushing their eggs and flushing their fish. Art and Ted would also pin me down on the floor, lean over me, dribble spit towards my face and, when it got right close, they'd suck it back up. All part of their early torture.

In those days, England was a place of grime, dust, dirt and booze-soaked odours. One of our neighbours just happened to have the filthiest house in Yiewsley, maybe even in the entire south of England, and I used to think it was great sneaking into their kitchen, nicking food and scoffing it under the table.

Everyone wondered how I survived, filling my belly with that rot.

At night I'd hear noises in my parents' room, sounds I didn't recognize, and think they were fighting. I'd climb out of my box room and get into bed between them, hit Dad and say, 'Stop beating my mum up.' It must have been a nightmare for them, having me come into their room when they were getting down to it. But I didn't know better.

Everything we needed was just there: our school, our shops and our family. Today, Yiewsley is developed because of the airport, but in those days it was a little village. Everyone knew everyone's business, everyone cared for everyone else, neighbourhood watch worked and grudges never lasted. Most families had an air-raid shelter in their back garden (Dad put our Anderson shelter inside the house until the war got 'serious') but God smiled on Yiewsley during the war. Even though the German bombers flew overhead, they missed. A pub once got blown up, but no one was killed. One night a bomb dropped near the 'Hut' pub. Mum felt Ted go stiff in her arms as the train of the blast ripped through the town. Some of the windows on the houses on Gran's street were blown in and she marched up and down the road telling fellow residents, 'Don't pay any rent till we get this settled.' On that particular night, Dad was on his way to the Nag's when the sirens sounded and the bombs started falling. He jumped into the nearest dustbin, put the lid on and safely waited it out.

Yiewlsey was relatively unharmed, but Mum's workplace in nearby Hayes (EMI's main manufacturing plant) was annihilated on one of her rare days off. These were hard times. Even when I was growing up, I recall that some people still didn't have toilet seats because they'd burnt them during the war for heat. Mum recalls frequently queuing for a whole afternoon to get just two ounces of sugar, a banana and one egg, which she'd rush home with to spoil us.

9

The green just off Whitethorn Avenue was where everyone on the estate celebrated life together. That's where they had their VE and VJ Day parties, and where I went to celebrate the Coronation. I remember that party because everyone on the estate came out with food and there was music, and it was the first time that I had ice cream, jelly and blancmange.

Everyone at school had to go to church. I found Sunday Mass at St Matthew's to be claustrophobic and hated the musty smell of the place. I hated that I couldn't move, that I was expected to sit perfectly still and be quiet. I once let everyone know just what I thought about church by vomiting. On that particular morning, I grew very faint and knew what was going to happen so I tried to catch it with my cap. I missed and covered three rows in front of me.

Not long ago, Art, who never threw anything away, found my old church stamp book. I hadn't seen it for forty-five years. Every time I attended Sunday school they would give me a little stamp with a picture of a saint or a heavenly, El Greco-type scene, to put in the book. I'm sure the reason I loved looking at the stamps was because they were like little oil paintings.

Once I'd grown up a bit and stopped being wary of her, I started to think Cousin Rita was like a little oil painting too. We were close. Her mum used to sing me to sleep with comforting, beautiful songs, and her dad, Mad Uncle Harry (or the 'Stag man' as we used to call him) would freak us all out as kids. He worked at the film studios as a prop man. He wasn't so much scary as he was, well, strange. He used to come in the back door of the house and simply walk out the front door, sometimes without saying anything. There goes Harry. Other times he'd walk in the back door, whistle a little birdsong, dance and then leave. There goes Harry again.

Sometimes when Rita and I were alone, we'd roll up pieces

of the *Daily Mirror* to look like cigarettes, light them on the fire and puff away, pretending to smoke. As the parties at Number 8 rumbled on, we were told to go to bed and we'd stop at the top of the stairs and sit there listening to the music. Then, as soon as we could, we'd sneak downstairs, dive under the table and hide behind the tablecloth. If there was a little drop of Guinness left in a glass on the table, we'd have it. We'd get caught under the table and be banished again, and eventually I'd wind up in bed with Rita. I must have been about ten, making Rita fourteen, and I was very aware of her. She was a scorcher, a real beauty in my mind, and I didn't hide my curiosity. I'd heard the expression 'doing it' and as we cuddled up I'd say to her, 'I want a do,' and Rita would say, 'You're not having a do . . .' and I'd try to convince her, always unsuccessfully, until we fell asleep.

So on those nights when it was just the two of us sent to bed, I couldn't wait for her to go into the toilet. That was the most exciting time, when I used to spy on her. I thought it was my secret, but she told me recently that she knew all along. We had loads of fun and mischief together.

The most vivid images I have of my childhood are happy ones. They are of parties, lots and lots of parties, and of music constantly playing everywhere.

Each evening after dinner, the adults in my family would 'go up to the top', meaning that they would head for the Nag's Head. Somewhere in my mind I can see myself sitting on the windowsill outside the pub with a Coca-Cola and a packet of Smith's crisps, and I'm staring in through the window at the old barrelhouse piano. Everyone from all walks of life is there. I can hear Dad singing and pounding the piano keys, and I can always tell it's him because there are so many bum notes. Everyone is sitting on long wooden benches, and when a fight starts and someone jumps up from the end of the bench the bench tips over and everyone winds up on the floor, with legs kicking up and bloomers in the air. It was a place of bottles and song, fighting, ale and fabulous faces. It was straight out of a Dickens novel.

The sun does not forget a village just because it is small.

African Proverb.

I would listen to them having a great time, cooking up riffs in my head for future reference and after a while some auntie or uncle or friendly neighbour would realize I was still on the windowsill and take me home. The next morning I'd hear that my dad took a wrong turn home, fell through someone's hedge and wound up sleeping it off in a string-bean patch. That was nothing new for him. We often found him asleep in our vegetables, amongst the cabbages or the potatoes. He would have all sorts of things crawling over him, like woodlice and spiders, but he couldn't have cared less. He didn't care if it snowed. Whenever he had to make a powerful, earth-shattering decision of a personal or worldly matter, he would just say, 'Qué será será,' whatever will be will be.

He had a bicycle, and I can remember being very young, three or four perhaps, sitting on the crossbars and him pedalling pissed. Even at that age I knew I had to steer if we were ever going to get home. I still remember the texture of his stubble, which he'd rub across my face to tease me while he was pedalling.

When he wasn't on the boats he was working in the timber yards right next to the canal, loading timber on to the boats.

He gave me a little handmade fishing rod with string and a worm on the end of a handmade hook, and I'd happily sit on the bank all day while he was busy working over the other side of the fence.

There were parties every weekend. When the crowd got turned out of the pub at half-ten, my dad would shout, 'All back to Number 8!' Everyone would bring as many bottles of Guinness, pale ale and brown ale as they could carry, pack out the house, wedge the piano in between the front door and the front room. People were always crawling over and under it to get in and out, and the singalong would begin.

Everybody in the family played music. Dad never went anywhere without his harmonica in his pocket, right up to his dying day. His sister, Auntie Ethel, had worked as a piano player, pounding out music in sync with the silent movies. She was an exceptionally fluid, gifted player. In fact, everybody in the family had a piano at home, because you never knew for sure where the party might be when the pub closed.

In addition to all the Guinness, everybody brought instruments, which meant there were combs and paper, kazoos, accordions and spoons. And it wasn't just family at these parties. Dad had a bunch of mates with weird names like Onions, Tatters, Dingle, Treacle, Patsy, Chalky, Benny, Knobby, Butcher and Bongo. Some of them were water gypsies and some of them were racetrack refugees, but all of them were musicians, all of them were drunk and all of them were fucking nuts. They'd show up at the party on a Saturday night and come Sunday morning, when I'd appear for my breakfast, these blokes would still be there, passed out all over the place. Draped over any available furniture, doused in a stale cloud of alcohol. My mum would come down and shout, 'Get out, all of you, out . . .' and they would start moaning for Archie to come to their rescue.

He'd struggle downstairs, still half asleep, and beg Mum, 'Be nice, they're my mates.' She'd shout that they had to leave and he'd explain, 'They can't possibly leave yet because the pub isn't open.' He'd sweet-talk her and she'd give in and wind up cooking them breakfast.

In those days, the *News of the World* published a song on the middle page of the newspaper every Sunday, with the notes and words to tunes like 'Right in the Middle of the Road'. That song seemed to have a million verses and go on forever and as soon as they got into it, you knew it was going to be a very long night. Everybody in the family spent a little time on Sunday morning at their piano with the latest song from the *News of the World*, getting ready for the next singalong. Dad would prepare such beauties as 'Yes We Have No Bananas' accompanied with 'Get Off Me Barrow' and, when washing, he would always say, 'Never shove your granny while she's shaving!'

Even though the parties were usually Friday and Saturday nights, if they could collect enough empty Guinness bottles by Sunday afternoon, they could cash them in to get their deposit back and have enough to buy a few more bottles, which meant there was a party on Sunday night, too.

Dad not only played the piano, but also fancied himself as an entertainer and did the shimmy. He used to sing 'Ragtime Cowboy Joe', and pretend that he was riding a horse. In his spare time, when he wasn't doing his solo act, he also had a band – a 24-piece harmonica band made up of his playing mates. They would pile into the rear of a big truck (except Archie would sit in the cab next to the driver) and they'd tour the racetracks of England. Once in a while, the truck would hit a bump and they'd lose a member off the back.

I don't know if the band ever had a name, but the 'honkestra' always played right by the winning posts, hanging out there with Prince Monolulu. He was a black hustler from Guyana named Peter Mackay, who had failed as a fortune-teller, a boxer and a fake opera singer before he started wearing flowing headdresses with ostrich feathers and outlandish waistcoats. He introduced himself as Ethiopian royalty, sold tips to punters while shouting, 'I gotta horse!' and became a British racecourse institution during the 1940s and 1950s. Wherever Prince Monolulu was, that's where Archie would be with his harmonica-playing mates. Whatever money Archie and the band collected by passing the hat, they blew on Prince Monolulu's tips, or spent on the way home from Goodwood or Epsom. Their lorry couldn't pass a pub without automatically turning in. Years later Benny, the accordion player, told me that my dad had a habit of jumping out of the truck as it pulled up to a pub and for some unknown reason climbing straight up a tree. 'And there would be your father up a tree.'

The neighbours could always tell when the Nag's Head was opening, because Dad would walk past. As soon as he got there, the other patrons would say, 'We're in for a good night, Archie's here.' And they could always tell when the Nag's Head was closed because Dad would stumble by in the other direction.

Then, one day, tragedy struck. Dad got barred.

Apparently the landlord of the Nag's found out that Archie was also drinking at the Red Cow down the High Street. So in a fit of jealousy, he tossed Dad out of the Nag's and told him he wasn't welcome any more. Archie protested, 'The Nag's belongs to us. The Woods and the Dyers [Ma's maiden name] have paid for the place two times over.' But the landlord wasn't having it, so Dad was barred from the Nag's and had to drink at the Cow, which didn't last because he had a row with the landlord there as well. I don't know what the argument was about, but before long he was barred from the Cow too.

Luckily, by that time, the landlord at the Nag's had come to his senses, realized that the atmosphere and takings had gone down, realized that Archie was too good a customer to lose, and that the Woods and the Dyers really had paid for the place two times over. So the landlord lifted the ban and welcomed Dad back by giving him a job as a bottle washer. To Archie, this meant he was allowed to be in the pub before opening, and couldn't leave until after closing.

Like Grandad Fred, Archie also lost his leg late in life. He was about seventy when it happened and he lived that way for another eight years. When he asked the doctor why his leg had to come off, the doctor replied, 'Age, Mr Wood.' Archie replied, 'Why? This leg is just as old as that one.' The first or second day after his operation, he got out of bed, forgot he didn't have two legs and fell on to the bed next to him. He landed right on top of the bloke lying there. The two men stared at each other until Archie asked, 'What are we going to call the baby?'

Everybody in the family and all of Archie's friends (which was hundreds of people) came to visit Dad in hospital, and he asked everybody who showed up, 'What's got two heads, four arms and three legs?' When they said they didn't know, he answered, 'Mr and Mrs Wood.'

Missing that leg didn't slow Archie down. But then, nothing could have stopped him from getting to the Nag's. Once, when a friend was helping Dad out of the house in a wheelchair, something happened and Dad rolled into the street and got hit by a car. It bounced him all the way back on to the green opposite. Everyone was concerned that Archie was hurt, but Dad's only concern was that, by now, the pub was already open. It wasn't until he was on his way home after closing that he started complaining about aches and pains.

I didn't see much steak, except rump, until I was fourteen

because we couldn't afford it. But Mum still managed a Sunday roast, and that meant bubble and squeak on Monday. Turkey was rare, so we had chicken for Christmas. We had lots of stew, lots of cabbage and parsnips, and plenty of fresh vegetables, which I picked from our garden when Dad wasn't sleeping there. Fruit was plentiful, too. The area around Heathrow Airport was just fields and we would go scrumping there for apples, raspberries and blackberries. They were free, so growing up I had a lot of them.

It wasn't until some time after 1960 that we got a television, but the old girls Dinah and Ethel next door had a tiny eight-inch set and I used to go over there to watch theirs. When I think back they were defo a lesbian couple. When we did get a TV of our own, you actually had to be staring at the screen or Dad would decide you weren't really watching it. He would come into the room and turn it off. The conversation would go like this:

'Why'd you do that?'

'Because you weren't watching it.'

'I was looking at you, Dad, that's why.'

'You weren't watching it.'

And that was that. I think wasting this newly acquired thing called electrical power was at the foot of it.

Instead, I would go to the tiny room off our kitchen called the 'coal hole' and do early photographic experiments with a pin-hole camera. A converted shoe box, a sheet of bromide paper, developing fluid and a red light bulb became another world where I could escape into the realm of the great photographer. Some of the pictures were quite good. I wonder where they are now?

Before long I was at Ruislip Manor School, playing basketball at the nearby US airbase. We had light blue satin uniforms and Converse sneakers. I was the shortest one on the team but they let me play because I could run under everyone else's legs. All of us on the team idolized the Harlem Globetrotters, and whenever they came to Wembley, Art and Ted would take me to see them. I thought that they were wizards, not just for the way they played basketball, but musically, too, for the way they used 'Sweet Georgia Brown' as their great jazz standard theme song.

Art ran the hurdles when he was in school, so I joined the track team and ran long distance. It was something like six or seven miles and I loved it, drumming out rhythms and riffs in my head as I ran, like you do.

Both of my brothers went off to Ealing Art College. By this time I was winning prizes for my drawings. After St Stephen's, my first ever school, I had painted a mural of St Francis and the animals while I was at St Martin's and the headmaster, Mr Scholar, liked my talent. Another teacher, Mr Reasey, would greet my mum as the 'Mother of the Artist'. I won the art cup and wanted to take A-level art, but the school told Mum I was wasting my time and talent at their school. So off she went to see the headmaster at Ealing. He asked why her youngest son wanted to come there and she said, 'Because my other two sons came here and I want Ronnie to have the same chance.' That's how I got in. Mum and Dad supported us like that. Whatever crazy job we wanted to go into, or whatever silly hairdo we had, they would both smother us in love, offering constant support.

Ealing was the right school for me because, after music, drawing is what I did, and I was always doing it. Besides music, I was always drawing while I was growing up, and sending my artwork into the BBC's *Sketch Club*. That was the first art show on TV and starred a man named Adrian Hill. On Thursdays, just before dinner time, he'd stand in front of an easel in his

white smock and talk about watercolours and oil painting while showing the viewers how to draw. I watched him on our tiny black and white telly, and when he asked kids to send in their drawings I bombarded him with mine. I was ten years old at the time and he started showing my drawings on the telly. A few years later, I won the show's main prize for a picture of an audience in the cinema, shocked and scared, looking at them from the screen out, as they reacted to a horror film. Winning that prize got my drawings into an exhibition and that was my awakening to art. I sometimes look back to this picture as the seed to both the worlds I ended up in. Depicting an audience in shock and awe meant my two worlds of art and performance came together in this little picture and preceded my night and day jobs.

Whenever I ran out of paper, and had to wait for Dad to bring some home from wherever he was working, I'd draw on anything I could find. Dad would say, 'A horse wouldn't walk like that. Look again.' Until Art brought home an easel, I used a block of hardboard propped up against books. I especially loved to draw horses and was inspired by the early Buffalo Bill annuals. After school, I worked for a while as a commercial artist, just like Art and Ted both did.

At one point I also worked as a potato picker in fields owned by a big Irish guy who demanded I show up in the freezing cold at seven in the morning, yelling at me, 'Jesus Christ and his blessed Mother Mary, pick up them damn potatoes . . .' That job didn't last long. Neither did my work as a Formica cutter, which was awful because when you handle Formica it cuts your hands back. Then I became a butcher's boy, delivering meat on a bicycle. I was always the last one to arrive at the shop so I always got the worst bicycle. It had a big basket in the front and even though I was the smallest, I had the most meat to carry. I'd fall off the bike and the basket would spill on to the ground and I was forever picking shingle and gravel out of people's sides of beef. Finally I got a job as an artist, well, sort of. I worked for a real-estate agency painting placards that read 'For Sale', 'Sold' and 'For Rent'.

Art was the most fun I ever had in school. We did action paintings like driving bicycles over canvasses. The first time we did that everyone laughed, but when I saw it I said to myself, hold on, something's happening here. A new form of expression was being explained to me. Some of the kids couldn't be bothered, they'd leave school and go home, but a few of us used to stay back with the bonus of being allowed to smoke and hang out because we were the ones looking for something. We studied technique, colour, texture and line, and that got me started reading books about artists, which is how I discovered Picasso and Braque. It was a very exciting time, but then, these were the early 1960s and things were changing rapidly.

Some traditions weren't going to change at Number 8 Whitethorn though, even if it was the 1960s. I remember gathering the courage to speak to my first girlfriend, Linda, by constantly riding my bike past her house until she came out and I'd crash into her. Then coming in my pants in the cold night air in the dark with Taffy, a Welsh beauty. My parents once allowed a girlfriend of mine to stay over at our house. Naturally, they assumed I would kip in the other room, but after they went to bed I snuck into her room and we soon fell asleep in each other's arms. The next morning, when Dad came in to wake her, I was still there and all three of us got a shock. He looked at us for an eternity before finally saying, 'I suppose that's two cups of tea then . . .'

Later that morning he pulled me aside with some stern words.

'I'll have you know your brothers never did this.' He shook his head to show his disapproval. 'Where do you think you are, on yer father's yacht?'

I later found out both my brothers had done it at one time or another.

Years later, when I bought my house in Ireland, I redesigned one of the outer buildings to make it just like an old-fashioned pub. The sign that hangs above the door is a painting of Archie wearing a naval uniform with the name of the pub, in big bold letters: 'Yer Father's Yacht'. My brother-in-law Paul very kindly painted it while I was busy breaking in the bar. On the other side it reads 'Purveyors of fine wines, beers and spirits for absolutely nothing.'

Whenever any of us came into any money, like when I got

that job picking potatoes, or when Art and Ted started playing gigs, we'd go fifty-fifty with Mum. Dad brought his wages home, faithfully gave Mum her housekeeping money and then, equally faithfully, spent whatever was left at the pub. If you'd told me then, I'd never have believed that one day I'd fashion my own pub in the style of these early days, or that the alcohol contained within would play such a tricky role throughout my life.

The back room at Number 8 Whitethorn could have been a dining room, except for the fact that it was filled, floor to ceiling, with records and instruments. It was our music room, and that's where my brothers had their parties with all their beatnik art-school friends. My uncle Fred knocked a few bricks out of the wall between the kitchen and the back room, creating a little hatch for my mum to feed cups of tea and coffee through without disturbing anyone. It was like a speakeasy.

I loved being at my brothers' parties and couldn't take my eyes off the girls who showed up. They wore bright red, yellow and green dresses, together with bangles, and they all had long earrings. Viv was an Egyptian goddess, Helen a young Audrey Hepburn and Jackie a pouting Kim Novak. Maria, Doreen and Julie were just a few of the others I can visualize draped decadently over the sofa. They were superb, bohemian, truly beautiful, and I fell in love with each of them. Unfortunately, they were seventeen or eighteen and I was seven or eight and still in short flannel trousers.

Everyone played skiffle music in those days, but there were also R&B and deep traditional jazz jam sessions played by guys wearing drainpipe trousers and dark glasses. I desperately wanted to hang with them, to be part of the gang, but Art and Ted needed to get rid of me because nobody felt like snogging as long as I was there watching. So Art or Ted would hand me some coins and say, 'Ronnie, nip down to the off-licence and get us a bar of chocolate and a bottle of lemonade.' The shops were only at the bottom of the road, not far away at all, but far enough that it should have given them ten or fifteen minutes. Instead I'd say, 'Sure, okay. Time me and see how quick I can be!' I didn't want to miss anything. Art would beg me to take my time, and Ted would assure me that I didn't have to go back and forth at some record speed, but I didn't understand and I would pretend that I was an Olympic runner. Before they could get it on, I'd be right there in the music room with the lemonade and chocolate, all proud of myself four minutes later.

The music, the art, the theatre, the humour and the girls were what made my brothers' lives so appealing. That's what I wanted to do and I wanted a bigger piece of it, so I took it upon myself to learn how to play all the instruments that my brothers' friends brought with them to the parties. There were clarinets, cornets, banjos, guitars, saxophones, trumpets, the comb and paper, kazoos, harmonicas, a home-made drum kit with Chinese wood blocks and the washboard, which became my first instrument. I learnt it well enough that in 1957, when Ted got a gig with his Candy Bison Skiffle Group at the Marlborough Cinema in Yiewsley High Street, he brought me along. Skiffle was another musical import from America. Black musicians in the South in the very early 1900s got hold of whatever regular instruments they could find, and because they couldn't afford anything else, the rest of the band played home-made instruments like kazoos, spoons, pots, pans, glass jars, box-crate basses. We all played skiffle in the beginning, even the Beatles.

I thought I got a chance to play that night because I was now part of the gang. It turns out that Ted's washboard player was sick that day and you can't play skiffle without a washboard. That was my first live appearance. I was nine. We were the interval act, between two Tommy Steele films. I was very nervous walking out on to the stage, but once I was there and got into strumming my washboard, and saw all the threatening potential of an audience, I knew this was a very good job.

Art's real love was R&B while Ted's real love was traditional jazz, so I grew up listening to Gus Cannon's Jug Stompers and Paul Whiteman, Leadbelly, Bix Beiderbecke, Sidney Bechet, Django Reinhardt, Louis Armstrong and Chuck Berry (whom I later got to know as one of the greatest nutcases on the planet). It was a wonderful mixture of influences.

It was Art who bought my first record player for me, a grey and maroon Dansette. This was modern technology, with a swing arm so that you could stack records to play automatically, one after the other. Except that, more often than not, two or three would drop at the same time. But the Dansette could play 45s, 33N s and 78s, which my mum used to call 79s. This Dansette became a doorway to a world of sound for me. Art bought me my first few records, including Jerry Lee Lewis singing 'Great Balls of Fire' and the first record I ever bought was Big Joe Williams with Count Basie. The first time I ever heard Elvis was when Cousin Dougie came by with 'Hound Dog' and 'Blue Suede Shoes' and put it on. I also heard one of the first fade-out records on that Dansette. It was 'I'm Walking' by Fats Domino. My cousin Rex brought it round. Tragically, he was killed just a few weeks later at the age of eighteen when an oxygen tank exploded at the factory where he worked. Not much health and safety in those days.

Legend has it that Fats wrote the song after his car broke down and some fan called out, 'There's Fats and he's walking.' Fats thought to himself, yeah I'm walking, and wrote the song.

The thing about it was that it didn't end like any other song we'd ever heard, it simply disappeared. I can still see my mum and Rex leaning over the Dansette, with their heads close to the built-in speaker at the front, wondering where the music went. And I can still hear Mum tell Rex, 'Take the record back and get one that finishes properly.'

It wasn't until Art was called up for his national service in 1955 that we discovered Fats. It was just after basic training, when the army sent Art to Devizes. I thought my big brother had gone off to some foreign country, even if it's actually only in Wiltshire, not far from Stonehenge. To me it might have been on the other side of the planet because now the house was a lot emptier. Art formed a skiffle group in the army called the Blue Cats, when he heard Fats for the first time on the base jukebox and decided he wanted to sing like Fats.

Maybe thirty years later, after I got to know Fats, he was showing me around his house in New Orleans, and in his bedroom he had exactly the same old grey and maroon Dansette that I did.

There was a record shop on Yiewsley high street called Franklin's and Ted had an account there, which is how he bought all his jazz records. When Art came home from the army, broke, he'd pick the records he wanted and stick them on Ted's account. And I'd pinch them five minutes later.

It was clear to everyone how interested I was in music from an early age, and how anxious I was to learn chords. Two of my brothers' friends, Lawrence Sheaff and Jim Willis, noticed this and kindly drew stripes and frets on a piece of paper for me, putting little dots on the stripes so I would know where to put my fingers on a guitar. I always carried that piece of paper around with me, and my son Jesse would eventually learn that way too. They let me practise on their guitars, until Art gave me one I could experiment on. I thought it was mine to keep, not knowing that it belonged to his mate Peter Hayes who lived down the block. No one told me that Peter had only loaned it to Art. I was just getting used to it when Art said sorry, you have to give it back. I thought I'd never get a guitar of my own. Art and Ted must have seen I was gutted and chipped in to buy me my own guitar. It was a lovely acoustic, and a blessing from above, although the action was a bit high on the neck and it hurt my fingers to play it. My hands were ready to deal with the blisters and cramps and I wasn't going to let the pain stop me from getting to know my new spokesman. When Art handed it to me he said, 'This one is not going to go away. It's yours.'

There is nothing to it. You only have to hit the right notes at the right time and the instrument plays itself.
Johann Sebastian Bach.

By then I was watching Art's and Ted's friend Lawrence Sheaff very closely because his style was amazing. I wanted to play like that, I wanted to deliver like that. He tried to teach me 'Guitar Shuffle'. I say tried, because I watched him play it a million times and to this day I'm still trying to figure out how he played it. Lawrence was born knowing how to play a guitar – six-string, twelve-string, it didn't matter – and like my dad always used to say, 'He could make that banjo talk.' I know now, after all these years of playing with the world's best musicians, that Lawrence was up there with them, but I'm sure he never realized how wonderful he was.

Lawrence introduced me to the sound of Big Bill Broonzy,

who still remains an influence to me. I know he is to Keith, and Clapton too, as well as just about every other really good rock guitarist of my generation. Big Bill was one of the most important musicians who helped to create the early Chicago sound, even though he was born in Mississippi in 1893 and grew up playing the fiddle. He switched to guitar when he could get one, and by the 1930s he was right up there with all the big names of the day including Memphis Slim, Washboard Sam, Sonny Boy Williamson, Tampa Red and Blind Willie McTell.

Until I was thirteen or fourteen, I was still playing the guitar that Art and Ted bought me. But once I had some odd jobs, I started saving some money. I went to Franklin's music store and bought myself a new guitar on what we used to call the never-never; instalments so small with interest so high that you would never-never pay it all back. My parents signed for me and I faithfully paid Franklin's two and six every week for the next however many years. The guitar cost £25, which was a fortune at the time.

It's going on forty years since any of us lived at Number 8, and today there's a little porch built on to the front of it. The man who lives there now told Cousin Beryl that everyone still refers to it as 'the Woods' House'. He dug up the back garden one day and found 1,700 Guinness bottles. I'll admit to using a hundred of them to build homes for my terrapins but the rest are down to my dad.

My mum was a great judge of character. I remember her once asking the police politely to leave our house, after they had my autograph. She turned to me and said, 'I know I don't like someone when they make my feet ache.' Just before Mum died, just before she had her last sip of Jameson's, she told me that number 8 Whitethorn Avenue had a crack down the middle of it. She said she thought it came about when the house breathed a sigh of relief when the Wood family finally left. But I don't think so. It might have been a tiny house, but it was a happy, rocking house and I think the crack is one big smile from all the parties.

2
Conception

With all the different music swirling around me, I needed a band. Dad had his one, Ted had Candy Bison Skiffle Group and Art was singing with Blues Incorporated, Britain's first R&B group. These were a bunch of white guys who sounded like black guys out of Chicago. It was Art, Alexis Korner on guitar, Dick Heckstall-Smith on sax, Spike Heatley, Jack Bruce on bass and Charlie Watts on drums. They started at the Marquee Club on Oxford Street in central London, but soon moved to the Ealing Club, which, thanks to them, became the traditional home of British R&B.

It was a narrow basement room with a tiny stage at one end, a bar at the other and always more than a hundred people crammed in between like sardines. It used to get so hot that sweat would come off the ceiling. This place, the 'Moist Hoist', oozed ready-to-rock musicians.

The deal was that anybody who wanted to join in could, as long as the band approved. Which is how Mick Jagger came to sing with my brother Art before hooking up with Keith Richards and Brian Jones. Long John Baldry also sang with Art's group before discovering Rod Stewart and forming Steampacket. The Ealing Club and Blues Incorporated were heavy influences on just about everybody, but especially on Fleetwood

Mac, Cream, the Yardbirds, Manfred Mann, John Mayall and the Pretty Things.

As much as I wanted to hang out with my brothers and be part of their musical adventure, I also wanted to embark on my own one. Ted and Art would come around and show me photographs of their crazy nights, thinking that they were just being kind to me, but in my head they were rubbing it in. 'These are the members of my band,' they'd say, and I'd open my eyes wide. Mitch Mitchell played with Art before joining Jimi Hendrix, Ronnie Lane used to test the amps for Art, and Keith Moon was also always hanging around. I would see Moonie on my way home from Ealing Art College as the train went by a field, and there he'd be kicking a football around on the other side of a chicken-wire fence.

By 1962, Art was backing some fantastic R&B stars who were over from America, including Howlin' Wolf, Little Walter and May Mercer. Art was also playing at Klooks Kleek, a big old club in West Hampstead, where all the flash guys got to play. For a while Art's Blues Incorporated was also the resident band at the 100 Club.

After moving from the Marquee to Ken Colyer's Club, Charlie Watts decided to quit the band. He went to Art and said, 'I've got an offer to join an interval band,' which was some unknown group playing in between the main headline band and the second headline band, kind of like what Ted and I once did at the Marlborough.

Art shrugged, 'If you really want to give it a try, I'll give you a hand with your drum kit,' before asking, 'Who are they?'

Charlie answered, 'They're called the Rolling Stones.'

As far as I was concerned, my world was Cowley, Uxbridge and West Drayton. In this neck of the woods, Brian Poole, Cliff Bennett and Roy Young were as near as we could get to Elvis.

But round there could be dangerous for anyone who played live music because the local hoodlums, Lord Rat and his gang, would show up and start a fight. He was a rocker who wore a leather jacket with studs and carried knives, and he used to terrorize the neighbourhood because, well, that was his job. He ruled the roost at the Two Sisters Café on the high street and when I was growing up, we'd walk on the other side of the street instead of going anywhere near him. Lord Rat especially liked to get into fights with the Americans from the airbase at Ruislip and I was always hearing stories about people flying out of the Two Sisters' front window. You simply did not tangle with Lord Rat and his gang.

By this point I had really long hair, which was different because almost everyone else I knew had theirs really short. People in the street used to ask, 'Are you a boy or a girl?' I didn't mind because long hair was one of the ways I was being me. My parents didn't mind, either. My dad never told me to go and get a haircut. In fact he actually said to me, 'If you want to look like that, son, it's up to you.'

He made sure that I knew a lot of things were up to me, so I started recruiting friends for a band. I didn't have to look far though. Kim Gardner was round the corner, Tony Munroe was up the other end of the street, and Ali McKenzie was just down the other block. I decided we would call ourselves the Thunderbirds, after the 1960 Chuck Berry song 'Jaguar and the Thunderbird'.

Tony and I were the first ones to join the band, but we had only one amp between us, which had to work for the vocals and the two guitars. That's why we let Kim into the band – he had his own bass amp. And as a two-amp band we rocked Birmingham, Leicester and Manchester, but mostly we rocked Yiewsley. We played Motown, songs like Marvin Gaye's 'Ain't

That Peculiar', and 'Baby Don't You Do It', and the Velvelettes' 'Needle in a Haystack'. We played Bo Diddley, the Temptations, the Beach Boys and Jimmy Reed, all in one set. I used to sing the Chuck Berry numbers 'Talkin' About You', 'Maybelene' and 'Too Much Monkey Business'. Tony would also sing, but Ali was really the singer so he'd do most of them. We'd rehearse in whoever's garage was free and jam until we were moved on. Eventually we got another rehearsal venue when a really polite old gentleman who ran the Rainbow Record store next to the Nag's Head said we could rehearse in his shop window. He would look inquisitively at us and explain the situation to his customers as we boomed in his shop, bounced off his window and made all sorts of noise. Anyone who walked past that shop got a free gig from us, we built up a small following, and it wasn't long before we had a proper stage.

It was just over a mile from Whitethorn Avenue to the Nest, which is where we got our start, playing every Friday and Saturday night. Ali, Kim, Tony, Bob Langham (who was our original drummer) and I had to walk to work because none of us had a car. But we did have a wheelbarrow and a cart with flight wheels on it, so we'd pile our equipment up high and push it right down the middle of the high street, dodging cars, buses and taxis as we went. To get down Tavistock Road (good Tony King country) we had to cross over a bridge, which is inevitably where the wheelbarrow would tip, spilling the amplifiers, drum kit and everything else we owned on to the road. But once we set up at the Nest our mates would come in, plus our girlfriends, and we'd vibe up a show.

As word got out about us, more and more people jammed into the Nest, to the point where it regularly got packed. I guess we were doing all right because when Memphis Slim came to England without a backing band, word had got around that we would fit the bill just right, he came and saw us and after the show he asked if Kim and I would play with him at the Ivy League Club, which was just up the road from the Nest. I didn't realize how special Memphis was at the time but remember he sang and played piano real sweet. I wasn't sure if we were going to get any money for the gig. We didn't. Instead, Memphis paid us with a bottle of whisky and a big hug!

It was during this exciting time that I was stopped in my tracks by one of life's brutal, unexpected trials. The kind that never gets easier with age, but the kind that really knocks you for six when you're seventeen.

Stephanie de Court was a childhood sweetheart of mine who I would walk home from school. She was beautiful. It was all very innocent – talking, hand-holding, the occasional kiss. But there was an unmistakeable bond between us. I really cared for her. Whenever we went out, I'd hide in her garden waiting for her to leave, because she didn't want her parents to know about our little romance. Then, when I'd bring her home, I'd hide in the garden until she went inside. If we were one minute late, I'd hear her getting all sorts of grief from her parents. It was the special kind of romance that stays with you, and I was always so pleased it happened with her.

On 31 May 1964, the band and I were playing a gig, and Stephanie and three of her girlfriends were coming to see us, but they never showed. We did the gig and I went home to my parents' place.

My dad woke me the next morning. It was my seventeenth birthday, but I knew from his expression that birthday wishes were far from his mind.

'It's something about Stephanie being killed.'

Her uncle was waiting downstairs. He told me how the girls had been travelling through Henley-on-Thames in a Mini, en route to our gig, when the accident occurred. Somehow, they were hit by an oncoming car. I have recently spoken to one of her friends, Diane, who never went that night, and therefore lives on to reflect the treasure of the times we spent together, and, being Steph's best friend, remembers how close we were.

I wasn't allowed to go to her funeral because her parents decided they hardly knew me and didn't want me there. So while they were burying Stephanie, some friends took me to the pub. That's how I discovered that alcohol could help me hide my feelings. They got me drunk because it was the only way I could accept the fact that she was gone from my life forever.

Although I missed her funeral, I did visit the accident black spot, and several days later her grave. Despite this, I was unable to accept what had happened to Stephanie; but in the bottle I had discovered a way not to think about it. I know that anger and disappointment blow out the candles of the mind. I would never let them get the better of me.

3

Scene

Music was exploding all over England and there were local bands, like ours, up and down the country trying to make it. But unless you had a manager you remained a bunch of neighbourhood friends with guitars and drums. We knew we needed someone to guide our careers, which is how I hooked up with the first of my occasionally dodgy managers, Leo de Klerk. Don't get me wrong, I had some good managers but Leo told us he was a South African businessman and bragged about all his connections in the music and entertainment industry. It turned out he was actually an East London wideboy whose first name was Lionel.

Leo was in his thirties when we met him, and in great physical shape because he worked out a lot. He was a bit of a ladies' man and I remember he was trying to be an actor. Every now and then, he'd land a bit part in some drama on the telly. I'm not sure if we found Leo or Leo found us, but the connection was a good-lookin' hard nut named Colin Farrell. He and his brother Tony did odd jobs for Leo and Colin thought we were cool so he got Leo to come to the Nest to check us out. Leo told us he owned some clubs, including the Zambeezee in Hounslow plus the Caverns in Windsor and Reading. Whether he actually owned them, or just ran them for others, I don't know. But that didn't matter to us at the time because Leo's venues meant we always had somewhere to play. For Leo, booking us in his own venues meant he could easily control the bookkeeping.

It was around that time when we had to change our name. There was already a group called the Thunderbirds, and even though they were officially called Chris Farlowe and the Thunderbirds, they got angry with us. I took that to be a good sign because it meant someone had heard of us. But we got the message and shortened our name to the Birds.

The next thing we knew, Leo offered to put us on the road and to pay us ten quid a week. He said he would get us a van and a roadie (Colin) to look after us, said he would pay for our petrol and promised that he would get us gigs in foreign countries. None of us worked out how much this was going to cost Leo but we didn't care.

So now we had a manager. Leo's solution to our transport problem was a knackered old blue transit van, and one of my last signpainting jobs was to write 'THE BIRDS' in big letters on the side of it. Colin, who turned out to be a slave-driver, would chauffeur us to wherever our gig was, then shout orders at us as we unpacked all our equipment and carried it up God knows how many flights of stairs, especially at the Blue Moon in Cheltenham. Colin was a friendly bloke, but he was also large enough to be threatening and wasn't somebody you'd argue with. He never lifted a finger so we all had to do manual labour before going onstage.

We may not have been a very good band in the beginning, but we were very enthusiastic, and we were getting better all the time, finding our feet, experimenting with Motown, soul and rock, and building up a following.

Until Leo came along, I was holding down a day job at Solet Signs. I painted 'Bush Radio' along the wrought-iron stands at the local football club. Actually, that was pretty cool because there I was, just like Michelangelo, up on scaffolding doing the entire football stadium, and got paid £70 for it, which was a lot of money to me. My next job gave me £150, and that was more than my dad earned in a long time. I was bringing home the bacon and my parents couldn't believe there was suddenly all this extra money in the house. Anyway, painting signs drove me mad, so when Leo offered us a contract I retired from that career to concentrate full-time on music. Not that Leo missed an opportunity to take advantage of my abilities with a paintbrush. One day he asked me if I would come over to help him decorate the Zambeezee Club and I thought he was just looking for some artistic advice. Instead he handed me a brush and I spent the day painting the insides of the place black. I thought doing that for Leo for free was what musicians did to keep their manager happy. Keith told me once that he walked into the famous Chess Studios in Chicago, noticed a black guy on a ladder painting the walls, did a double take and realized it was Muddy Waters. So I'm in good company.

The contract we had with Leo was neatly typed on several pages and looked very professional to us, but as we were all under twenty-one he insisted that our parents become our guarantors. None of us in the band knew better and our parents didn't understand it, so none of us really knew what we were getting into. All I knew was that, if I wanted to be in this evergrowing thing called a band, my mother and father would have to sign for me on the dotted line. Of course they did, not understanding that the deal with Leo could give him everything and us nothing.

The contract basically said that Leo had no liability whatsoever, and couldn't be held responsible for anything. The only member of the Birds who didn't sign was Bob Langham. His dad refused. The Langham family wouldn't take the risk so we had to get a new drummer, which is how Pete McDaniels joined us.

Once our parents signed Leo's contract, he began working us seven nights a week. From £10 a week, I seem to remember we went down to £5 per gig and then, after months and months on the road, slowly worked our way up to £30 a gig. It might sound like a lot of dosh for that time, but this is what Leo was paying the band, not each of us separately, so we had to divide it by five as well as paying for our own food on the road, plus our clothes. Some weeks it was actually costing us money to be in the band.

Not only was the money hardly worth it, but life on the road in the blue Ford van was fucking horrible. Colin drove while the rest of us were crammed in the back with the equipment. It used to take five hours up to Manchester. We'd put cushions on top of the amplifiers and try to sleep, but the cushions always slipped off and we'd wind up on the floor. We'd get up north, crawl out of the van stinking and farting, and Colin would order us around.

I didn't know it at the time, but just about everybody in the music business went through the same kind of misery when they were starting out. In the early days of the Stones, their now sadly departed keyboard player Ian Stewart would drive them everywhere in a minivan. They'd be booked somewhere up north on one night, then down south on the next, then back up north on the night after that. Stu was a killer driver and would never stop, no matter what the others wanted. So Mick, Keith, Brian and Charlie would pile into the rear of the van, while Bill had everyone conned into believing that he had some sort of condition which flared up if he sat in the back and could only be cured if he was up front with Stu. The others would all be rolling around in the rear while Bill was comfortable and Stu careered along, criss-crossing England. If anyone wanted to pee, they had to do it in a bottle. That was their apprenticeship.

Jesse Ed Davis, the guitar player for Taj Mahal, used to play with Conway Twitty and he told me a similar story. He said that when they were riding in vans, Conway would never stop when someone wanted to pee. Jesse Ed, or someone else in the band, would beg Conway to pull over but he would just drive on, shouting, 'I ain't fucking stopping, go pee in a bottle.' It got so bad one day that Jesse Ed pissed in a bottle, didn't know what to do with it, thought the shiny van window was open and tossed the bottle out. Except the window was shut, and the bottle came bouncing back all over Conway. Jesse Ed got fired for that.

The main reason bands drove through the night was because hotels cost money and managers never willingly spent it. One of the few hotels where we did sometimes stay was the Altrincham, outside Manchester, but only if we were appearing somewhere nearby the next day. Ali had pulled the daughter of the fellow who ran the place, so we were always happy to go back there whenever we could. One night at the Altrincham I pulled a bird and brought her up to my room, not knowing that the guys were hiding in my closet. We were always pulling jokes and pranks on each other, because that's what you do on the road to keep from going crazy. By the time Kim, Tony and Ali jumped out of the closet, I was just about finishing the job. They started laughing and teasing me, not because they'd caught me in the act, but because while I was in the act I still had my red socks on. But I always did that – it's an old English habit. I only started taking my socks off much later when I began meeting girls who were naughty.

Red socks included, one of the best things about being on the road was all the girls who were around the band. We used to get mobbed in Salisbury and we were very big in Cheshire. The girls would yell, scream and try to pull our hair out and, better still, try to rip our clothes off. The girls would also write all over the van in lipstick.

Leo now got us booked into a regular gig, making the Birds the Monday-night band at the 100 Club in Soho. I liked that because my brother Art played there regularly. Tom Jones and the Squires were there on Tuesdays – Tom was a big-nosed Welsh labourer yelling the blues and bumping and grinding for the girls – and Jeff Beck and the Tridents were there on Wednesday nights, although I never met him then. On weekends, the 100 Club always featured some big-name American stars like Muddy Waters and Chuck Berry. It was a wild place to be. When Bo Diddley came over he needed a backup group, so they asked us if we wanted to do it. That was the beginning of a life-long friendship with Bo that would even, years later, put us on the road together. After our show with him at the 100 Club, Bo wanted to know how things were going and we spilled our hearts out to him about Leo. Bo was the first person to give me really good advice about the managers. He said, 'Tell your manager if he ain't gonna shit, get off the pot.'

Our venues and crowds were getting bigger, and we thought we'd finally arrived when Leo announced that the Birds were going to play the Glad Rag Ball, on the same bill with the Kinks, the Hollies and the Who. We were now considered a UK Top Twenty live act. This, without even having a hit record.

That was what was supposed to come next. We wanted to record, and so I wrote my first song for the Birds, 'You're on My Mind'. I just picked up my guitar, turned on the tape recorder and played what I felt. Of course, I was heavily influenced by the music I was listening to at the time, but I believed then, and still do today, that it's not what you steal, it's how you steal it.

So I nicked tunes off people whose music I loved, and extended those tunes and turned them into new songs. I was very influenced by the Yardbirds' version of 'There's a Certain Girl' – as soon as I'd treated the song in my own way and used that as my starting point for 'You're on My Mind', I wrote the words, too.

I did study some musical theory at school but I never really used it. Sure, it's nice to know the rules and yeah, I can read music, but I don't want to read it, I want to feel it. I believe that there's a basic rule which runs through all kinds of music, kind of an unwritten rule, that's adapt to your musical surroundings with whichever instrument you choose, blend right in and kick it. Learn the roots of the song then improvise.

I played the song for the other guys; I wanted to show it off because I was excited about my stuff – it was basic R&B with a thumping beat and lots of harmonica, which I loved to play. They loved it and we wanted to record it. Leo didn't have much choice, which meant he had to spend some money on us, so he found a little place that didn't cost much called the Tony Pike Studio in Putney, and that's where we cut our first vinyl. As long as we had the studio, we also did a song called 'You Don't Love Me, You Don't Care' written by Ellis McDaniels (Bo Diddley).

For me, that recording session was fascinating and so new. I soaked it up and sucked it in. I went through all the motions and started learning the fundamentals of overdubs. It's a bit like doing a silk screen, where you put down one colour, and then put down another colour and continue like that until you've got a painting. We'd lay down the basic wash with drums and bass, a guitar track, then lay down the second guitar track, then the vocal and little by little we had a song. Now, this was the 1960s, so the equipment was primitive – sometimes four tracks but more likely two. From that they made one big 78 rpm vinyl master, then used the master to make 45 rpm records – you know, the small ones with the big hole in the middle. We each got one white label 45 rpm, and two spares. I took mine home and played it for my parents, all my friends and all my parents' friends. I discovered the hard way that you couldn't play those records too many times before they wore out. I was so hungry to squeeze more songs on to vinyl.

Our demos got us a deal with Decca. So sometime in November 1964 we went to their studio in Savile Row and did both our songs. This only encouraged my craving to spend as much time as I could in these soundproof creative holes. A few months later we went back to Decca to record 'Next in Line', which I wrote as the B-side for the Eddie and Brian Holland song 'Leaving Here'.

That record earned us an appearance on a battle of the bands television show called *Ready, Steady, Win*. Consequently the song charted within the Top Fifty – this at a time when getting in the charts meant something. Understandably it was a big deal for us, as we could hold our heads a little higher alongside the bands we were rubbing shoulders with. But it also made me hungry to make better records. That's the problem with tasting success; you want more, to gorge on it.

Charting when we did threw up another issue as an American group called the Byrds had a really huge Number One hit on both sides of the Atlantic at exactly the same time. Their song was 'Mr Tambourine Man', written by Bob Dylan. *Those* Byrds, featuring Roger McGuinn on a twelve-string Rickenbacker guitar, backed up by Gene Clark, David Crosby and Chris Hillman, were about as big as you could get in America. They were always being compared in popularity to the Beatles, although they were a folk-rock band and had a very different sound. They planned a UK tour and laid on tons of publicity. Even though our name wasn't the same as theirs, they didn't see it that way and threatened to get nasty. Leo conned them out of that idea by greeting them at Heathrow Airport with writs that demanded they change their name because they were now infringing on our territory. The Byrds had lawyers, and their lawyers had lawyers, so Leo's writs didn't accomplish anything, except to create a lot of publicity for us. What it did do was get us on the front page of *Melody Maker*, the hottest music publication of its time.

The Byrds tour turned into a disaster when several band members took ill. They left Britain, we were still the Birds, and along the way Leo persuaded the BBC to book us on the *Millicent Martin Show*, which gave us some more credibility. We followed that with an appearance on a pop-music programme called *Thank Your Lucky Stars*. For some reason, our drummer was lowered from the ceiling behind his kit with the aid of Royal Ballet stage props. Obviously he missed his footing and went sprawling elegantly across the stage. I'd love to see the TV out-takes.

Leo also got us our one and only movie. The film was called *The Deadly Bees*, and we were extras playing a band in the background. A very forgettable scene. It was years later before I actually saw the film, and there I was, wearing a horrible polo neck, holding a guitar decorated with Fablon (a frightful sticky plastic covering). But who cares, the Birds were doing their best.

We survived the costumes – and the Fablon – and made a few more records for Decca. Our third single was 'No Good Without You Baby', a rare Marvin Gaye song, with 'How Can It Be' on the flip side. 'Say Those Magic Words' with 'Daddy, Daddy' followed.

But the end came for Leo when he booked us into a New Year's Eve gig at the Starlight Ballroom in Sudbury in December 1965. Normally, Leo or Colin or someone would show up at the end of the evening to see that the management settled up. But that night Leo didn't show. No one did. So Ali, who was the only one in the band with even a slight business sense, went to pick up the takings. When he saw how much it was, he couldn't believe it. The rest of us couldn't believe it either. It came to nearly £1,000. We were dumbfounded. Leo was paying us next to nothing and we had no idea how much money he was making out of our performances.

We decided we had to get rid of Leo.

We called a meeting at Kim's parents' house on Edgar Road. We wanted to make sure we had something on Leo, so Kim and I hid a tape recorder under the table in order to secretly tape the meeting.

Leo tried everything he could to convince us that he had our best interests at heart and even offered us clothes – a definite perk. I knew full well that the Small Faces could go down to Carnaby Street and buy whatever they wanted and their manager, Don Arden (perhaps more well known as Sharon Osbourne's dad these days), would take care of the bills. I didn't yet realize that this was an old trick – while the band is getting new clothes, the manager is still taking the money. The Birds earned a lot of money for Leo. He got married and opened a chain of grocery stores on us.

The music scene in England back then was vastly different to how it is now. Today, groups like the Rolling Stones are big businesses and isolated from other groups by private jets, managers, lawyers, accountants, roadies, crews, hangers-on and bodyguards. In those days we were just in vans, all hitting the same road and, on that road, always bumping into everyone else. Everybody knew everyone else and we would play on each other's records without even being credited.

There was an old hotel on Eel Pie Island, in the middle of the Thames near Twickenham, which became a famous venue that everybody wanted to play – Long John Baldry and Rod Stewart, John Mayall and Eric Clapton, Jeff Beck and the Tridents, the Who. When you weren't playing at the Eel Pie Island Hotel, you went along anyway to see who was. It's where you found Cyril Davies and his R&B All Stars – to hear Cyril play 'Country Line Special' on his harmonica was a sight and sound to behold. It made me take up the harmonica. Jagger went up to him when onstage once and said, 'How'd you bend a note?' 'Well you get a pair of pliers . . .' Cyril replied.

There was the Crawdaddy in Richmond, which was named after the Bo Diddley song 'Doing the Craw-Daddy', and where the Stones played from February 1963. The band got so popular by playing there they had to move to a bigger location.

There was the Railway Club in Harrow and Wealdstone. The fellow who ran it had gone to Ealing Art College with Pete Townshend, so the Who became the Tuesday-night resident band there. There was Pete Townshend, Roger Daltrey, John Entwhistle and Keith Moon, and there was all that wreckage, as well as all that noise coming out of all their amps, which were turned up to the max. The first time I heard them I kept asking myself, 'What the hell is going on here? It's fantastically great.'

The club scene in those years was really rocking, and so were the record companies, which were all within staggering distance of each other along Oxford Street. You'd get invited to Christmas parties at all of them and go from one to another – Warner Brothers, Immediate, CBS – right on down the block, bumping into the Stones, the Small Faces, the Pretty Things, the Kinks, the Beatles and the Dave Clark Five. Anybody who was anybody was crawling Oxford Street at Christmas time. It was a mad, special era in British rock. Everybody was interchanging. The Birds would play the Ealing Club and the Who would walk in and tease us with their success. They had hit the top of the charts by then with 'Can't Explain', but that never stopped Keith Moon from jumping up on our stage and jamming with us. When we played the NME (New Musical Express) Poll Winners' Concert in the mid-1960s, we were on the bill with a host of bands including the Beatles, the Stones and Cliff Richard. There were a series of stages, and one band would play one song then the next band would take up when they had finished, and then suddenly it was your turn. It was good fun, essentially a massive jam, being out in front a sea of people.

Speaking of wreckage and noise, another group we used to run into was the Move, and they were something. They were an outrageous psychedelic rock group from Birmingham who were very slick, turning out hits like 'Flowers in the Rain', 'Do Ya' and 'Night of Fear'. The Move were wicked-sounding, they were clever in their playing and great live. But their claim to fame was getting sued for libel by Prime Minister Harold Wilson – they depicted him naked on a flyer. The band responded by saying stuff like, we voted for Frank Zappa and Jimi Hendrix, but the PM won. Soon after, Jeff Lynne, Bev Bevan and Roy Wood left and went on to form Electric Light Orchestra.

The Blue Boar. A motorway services station on the M1, near Watford Gap. Every band always stopped there for food and coffee on the way home from a gig in the middle of the night. There was no live music at the Blue Boar, just a jukebox, but it was the most wished-on jukebox in England because every musician who ever went there wished that he was one of the

Walker brothers, or would one day hear his latest song being played on it when he walked in. The Blue Boar was so much a part of British 1960s rock legend, and word spread so far and wide about it, that when Hendrix first came to London he thought the Blue Boar was a club and wanted to know who was playing there that night.

The Blue Boar was one of the best places in England to meet other musicians, but it could be a dangerous place because this was the mods versus rockers era, a bizarre time which was all about how you dressed, what you rode and the kind of music you listened to. The rockers thought the mods were stuck-up rich kids who drove good motors or rode Vespas or Lambrettas, and could afford to get high on the uppers known as 'purple hearts'. The mods thought the rockers were working-class troublemakers who rode around on Triumph bikes and got drunk on cheap beer. Mods dressed sharp, and liked jazz, blues, soul, R&B, Jamaican bluebeat and ska. The rockers wore jeans and leather, thought they were the British version of the Hell's Angels, slicked back their hair, rode souped-up bikes and were totally sold on Elvis, Gene Vincent and Eddie Cochran.

That would have been fine, as far as I'm concerned, except that whenever the two groups met, they'd fight. The most famous confrontation was on a 1964 bank holiday Monday along the south coast. More than 600 mods and rockers turned Brighton, Margate and Broadstairs into a battlefield. When the smoke cleared, fifty kids got arrested and a few of them got stabbed.

The further north you went on the M1, the more the rockers would attack the mods. The further south you went, the more the mods would be after the rockers. If you didn't play the music the crowd wanted to hear, you'd get glass bottles thrown at you, or they'd toss those big old pennies at you which, apparently, hurt a lot if they hit you. Luckily, we didn't get that with the Birds, or even later with the Jeff Beck Group, because the crowds generally liked what we played. But I knew plenty of bands that did get it, got booed off, and got hurt too, especially in Scotland. Glasgow was the toughest venue. My personal philosophy whenever fights broke out was, I'm getting the hell out of here. With the Birds, we had Colin to help us escape before anything serious happened. Or, if necessary, do the fighting for us. I stayed out of mods and rocker arguments and remained a 'mocker'.

Both sides knew that all the bands stopped at the Blue Boar, and they used to lay in wait there just to start a fight. One night at the Blue Boar with Jeff Beck, we were eating when we noticed these rockers out by the petrol pumps, ganging up with clubs, baseball bats and tyre irons and looking straight at us. I knew this was going to be trouble and wanted to sneak out before anything happened, but Jeff started antagonizing them, yelling from behind the window, 'Fuck off, you cunts,' and making all sorts of gestures.

I asked Jeff if he had any other bright ideas, like, 'How the fuck are we going to get out of here now?'

The only thing he could think of was to make a run for it. So we dropped our food and raced out of the café, heading straight for the car. Our driver on that night was a delicate woman and by no means a getaway driver. The rockers came after us. Jeff got behind the wheel and revved up, the woman slid in the passenger side, and when I saw the back window open I leapt straight through it, head first. Those guys in leather got to the car and started banging on it so Jeff threw the car into reverse, which pinned one of the rockers against the petrol pumps, then put the car in forward gear and pinned another rocker against the wall. These guys were furious now and were still climbing and hammering on the car as we skidded out of there. The same scenario happened on a train in Italy, in Italian. We scarpered again.

After a time, my success with the Birds had made me just about enough money to buy my first custom guitar. I had it made at Jim Marshall's of Ealing and Terry Marshall (he used to accompany the Everly Brothers and was a man to admire) sorted it for me. Mine was a converted Fender Telecaster body with a Danelectro twelve-string neck which I ordered in emerald green. I also got a double cabinet speaker stack made there, a huge thing with eight twelve-inch speakers in one cabinet instead of the usual four. In those days, Pete Townshend was getting famous for having all his speakers in big stacks. I was in Marshall's picking up mine when he came in and the minute he saw my double cabinet, he looked at me and said, 'You bastard.' I beat him to it. To take it a step further I customized my amp to 200 watts. The control did indeed go to eleven.

So all of us spent our time playing music together and getting to know each other. When some people reminisce about the good old days, they claim not to have realized how exciting the time was, but *I* knew. I knew how good Clapton, Townshend and Richards were when they were first breaking it. It was easy to see they were stars in the making.

Speaking of Clapton, I was watching his band the Yardbirds at the Crawdaddy when I met Krissie, the girl who would go on to be my first wife. She was with Eric at the time and as the Yardbirds were the Sunday-night house band, she was watching them perform. I was there because I liked their music, especially Eric's playing. It was the night their harmonica player, Keith Relf, failed to show because he was sick. One of the band asked, 'Anybody here play the harp?'

My mates pushed me forward, shouting, 'He does, he does,'

and just like that I was jamming with the Yardbirds. We did 'I'm a Man', and they must have thought I was pretty good because they gave me a few solos.

After the gig they were all saying, 'Get that guy backstage, the one who looks like Cleopatra,' because they liked the way I played, which really boosted my confidence.

Somehow, Krissie became my girl, and Eric used to remind me of that whenever we met. 'You pinched my bird, Woody.' Krissie was my girl and I knew she was special, but I can't pretend she was the only one.

Pete McDaniels had a flat in Westbourne Grove with a lot of extra rooms where we would party, so my London-based philandering went on there. When I moved out of my parents' place, I got a flat with a few friends on Edgehill Road in Ealing near where Krissie was still living with her parents. Not long after I moved in down the block, her parents moved up north. She insisted on staying in the family flat and as soon as they were gone, I moved in with her.

One day in 1965, I was hanging out at the Intrepid Fox, a pub on Wardour Street where a lot of musicians used to hang, when a fellow walked in wearing a big checkered Coco the Clown jacket, with his hair sticking up – almost exactly like mine – and sporting a real shiner of a black eye. We looked at each other and that's when he just walked up to me and said, 'Hello, face, how are you?' The bloke with the black eye was Rod 'The Mod' Stewart. We turned out to be kindred spirits. He'd just had a record out called 'Good Morning Little School Girl', which was starting to climb up the charts. I knew his music and admired what he was doing. He told me the same thing about my music. Back then, two blokes with the same haircut couldn't escape each other for long.

We started drinking and talking and it was as if we'd known

each other forever. We talked about bands and exchanged influences – vocalists like Sam Cooke, Otis Redding, Arthur Connolly and Jo Tex, and on the guitar side Buddy Guy, Robert Johnson and Broonzy. We sat shooting port and brandy and discussed various clubs we'd both played in, and the people we knew in common, how we had the same middle name and agreed that our favourite group was the Small Faces.

Several months after meeting Rod, I got a phone call at Whitethorn Avenue from Mick Jagger wanting to know if I'd play on a session. Yes, no doubt. He said he was producing a record for PP Arnold. She was a terrific singer and had been Ike and Tina Turner's backup vocalist. I would have been happy to play on any session for her, but this was even better because she was to do a duet with Rod. They were going to do the Gerry Goffin and Carole King song 'Come Home Baby'. Mick said he wanted me on the session because 'Rod likes you.'

I was there in a flash. Mick and I hit it off really well from then. The session was at the Olympic Studios and it was the first time I really met Keith (the swine who would become my lifelong weaving partner, brother and mate). He was at the studio, listening to a freshly laid-down track. I grabbed a drink, took a sip and went over to say hi. Just as I approached him, I stumbled a little and poured my drink on him. We laughed it off and cracked on. The manner in which our relationship started pre-empted how it would go on. Him with the upper hand. Conquering Buccaneer. I think for the next forty years I have been the little brother, his sparring partner and the new boy.

The other guys on the session included Keith Emerson on organ and, of course, Keith on guitar. That left me to play bass, which I hadn't done before. But that didn't matter. There was no way I was going to miss out on the session.

The next thing I knew, Rod was seeing Krissie's friend Sara Troupe. So Krissie and I started hanging out with Rod and Sara at her tasty flat just off the Fulham Road, and the four of us spent days and nights laughing, singing, watching Jacques Tati films and going everywhere together. In those early times with Rod, our friendship was clearly cemented by our taste in music. We had the same yearning, that eye of the tiger, and knew we were going to make a statement. We were also brought together in constant competition over our appearance. I used to go shopping with Marc Bolan, normally to a shop on the Fulham Road called Alcazura, where we would purchase the most outrageous stuff available. When Rod and I started hanging out we would go there too, but also to an Aladdin's cave called Granny Takes A Trip on the King's Road. We'd run around the shop causing mayhem and trying on outfit after outfit, each attempting to be more extrovert than the other.

'*I* want that one!'

'No, Bowie's got that. You can't wear it.'

'You've nicked the jacket I wanted!'

And so on. Laden with clothes we'd normally jump into Rod's car and speed off. Rod has always loved motors. He started with a Spitfire but as soon as he made a little dosh, he bought a Marcos, then made more cash. The cars got better and better – until finally, with the help of 'Maggie May', he hit the realm of the Lamborghini.

The Birds, filthy from all those trips up the M1, had shot themselves from the sky and were just floating on thermals. We had left Leo and escaped into the arms of Robert Stigwood.

He was a wonderfully over the top Australian impresario, who paraded though the London music and theatre scene, making and losing his fortune three or four times over. Robert

ROD STEWART

DECAY ON THE HORIZON

HAPPY BIRTHDAY RON FROM ROD

And as life's thread becomes diabolically thin
Through riotous rape of hemp and gin
With retirement's shadow short fifteen years away
When knee and vest become bent and grey

For as the trumpets herald the coming party
Let us not get too arty farty
But remember 'pon days of feeble beginnings
When Father would prod to begin the innings.

C. Findlay may recall it quite profusely
With flared loon pant worn around Yewsley
Between the sheets you always left a puddle
Which Mother would remove with chisel and shovel.

And so Ronaldo, my dear old thing
You must strum and I must sing
No more chasing of skirt and kife
For this be the tea time of our life

While postage stamps may come and go
Our flea infested friendship will neither wither nor bow
While some may mock and suggest incontinence
Let this night not be spent in toilets and the like,
    talking nonsense to anybody who will listen and therefore,
    without due regard I must wilfully beg indifference to any
    blotch left on my character, because of ill fitting dentures.

Yours, R.S.

15th June 2007.

To Roderick and Penny ～
　　　　～ on their wedding day!!!

　　Being blessed with exceptional fortunes and outstanding slitherings on this day of much aptitude. One cannot help thinking how great it would be, (if like me and my wife), you two got married as well!!!

　　What better choice to pick a woman, who, (like my wife), was born on the 15th of March.

　　This noble binding of woman and beast has indeed not gone unnoticed by me, as I sit in my historic Parisien surroundings wishing I could be with you.

　　Please be blessed with all the hapinness you can muster and may your union withstand the utterances of time and last forever!!!

　　　your oldest pal in the world.....

　　　Ronnie (and his wife Josephine)
　　　　x x x

was then only about thirty-two years old. He'd been partners with Brian Epstein, who managed the Beatles until he died, then formed his own company and handled just about everybody from Mick Jagger, Rod Stewart, David Bowie and the Bee Gees to Blind Faith, Cream and Eric Clapton. From there he went on to produce plays in the West End such as *Hair*, *Jesus Christ Superstar*, *Evita* and *Oh! Calcutta!* Robert had a great sense of humour and I liked him a lot. It was difficult to get close to him though; he was always plotting mad schemes and flirting with the pretty-boy actors he managed alongside us (or trying it on with our bass player, Kim).

It was very cool when Stigwood signed us for the Reaction record label in late 1965, which he also owned, because that meant we were in seriously good company. We especially liked going up to his office because you never knew who you were going to meet there, or what was going to happen. One afternoon while we were there Cream's mad drummer, Ginger Baker, strolled in, went up to Stigwood and announced, 'I hate that tie you're wearing,' grabbed a pair of scissors and cut it off.

We knew we weren't huge stars but we thought of ourselves as a relatively successful group. Yet for some bizarre reason, Stigwood saw things differently and came up with the high-blown idea that we needed to be repackaged. He said he wanted to change the group's concept and the first step was to change our name from the Birds to the Birds-Birds. Huh?

To this day I'm still asking myself why. It didn't make sense to me, or to any of us, but he assured us, 'You're with new management now,' and promised us the world if we went along with his scheme. We were confused and kept asking if he was sure. And he kept telling us, believe me, trust me. So we did.

Unfortunately for us, nothing wonderful ever happened. We did one record for Robert at Reaction – a cover of 'Say Those

Magic Words', which had been a big hit for the McCoys – but it failed to chart. Our name change simply confused those fans we once had. By the end of 1966 nothing was happening for us any more. We were finished. The remaining four of us split up because there was nowhere else to go, nothing else we could do with the band and we felt that this particular dead horse had been flogged enough.

I still get cheques for Birds' royalties. I think the last one was £17.06.

4

Apprenticeship

My move from band to band has been determined by my uncanny ability to be in the right place at the right time. Fate, luck and talent seem to come round just when I need them, putting a deal on the table right in front of me, on an irresistible plate.

The group that was called the Yardbirds when we were called the Birds only lasted a little longer than us, but they remain legendary in the story of rock and roll because they boasted three of the world's greatest ever guitar players – Eric Clapton, Jeff Beck and Jimmy Page.

Clapton came in to replace the original lead guitar, Anthony 'Top' Topham, and Jeff Beck came in to replace Clapton. Actually, the band's first choice to replace Eric was Jimmy Page, but he wasn't available so recommended his mate Jeff. Then, when the group's original bass player, Paul Samwell-Smith, the 'screaming skull', decided to leave, Jeff recommended that they bring in his mate Jimmy. So Jimmy started on bass but almost immediately moved up to share lead guitar with Jeff, which wasn't exactly Jeff's idea of a good time because he couldn't handle sharing guitar with Jimmy (or anybody, for that matter) so he quit. Still following? Good.

I used to see the Yardbirds whenever they came to Richmond, and always admired the way Jeff played. He was one of the first people on the music scene to fool around with electronic distortion, he milked foot pedals, fuzztones and feedback, and in a way he set the stage for the kind of sound that Hendrix would make famous as his own.

I met him pretty much at the end of his Yardbirds career, at Peter Stringfellow's Mojo Club in Sheffield. It was perfect timing. The Birds were finished, I was looking for a gig, so when I heard Jeff had left the Yardbirds I rang him up. I didn't know if he'd remember me, but he said he knew exactly who I was, and I breathed a big sigh of relief before asking him, 'What are you going to do?' He shrugged before asking, 'Do you fancy getting a band together?'

Before long we were speeding along in his Corvette Stingray, blaring out music, showing each other the sounds we loved. Buddy Guy, Vanilla Fudge and Chicago blues were devoured as we gathered riffs and licks on the guitar. I'd lost none of my enthusiasm for creating and was ready to grab the next opportunity. We spent the first two months of 1967 together, rehearsing at a studio on Gerrard Street in Soho before going out on the road.

The line-up was Jeff, me, a vocalist Jeff brought in called Roderick David Stewart and his choice of drummer, a paranoid Woody Allen type called Mickey Waller. We were ready to rock, target and conquer America with our new band, and with Jeff's experience in America we felt nothing could stop us.

Rod Stewart was born in London a couple of years before me and originally hoped to be a footballer. As a kid he tried out for Brentford but didn't make the team – not that it's stopped him hoping, or supporting Scotland and Celtic. Today Rod has his own football pitch to practise on at his treasured Los Angeles home, Celtic House, just in case Brentford ever ring back.

Soon after we first met, I loved watching him play with his extensive model railway extravaganza at his parents' house in

Highgate, North London. Rod had a collection of Hornby 00 train-set models and accessories that was second to none (apart from perhaps that of Sir Bob Pridden, the Who's most reputable roadie). I actually spent a few vividly uncomfortable nights sleeping underneath that train-set construction.

Rod sang and played harmonica for a band in Birmingham when he was eighteen. I think they made one record, and he sometimes found work as a session musician. The rest of the time (besides football) his interests were sports cars and women, but not necessarily in that order. In his mind, a sports car was what you needed to get the women. He decided that he would be able to buy himself a sports car if he started busking. So he played wherever he could, often along the beach in Brighton, then passed the hat.

It was while he was busking one night on the platform at Twickenham station that Rod was discovered. The great British blues singer Long John Baldry was waiting for a train on the other platform and heard Rod, who was wearing all his scarves, singing a Muddy Waters song and playing the harp. Long John called out, 'Hey, you, that bundle of rags over there, you got some talent,' crossed over to the other platform, introduced himself and asked Rod if he wanted to join his band, the Hoochie Coochie Men.

Rod couldn't believe his luck, especially when Long John offered him £35 a week, which meant that six months at that rate would buy him his Austin Healy Sprite, so he said yes on the spot. Baldry changed the band's name to Steampacket, and rehearsed only once before Rod's first gig at Manchester University. That night he sang the only song he knew all the lyrics to, Ray Charles' 'The Night Time (Is the Right Time)'. He was so nervous before he went on that one of the blokes in the band handed him some amphetamines, a pill known as a 'black bomber', and with that in his system, Rod kept singing the same verses over and over again, making the song last twenty minutes. Baldry found out about the speed, fired the band member who'd corrupted such a poor young boy, and then set about teaching Rod a bunch of new songs and how to sing them onstage.

Getting discovered in this way put Rod into great company because at various points in his career Baldry also worked with Brian Auger, Julie Driscoll, Ginger Baker, Jeff Beck, Jimmy Page, Nicky Hopkins, Brian Jones, Charlie Watts, Mick Jagger and a keyboard player named Reg Dwight. Reg was in Baldry's Bluesology band. He admired John Baldry and the group's saxophonist Elton Dean so much he decided to take their first names for himself, thus creating Elton John.

Baldry stood six foot seven, which is why everyone called him Long John, always wore a tie, had a proper English accent and a wonderfully deep voice. He was the most elegant gentle giant you could ever meet. In 1962 he had the trailblazing Blues Incorporated, the first blues band in England really. In the very early days of the Rolling Stones they opened shows for him and would eventually return the favour by having him open for them. He also performed with the Beatles in 1964. He wasn't someone you heard on the radio a lot, or saw much on telly, because he was a club performer. But he was the first white guy in Britain to sing the blues the way the black guys in America were doing it. When I heard he'd passed away in 2005 aged sixty-four, I thought about the effect he'd had, and how much we all owed him.

After Steampacket, Rod joined Mick Fleetwood and Peter Green in a band called Shotgun Express, which didn't last long enough for them to finish a song. That's when, in Feburary 1967, we joined forces with Jeff Beck.

It took a long time for our group to settle. Kim Gardner was brought in to play bass, Jet Harris was there for a day, and Jeff and I shared lead guitar for most of the rehearsal months. Then Roger Cook replaced Viv on drums, until Rod Coombs replaced Roger. The closer we got to our first date, the more Jeff was bothered about sharing lead guitar with me. We did one gig together at the Marquee with two guitars, and everyone told us we were real good, but Jeff couldn't live with it.

He'd handed over his lead-guitar job in the Yardbirds to Jimmy, saw lead guitar in this group as his rightful role and wasn't going to risk losing it to me. So he asked if I fancied playing bass. I looked at it as a good challenge and wanted to prove myself on a new instrument, so I started trying to master it in the week and was playing it by the weekend. *Carpe Diem*.

Taking over as bass player in the Jeff Beck Group presented two problems. First, it meant we would be without Kim. He was gracious about stepping aside and I got to play my four-string challenge. Second, I didn't own a bass guitar. I was still living at home and had no money to buy one. Instead, I did the next best thing and sort-of-borrowed one for twenty years.

We were rehearsing in Gerrard Street. Dave Ambrose (who went on to become head of EMI) was sitting in with us on bass, but Jeff was pushing me to get one of my own, so I went along to Sound City and found a Fender Jazz that I fancied. It didn't matter that I couldn't afford it, because the store clerk wouldn't sell it to me. He said, 'You're not twenty-one and you can't buy this guitar. The only way you can have it is if you get your parents to guarantee the purchase.'

I said, okay, yeah why not, and gave him my parents' names and our address, even though the purchase wasn't quite what I had in mind. I asked to see the manager and when he arrived I enquired, 'Could I please just borrow the Fender for the afternoon?' He gave me an odd look. I explained that I had this really important job, and that my entire career totally depended on me playing bass right away.

I got the guitar home and later I filed it down to the wood, shaved off the sunburst finish, and got it just the way I wanted it. Before I had a chance to return it, we went on tour. Over the years I guess I just got too busy to give it back. But every time I saw the bass guitar I felt bad because it reminded me how kind they were at Sound City to let me use it, and I still have it in my studio in Ireland.

There is, however, a happy ending. Many years after I sort-of-borrowed it, I went back to Sound City and told them about the guitar. They looked it up in their records and said, 'As a matter of fact that guitar was never returned.'

I admitted, 'I'm the guy who stole it and I've come here to pay you for it.' And I did.

Playing bass was funky and I always used heavy wirewound strings that gave me my own particular sound, which inspired others like Stanley Clark. I took to it, and started playing really well. On 3 March 1967 the Jeff Beck Group, with me on bass, opened at the Finsbury Park Astoria, the famous North London venue. The gig didn't go as planned. Right in the middle there was a blackout.

We thought it was our equipment that had knocked the lights off, but rumours have circulated since about one of the Small Faces, who were also on the bill that night. Supposedly their keyboard player, Ian McLagan, mischievously decided to pull the plug on our show. I should ask him really.

Jeff stormed offstage and instantly fired our drummer, Rod Coombs. I have no idea why. The papers slammed us the next day and because Jeff always took everything pretty seriously, he felt like pulling out of our tour and disbanding the group. Record producer Mickie Most (who was trying to mould Jeff into a frontman figure) stepped in and a few days after our dire opening night at the Astoria, we were back together again doing a radio show and things started moving. Mickie brought us into the studio to record 'Old Man River' and we had Keith Moon on drums and Jimmy Page on guitar.

At the height of the 'flower power' craze, Jeff made us all wear flowers and caftans at the Saville theatre. The rest of the band thought the craze was ridiculous and would don ridiculous outfits, wear far too many flowers and tie so many scarves around each other that we had difficulty moving. Mickey Waller came back to join the fun, we toured England, appeared on radio shows and turned out a few hits, like 'Hi Ho Silver Lining', which featured Jeff as vocalist and Rod as backup. Jeff hated playing this song live but it stayed in the charts for fourteen weeks and still remains the football stadium chant for QPR.

We were touring the country non-stop, making a name for ourselves with Jeff at the helm, and in my mind all those nights are all jumbled together as one very drunken, frantic, exciting long year.

I am an artist..... I am here to live out loud.
    Emile Zola.

One night, however, does particularly stand out as it was literally the most shocking of my life. We were playing one of the Starlight Ballroom venues up north and I unthinkingly moved a microphone whilst touching the bass strings with my other hand. With a VERY large bang I was catapaulted over the piano and ended up on my back.

The audience thought, yeah great, wow, do it again, Woody, but I had become the earth of an entire very loud gig, connecting the full pelt of all our equipment. A roadie realized what had happened and unplugged me. They took me to hospital in between sets. I had burns on both my hands and after the doctor heard what happened he looked at me and said, 'All I can tell you, Mr Wood, is that you've got a really strong heart.' Then they drove me back to the bingo hall and we did the second set. I played with a refreshed, somewhat recharged look on life.

So it was time to go to America with the band. It was my first trip there, as well as Rod's, and before we left England, we used to tell each other that America was overrun with guns, hookers and pimps. When we finally got there, we discovered we were right. For young English boys like us, the States were frightening, but musically we stormed the place. We played Fillmore East in New York, where Jimi Hendrix jammed with us and I asked Mitch Mitchell what it was like being in a band with him. 'Oh it's great, Woody, he's really easy to work with and really fair, there's three of us in the group and he splits everything down the middle.'

The US tour was Jeff, Rod, Mickey and me, plus Nicky Hopkins on keyboard. He later played the piano on John Lennon's beautiful song 'Imagine', and was also on Joe Cocker's first record, 'Margarine'.

We played the infamous Fillmore West in San Francisco, where Rod was so nervous that he sang the first three numbers from behind the amps where nobody could see him. We rocked just about every venue going, including another four or five dates with Hendrix as our guest. We blew everyone else off stage, including the Grateful Dead and Moby Grape.

A reviewer from the *New York Times* wrote that the interplay between Jeff Beck and Rod Stewart was like a Harold Pinter play. We had that review blown up and sent everywhere across the country where we were going to perform. We were established coast to coast.

The way tours got booked in those days meant you had to go for three months. That was the way promoters made lots of

money off your back. But three months is a long time to be away from home, and seemed even longer when you were travelling in a strange place without much money.

Our hotels were paid for, which meant the cheapest rooms in town. We paid for our own food, and to survive on the road without starving, we had to get very good and very fast at helping ourselves to extra portions. That usually meant stealing eggs and anything else we could get from restaurants like Horn & Hardart.

We also discovered red vermouth, and got fucking ripped on the stuff, because it was cheap and we liked it and it softened stage fright perfectly. Back home, we would play to audiences of several hundred people but in the States we were getting audiences of several thousand, and for a long time Rod found it terrifying. We drank before going onstage, but were sober as soon as we got up there because we were too busy concentrating on the music. The vermouth came out again as soon as we got off stage, this time to celebrate.

We were young and we could handle it. We had a funny kind of body clock. We didn't do anything all day, then got hammered every night. However, no matter what we did (or drank) we couldn't hide the boredom and the fact that we were all hopelessly homesick. Without any money, sharing a three-minute phone call to England was the most Rod and I could afford. Rod would get on the phone with Sara, or whoever, say I miss you and I love you, and I'd be there with a stopwatch, counting down ninety seconds. Then I would grab the phone away from him, get Krissie on the line and tell her the same.

Day after day on the road, our loneliness increased. It was terrible and everyone got depressed. I found myself in charge of keeping up morale, which usually meant more red vermouth. Everyone always wanted to abandon the tour, people shouting, 'I'm going home,' but none of us did because none of us could. We had no money to run away with, which is exactly how our manager Peter Grant had it worked out. We'd complain, try to get money out of him and he'd bark, 'You ain't going nowhere!'

Although Peter didn't treat the rest of us as well as he treated Jeff and himself, he did in the early days offer me the chance of being in a band other than the Jeff Beck Group. He told me that a bunch of blokes were putting a band together and intended to call themselves the New Yardbirds. Peter said, 'They want you as their guitar player.'

Well, I'd met a few of them up at his office, including the rude drummer John Bonham, who reminded me of a farmer, bassist John Paul Jones and the harmless enough Robert Plant, and I told Peter, 'No, I'm happy where I am thanks.'

He insisted, 'This is an offer you really must consider.'

I considered it for two seconds, and then told him again, 'No way.' The New Yardbirds hired Jimmy Page instead and changed their name to Led Zeppelin.

Peter Grant's dedication to Jeff made touring with them an endless uphill battle, though Rod and I both loved meeting the other bands we were bumping into all over the country. We'd be on the same circuit as Sly and the Family Stone, coming across bands like Cream and a group called Savoy Brown. We got to know Jethro Tull (we called them Jethro Dull, Bore 'Em at the Forum), the 'Grateful When', and we were always bumping into the Who. By now we were referring to them as the World Health Organization.

I also discovered southern California on those tours, and my first port of call became the Continental Riot House. It was real fucking mayhem there. The actual name of the place was the Hyatt House and it was the first rock and roll hotel in Hollywood. Everyone came through it. It was on Sunset Boulevard and someone told me the legendary cowboy Gene Autry owned it.

Things happened there all the time with bands moving in and out. There was music everywhere and wall-to-wall groupies. Keith Moon once got caught climbing the side of the building. He also drilled a hole through his wall so that he could get next door and into bed with John Entwhistle for a nap. Over the years I imagine more furniture wound up in the pool than they ever managed to put in the rooms.

On one trip through, I met The Mothers of Invention and fell for Suzy Creamcheese, who was part of that Frank Zappa band. Frank lived in Tom Mix's old house in Laurel Canyon. Tom was another old cowboy and had his horse stuffed and on display in his bowling alley in the basement. He invited me over and when I first met Suzy I asked her, 'Which one are you?' She said, 'I'm the present Suzy Creamcheese.' I still don't know exactly which number Suzy she was because there were three or four of them overall. Anyway, it didn't seem to matter at the time. She was stunning.

On the subject of women, on another Beck tour I fell for Kathy James, who is famous in rock and roll mythology because she was the original groupie. An absolutely gorgeous woman, believe me, she had a special feel for special musicians.

In those days we didn't have the money to bring our wives or girlfriends. I'd be gone for months, come home, reunite with Krissie, then head out on the road again. Nowadays, I'd rather take the wife with me than kiss her goodbye. Sorry, that's an old Max Miller joke.

It was beginning to become clear that our manager had seriously different agendas for us all. Grant was focussed on Jeff and Rod while Nicky and I had to make do. Krissie and I were living in the Old Forge at Henley-on-Thames and I was about to return to America with the group in March 1969, when a day or two before I was scheduled to leave, Peter Grant called to say, 'Woody, you're fired.'

I went, 'Oh really?'

He said, 'Jeff wants to get a new rhythm section so you and Mickey Waller are both gone.'

I said, 'Okay, if you think you can beat us, go right ahead,' put the phone down and thought, 'Bloody hell, what am I going to do now?' and then, 'Peter Grant is a shit.'

Jeff and the group flew out to America as planned, minus Mickey and me, and met up with a new rhythm section.

The new drummer, Tony Newman, hailed from Sounds Incorporated, but he could never play a shuffle like Mickey Waller, no one could. Mickey never owned his own drums, but could pick up any old kit and play shuffle better than anyone, including Mick Fleetwood. Mickey was the man.

The new bass player was Douglas Blake, a very pretty Australian boy who always wore a light-coloured raincoat onstage, and fingerless gloves when he played. I knew straight away he wasn't going to last long.

Just as I found myself unemployed, almost as soon as I put the phone down on Peter, Kenny Pickett rang up to say he had reformed the band Creation and wanted to tour Germany. The band was nearly complete but Eddie Phillips wasn't interested, so Kim asked me if I wanted to play lead guitar. That sounded like more fun than working with Jeff Beck (and definitely more fun than not working for anybody), especially because Creation were so huge in Germany – so big, in fact, that Diana Ross and the Supremes were billed to support them.

They wanted me to do the same tricks that Eddie Phillips used to do onstage, like playing guitar with a violin bow. That was strange, more of a gimmick than anything else, but it looked cool. So I was thrown in at the deep end and had to learn how to play with a bow very quickly.

Even more fun, Phillips painted onstage. I loved that. I would set up a big canvas plus a bucket of black paint, and every night while we performed I would somehow paint and play. I'm not sure how good my onstage paintings were or what happened to them, but I suspect they were trampled to death as soon as we left the stage. Painting while we played was way ahead of its time and added excitement to the show. Plus I got to do my two favourite jobs at the same time.

The band didn't last much longer than that tour because it was disorganized and everybody involved was pulling in different directions. Years later they tried to put it together yet again, but by then it was too late. Kim Gardner had formed Ashton, Gardner & Dyke, who hit big with 'Resurrection Shuffle', while Kenny Pickett had gone back to being a roadie (this time for Led Zeppelin).

Great timing though, because as soon as I got home I received a desperate call from Peter Grant saying the new rhythm section hadn't worked out and Jeff really wanted us back. The dispensable Mickey and Ronnie weren't so dispensable after all.

I loved hearing Grant squirm and said, 'Only on my own terms.' He asked, 'How much?' '£2,000 a week.' Which was enormous money then. To my surprise, Peter agreed.

So I went back to the States with the Jeff Beck Group for a fourth (and fifth) time, but with each trip life on tour become more and more miserable. This was mainly due to my feeling that Jeff had gradually become impossible to work with.

The only compensation, besides the money, was that Rod was getting more and more fun to hang out with.

We shared a room, and were always worried that one of us would see what the other was doing whenever we brought birds back, which was often. So as soon as we arrived in any hotel, we would construct a partition between our beds, piling up a mountain of chairs and cushions and anything else we could find in the room, so that we each had some privacy. That worked out fine, but we soon decided it would be hilariously funny if we had 'accidents' at exactly the same time, deliberately crashing into the partition and knocking it down. The chairs and cushions would tumble, we'd be all legs and arms everywhere, the girls would scream with embarrassment and shout at us that we were horrible, and Rod and I would be doubled over with hysterics.

Another game we played was 'Wood and Stewart Operations', featuring Dr Wood and Dr Stewart, plus any willing groupies in our room. Rod and I dressed up like doctors, with white blouses and even stethoscopes telling our 'patients' that we needed to carry out medical examinations and might even have to 'operate' as well. Some girls looked at us in horror and made a bolt for the door. But others were game, thought we were funny and loved playing along with us, gynaecologists at large.

5

Chuch

On our third tour of the States the Faces played two nights at the Grande Ballroom in Detroit, Michigan. The band was really huge there, and always loved coming to Detroit because it was then the best rock and roll city in America. Those Detroit audiences always seemed to recognize and appreciate that here we were, five English blokes under the influence of American R&B, who had grown up with skiffle, which had its roots in bluegrass and the blues, and were mixing up the two to make something new and different, something that white audiences in the States weren't hearing from American bands.

We also thought it was a terrific city because it was filled with girls looking for dates. Not that we minded at the time, but none of us understood until much later why there were so many available girls in Detroit – all their boyfriends had gone off to Vietnam.

Because we were too poor, or, more likely, because Peter was too cheap to shell out any money on us, we didn't have roadies travelling with us (apart from Peter Buckland, who introduced me to Zemaitis guitars), so in Detroit, like all the other cities we played, we had to hire locals.

Roadies have always been an essential element in every band, because roadies make everything work. They look after the guitars, the amps, the drums, everything we call 'the back line'. Each guitar has to be tuned differently, a bass guitar is only four strings and they're really fat, whereas rhythm and lead guitars are a different game altogether, so the roadies have to know which guitar is going to be used on which song and tune it accordingly, whether it's open E or an open G, whatever. Being a roadie has always been hard work, but in those days it was even harder because if a gig was scheduled for eight that night, the band might not get there until nine and then only go on at eleven, but the roadie might have to be there from nine in the morning because he had the whole stage to do and very often unions to put up with. Then he couldn't leave until hours after the show because he had to load everything into a truck so that he could drive on to the next gig. Those guys never slept. It's not like today when bands have packers and drivers.

The roadie I got for those two nights was a white guy with a huge afro from Marquette, Michigan, who was only a few months younger than me and who had the unlikely name of Royden Walter Magee. But nobody ever called him Royden, he was known to everyone simply as Chuch.

After our second show at the Grande I said, 'Thanks, Chuch, for taking such good care of me,' and then, never thinking that I'd ever see him again, made the usual offer of 'If you ever come to England, call me.'

A few months later, Chuch arrived on English soil for some reason. I'm not sure I ever knew what he was supposed to be doing here, but he promptly got mugged and lost everything, even his luggage. He had absolutely nothing except he did have my phone number in his pocket, so he rang me and told me what he'd just been through. I said, 'Then you better come over, welcome to England.'

Krissie and I were now living in Ravenswood Court, in Kingston Hill, which I'd only just bought for £12,000 the year before. We had a parrott called Sadie who lived by the front door and whenever anyone opened it, the bird would welcome guests with a particular greeting. Chuch showed up and Sadie gave him the usual welcome, 'Fuck off, fuck off.' Chuch stayed for thirty-two years. He became my permanent roadie, part of the Rolling Stones family, and a legend in rock and roll.

We moved Chuch into the minuscule second bedroom in what was already a very tiny house. There was a kitchen, our bedroom, that second bedroom and one bathroom. The rest of the house, the main room which we could have used as a sitting room and a dining room, was going to be my music studio. Until Chuch arrived I was building it myself, putting the rock wall in, and putting in the two-by-fours, doing everything. Now that he was there, we got it finished.

I hired Chuch as my full-time roadie and he stayed with me through the Faces and the Stones. It was unheard of in those days to have an American crew working with an English band in England, so Chuch was the first, but Chuch was also the best, in spite of the fact that he was tone deaf.

In the beginning, he tuned the guitars visually. He could see the tension on the strings, and I'd have to tell him when he was an octave out. But by the mid-1980s he was doing it perfectly, with the aid of a strobo-tuner, which makes it possible for a non-player.

So Chuch looked after my guitars and my amps, and during his years with the Stones he looked after Charlie's drum kit too. Charlie only travelled with one kit, plus a couple of spare drums, skins and cymbals if something went wrong, and because Charlie is Charlie, he's extremely choosy what he plays with and just as choosy when it comes to letting anyone near his kit. Chuch was the first, and maybe the only, person that Charlie ever really trusted with his drums. Stu (the founder key-boardist, road manager and trusted friend of the Stones) would always mess with the way he tuned his skins.

Chuch could also do a mean piano set-up, with all the pick-ups in the piano for Ian McLagan during the Faces years and Ian Stewart with the Stones. That's a very tricky job because you have to cover the bass, middle and top end of the piano in order to get the whole range. Chuch could also set up the sound system for the vocalists.

Come to think of it, Chuch could single-handedly do every-thing for the whole band, if it came down to it. He also wel-comed my wife Jo with open arms when she came on tour for the first time. He made the whole tour thing a lot easier for her, showed her the ropes and became a great friend of hers. He even initiated her into his roadie group 'the Hardcore'. This was a tough hardcore unit made up of only the toughest roadies including Johnny Starbuck, Gary Schultz and Ernie. Jo was the only girl member.

In July 2002, Chuch died of a heart attack at the age of fifty-four, during a Stones rehearsal in Toronto, while we were preparing to go out on the Forty Licks tour. All of us were dev-astated. He was our crew chief and our road manager, but most of all, he was our friend for more than thirty years.

The band and the whole crew went to his funeral in Mar-quette, Michigan. We bought him a maple casket because guitar necks and drumsticks are made out of maple. Mick, Keith and Darryl Jones got up with me as I played 'Amazing Grace' on my lap steel to him and his wife Clare.

There hasn't been a day gone by that someone in the band or someone in the crew doesn't talk about him. A few of the guys in the crew even have black T-shirts that they wear on the set, with five white letters across the front: CHUCH. He was the leader of the pack.

During the Bigger Bang tour, Chuch's mum turned up. Everyone drops everything when we know she's backstage. She treats us like family, and so she should. What a surprise. She'd come backstage, telling everybody, 'You'll have to get the cavalry out to keep me away from you boys.'

We all kissed her hello and were thrilled to see her, she's like ninety years old, and suddenly she peeled up her jumper to show us a T-shirt with a Japanese cartoon on it of Chuch and all the Stones. Fabulous.

I said, 'Mrs Magee, can you please put your tits away,' and she said right away, 'These aren't my tits, that's my son.'

Chuch is still rocking.

6

Faces

In between my fourth and fifth tour of the States with Jeff Beck, Steve Marriott of the Small Faces announced that being in that band was no good for him any more, and left to join up with Pete Frampton and form Humble Pie. I can't imagine why he did that, except perhaps because that's when he started to lose it. They'd just made *Ogden's Nut Gone Flake*, which is an amazing album. Rod and I used to listen to it all the time, so Steve's departure was a shock and made no sense to me.

I didn't know Ronnie Lanc from Adam, but Krissie had once worked as secretary to Don Arden, who'd managed the Small Faces until 1966, and she'd come home at night with stories about 'these funny little leprechauns' who hung out in the office. Krissie gave me the hot news from the office that Steve had definitely quit the band. Steve's departure put Ronnie, Mac and Kenney in the lurch, so risking rejection and braving the outcome that fate had presented once again, I got hold of Ronnie's number, just like I did a few years before with Jeff Beck, and rang him up.

I said, 'This is a crime that you're splitting up. You're Rod's and my favourite band. What are you doing now that Marriott's left?'

He said, 'I don't know, we're lost. Do you want to come over and have a play with us?'

I was still employed with Jeff Beck, but I knew by this point that I definitely needed to find something new, to escape the lurid grasp of Peter, so I said, 'Of course I do.' I drove over to Mac's flat and we spent the night playing with our backs to each other because we were all sort of shy. But I liked the sound, it had a great feel, and I started thinking there might be a future with these blokes and after this delicate beginning we knew something was there.

The next thing I knew, my brother Art asked me if I'd put together a studio band for a recording session. His Artwoods had split up but he still had a four-record deal that he wanted to finish. I figured this could be fun and that it would also be a good chance to get together with my new Small Faces friends. I convinced Rod to come along with Ronnie, Mac, Kenney, Art and me, and the six of us went into the studio. We called ourselves Quiet Melon and it was made up of passing personnel. And even though the four songs we recorded never amounted to anything, we landed some live bookings. We played a Cambridge University ball, then an Oxford University ball, and then we played the Surrey University ball. But by now Art had grown bored with the music business and decided to retire, which marked the end of Quiet Melon.

I still had that fifth tour of the States to do with the Jeff Beck Group, but the writing was on the wall. Jeff and Peter had become too much of a pain in the arse, and the tour was a disaster. It was also very brief. We left England in early July 1969 and Rod and I agreed to suffer through it because we knew that the group was finished and that this would be the last tour, but Nicky couldn't take any more shit from Peter so he called it quits and Tony Newman incited unrest against the management. The group collapsed two weeks before Woodstock festival. We were meant to be on the bill and in that film. It's clear to me now that we never got the chance to stamp our mark or really take off like we should have. The ironic thing is that Nicky immediately joined Jefferson Airplane, and played Woodstock with them.

Instead of being in the States for three months, we were back in England in three weeks. My friendship with Ronnie, Mac and Kenney now moved up a few notches, as the four of us started looking around for some club dates. I needed to keep working and by that time, Ronnie, Mac and Kenney were pretty much broke.

A few big agents controlled the music scene in those days, had it all sewn up, and were like a kind of Mafia because you couldn't get a really good paying gig without going through one of them, and then they would screw you out of the money and the song rights and the royalties from your albums. The Small Faces left Don Arden in 1966 when they understood that he was earning a lot of money with them and they couldn't figure out why they weren't earning anything with him. Same old story. They escaped from Don and ran right into the arms of Andrew Loog Oldham.

In 1963, Oldham was a nineteen-year-old failed pop singer who got himself a job as a public relations man in the music business and got hired by the Beatles manager, Brian Epstein. But a few months after he started promoting the Beatles, he also handled Gerry and the Pacemakers. Oldham went to the Crawdaddy and heard the Stones. He decided they were going to be his group, and spent a lot of energy doing whatever he could to make friends with Mick. When he finally convinced Mick that

he was the guy they needed, he took over the band's public relations, began shaping their 'bad boy' image, coined the phrase 'Would you let your daughter marry a Rolling Stone?' and soon became their manager.

He used the money he made off the Stones to form Immediate Records, which was a hip and happening place to be, the wild card of the labels and if you could get invited to the Immediate Records Christmas party, that meant you were important because all the really important people in the music business showed up. The Beatles, the Stones, everybody was there rubbing shoulders with everybody else.

Immediate wasn't a major corporation run by accountants and marketing men who had fixed ideas about what music the public should have and how it should sound, which is why everybody loved it and why it was so special. Oldham let musicians run wild and do their thing, and allowed his friends and clients, like Mick and Keith, to produce songs for their friends. Immediate's first big hit was 'Hang on Sloopy' by the McCoys, but their first big act was the Small Faces, and the money those guys brought into Immediate sustained the label for several years, that is until Immediate went broke.

Ronnie, Mac, Kenney and I spent time together jamming at the Stones' Bermondsey rehearsal studios in South London, because Stu was in charge of that. Having no money he took pity on us and let us use the place for free. We sort of became the Small Faces minus Steve plus Woody. We didn't have our own name, we didn't have a vocalist and we didn't have any original songs, so we played instrumental sets. The music of really funky American bands like Booker T and the MGs, the Meters with Al Jackson, Zigaboo Otis and the Blues, the Mar-Keys and the Bar-Kays. Earthy, soulful bluesy music.

We hung out like that for about six weeks, and it was during this that I missed a real important phone call. Jagger was trying to replace Brian Jones and he picked Mick Taylor to take up the mantle. Taylor was only twenty-one years old when he joined the Stones and had been in a few bands. One night in 1966 John Mayall, who had a band called the Bluesbreakers, rang Taylor to ask him if he could sit in for their guitarist, who was missing a gig. That guitarist was Eric Clapton. Taylor impressed Mayall enough that, a couple of years later, Taylor was brought into the Bluesbreakers permanently. That band busted up around the same time that Mick Jagger was looking to replace Brian.

We used to be on the circuit together, so I knew Taylor and have to say that he was a good choice, even though it didn't work out. What I wouldn't know for another five years was that Jagger phoned me first.

Sod's luck, Ronnie Lane answered the phone.

Mick asked, 'Would Woody join the Stones?'

Lanie told him, 'Ronnie is quite happy where he is, thank you very much.'

I wonder what would have happened if I'd answered the phone that day. It would have been hard to say no.

Rod had been curiously listening to us rehearsing from an upstairs room during those six weeks in the Bermondsey studios. I knew we needed Rod, but the others were worried about having a bossy singer, another Steve Marriot. Also, Rod wasn't so sure about hooking up with a group like this, after what he'd just gone through with Jeff Beck.

I had to convince the boys that we needed Rod and had to convince Rod that he needed us. Kenney went upstairs and brought him down from his listening room. That broke the ice. With all of us in the room we looked around, saw that

Rod and I were taller than the others, agreed that the Small Faces had grown up, and decided to call ourselves, simply, the Faces.

Rod gave the Faces a dynamic that we didn't have with the Jeff Beck Group, and the others never had with the Small Faces. Thinking back, trying to put my finger on the most important thing that made it all different: it was fun.

In 1971, for instance, we appeared on *Top of the Pops* with the famous rock DJ John Peel pretending to play the mandolin with us. While we played, we kicked a football around the stage (that was Rod's idea just in case some team needed him) and it was obvious to the audience that the good times were spreading.

That's what got us through the next four or five years. That's what the Faces were about, five guys who wanted to go up there and have a good time. We would make mistakes onstage and burst out laughing, and the audience was right there laughing with us and loving it.

Because Rod and I had already toured the States and the others hadn't been there yet, we knew the kind of fun we could have there, so we went off on tour to America as soon as we could. In all, there were eleven US Faces tours.

On one of our first trips to the States we discovered that Mac didn't know there was a difference between US and UK voltage, and when he plugged in his Hammond it played in a different key from the rest of us. We laughed our way through that, became the first band ever to have a bar onstage, complete with waiters in tuxedos so that we could drink our way through the set without ever having to go offstage, and built a reputation as a solid, but fun-loving group.

For a while, the Faces were the second most successful British group in rock, after the Stones. We also built a reputation for raising hell, because most of the time we were so fucking home-sick, and when we weren't homesick, we were sitting around a hotel room in some strange city, really bored. We would be eccentrically creative in filling our time. Days off would be spent picking on each other, terrorizing anyone who had the guts to come into our room, and ornamental nude displays of women were commonplace. The 'doctor's surgery' was open and hilari-ously thriving. Pharmaceutical cocaine abounded as did the local grog and spliffs which were daily bread to all except for Rod, who would only chew a little hash for a dare.

Evenings were filled with terrorized explorations of great dexterity. Local night haunts would be ours.

Unless you've been on a tour, travelling steerage class the way we had to, you can't possibly imagine how dreadful it can be. We'd be away for three months at a time and only barely have enough money to scrape by. The highs were very high, but the lows were very low, and each of us, often, got to the point of wanting to throw in the towel.

Rod used to say that we were so unhappy on those tours because we were scared shitless, and none of us thought we were very good. One day Lanie would announce, 'I'm going home,' and if it wasn't him, the next day it was Rod. I'd go to their rooms and talk them into staying. The day after that it would be Kenney. I remember sitting with him once when he was literally crying that he needed to go back to England because he hated being on tour so much.

Arrangements were always going awry. Hire-car companies didn't have enough cars for us. We'd lose our way from the air-port. We'd be late for gigs. Thanks to our workaholic record company rep, Rush Shaw, we made gigs we would never have made. He stuck by us even after we physically threatened him, pushing him up against a wall exclaiming, 'Make us famous or you die.' All the frustrations quickly build up and it doesn't take long before the stress gets to you.

In the beginning we'd share rooms at cheap motels, but no one kept the same hours so that added to the tensions and we took it out on the furniture. Later, when we had our own rooms, we'd go from Holiday Inn to Holiday Inn, and all those rooms looked exactly the same, so we 'personalized' them. We would put in quality additions, and spice up the interior decorating. My favourite was to improve the artwork over the bed by drawing bicycles or airplanes or phallic additions into the pictures. Rod would draw nobs on everything.

Having gone through America with the Jeff Beck Group, Rod and I knew what to expect and, especially, how to party. We knew we could have fun if we invited the audience back to our hotel, so in the middle of our concert we'd tell them, 'We're staying at the Holiday Inn up the road . . .' and after the concert hundreds of people would come home with us. Our parties usually always started with getting girls into the pool naked. They often ended when the manager threw us out of the hotel for tossing the furniture in the pool as well.

We needed to brighten things up, so we played a lot of football in the corridors, and we prowled through the hotel at night, changing people's shoes. Anyone who put their shoes in front of their door to be shined, forget about that if we were in the hotel. The next morning men would find themselves with women's shoes, or one shoe, or two left shoes. At one place we took all the furniture out of a room and set everything up in the corridor. Couches, beds, lamps, everything. We sat there reading magazines until the manager came along and burst out laughing. He had a sense of humour, so we put it all back where it belonged and promised to behave. That time. Other hotel managers weren't so lucky, and we quickly got a reputa-

A typical night in the front room at N° 8 with friends in Yiewsley, 1950's

My dad and his mates coming back from Goodwood races.

early 70's

The Birds circa 1963

The Jeff Beck Group circa 1969

With Eric, Rainbow concert, London 1973

Faces revving-up

Travelling Faces

The Wick

wearing as much as possible

with Krissy, George Harrison and Kumar
in Friar Park, Henley.

Hot fun with Eric, playing 'Mudguards'
our favourite dice game. Paradise Island
1975

tion for trashing hotels. The Faces were pioneers in that particular art.

Before long, we started trashing the stage, too. One night, Rod threw the microphone into the air, stand and all. The audience loved it, so he did it the next night. That audience loved it, too, so he started doing it all the time. It became part of the act. He kept doing it until one night in Detroit he threw the microphone stand so high into the air it didn't come down. It got stuck in some wires above the stage and just hung there.

Mac always wanted a Steinway wherever we were playing, and if the promoter provided anything else, Mac would axe it after the show. But mostly we trashed hotels whenever something upset us, and it didn't take much. Bad room service. Rude people. Too much noise. Mac especially did it a lot because just about anything could set him off fuming. He'd get over-scrambled eggs for breakfast and within seconds his entire breakfast would be up in the air and on the walls.

We were sometimes criticized for breaking up hotel rooms simply to generate publicity for one of our albums. That's rubbish. As Rod and I have both often explained, we didn't do anything to get in the papers, we did it because we felt like it. Perhaps it isn't surprising then that we were also the first group to get banned from the Holiday Inn chain. After our second or third tour of the States, they categorically refused to take a booking from the Faces. We couldn't afford to stay anywhere else, so we had to find a way to get rooms, and that's when we started making reservations at the Holiday Inn as Fleetwood Mac and the Grateful Dead.

There was one receptionist at a Holiday Inn in Detroit called Mona, and that's exactly what she was, a real moaner, and she was one of the few who figured out we weren't Fleetwood Mac or the Grateful Dead, that we were that terrible bunch of guys who wrecked hotels, so we had to get out of there a bit quick.

We also got banned from the Beverly Wilshire Hotel, in L.A. We were in town and heard that the Stones were staying there and got a message through to them. They invited us by to party and there were drinks and naked women everywhere. We actually wore out the carpets so that the rooms had to be completely redecorated. When Keith Moon showed up, he walked into the lobby and they wouldn't let him in to party with us, so he pitched a tent right there in the middle of the lobby and refused to leave. Another time he drove his jeep through the plate-glass windows, through the lobby and up the steps. He leant over and said to Reception, 'May I have my keys please?'

What a polite gentleman that Keith Moon is.
My mother.

I'm not sure if it was on that trip or at that hotel, actually I think it was the Beverly Rodeo Hotel, but there's a wonderful story told about someone getting even with Peter Rudge, for some long-forgotten reason, when he was managing the Stones. Peter went out for lunch and came back to find that his room had been invaded by 1,000 chickens. Do you know how much noise and what a mess that many chickens can make?

When we flew commercial, we would tear through airports, generally terrorizing everyone in them, pulling pranks and having some laughs. When we started flying private, we would always invite the pilots and hostesses to the show and then back to the hotel, and they would all eventually end up in the pool naked.

The Faces was an explosion of humour, vanity and boredom

on the road. The infusion of uncontrolled excitement with cheek and menace at airports, interviews and concerts, band management and record company meetings.

The air of mischief was ever present. So was the continual striving for our kind of musical perfection. Attained only by hours of dedicated attention to tempo, style authenticity and maximum impact. Genuine respect was our goal when attempting any cover songs as a tribute to the respective artists, like The Meters, with Al Jackson on skins, Booker T and the MGs, Zigaboo Otis and the Blues, through the backbeats of Francis Clay, Fred Below crackin' under the bass ground of Willie Dixon and the cry of Muddy Waters. My harmonica playing was influenced by Sonny Boy Williamson, Junior Wells and Little Walter. From rehearsals to stage we tried to carry this musical message through.

7

London Life

When you come to a fork in the road, take it.
Yogi Berra

I wanna tell you a little about what it was like between tours. I was settling into the London scene and it was nice to be home. I shared a house with Jimi Hendrix in Holland Park, on and off, for about six months when he first came to England. Actually, it was PP Arnold's house. She rented the basement to Jimi and the ground floor to me while she was in the big flat upstairs. He was in the charts with hits like 'Purple Haze' and 'Hey Joe', and she had a hit with 'The First Cut is the Deepest'. These were the days when she was going out with Jim Morrison and he was always bringing her diamonds. Ironically, he died a year after Jimi and at the same age. Two more guys for Keith's now infamous list of those who weren't meant to reach thirty.

Jimi loved London and seemed to fit in so well. Jimi also loved his hat, which he never took off. It was pretty sedated at our flat. He was pretty strung out most of the time, definitely more strung out than me. I was too happy buzzing on life, didn't want to fall out too much, and would have a 'lude once in a while for a laugh. But Jimi was permanently on a plain that was very stoned. We were also both real busy at the time, doing gigs, interviews, coming in and out of the country, so wouldn't see each other for weeks at a time, but on those occasions we were together, Jimi was a great, relaxed flatmate.

One night, he and I were lying around in our flat in a pillow-strewn room with incense and candles burning and we talked guitars. He showed me how he could play with both hands (years later Ronnie O'Sullivan would show me the same trick, but this time with a snooker cue) and I was blown away, this was cool as cool and he mesmerized me. But the thing that struck me about him was how he had so little self-confidence. I couldn't believe it. He confessed to me that night that he hated his own voice, that he couldn't stand singing and that he wished he could just stand onstage and play. That's what he really wanted to do. Just play. I told him to stop being ridiculous and think of his voice like another instrument. He must have liked that because after I said it he went to a shelf and pulled out two records and gave them to me. I hadn't heard either of these albums, so he insisted I take them. The first was *James Brown Live at the Apollo 1962.* The second was *BB King Live at the Regal.* It was recorded in 1964, when the Regal was Chicago's version of New York's Apollo.

I'd never heard stuff like this. They were so filled with energy. Both of these albums blew me away. This was the Americans taking on the Brits. This was soul versus rock.

James Brown fully hypnotizes the audience with a desperate plea as all the suffering, passion and ecstasy of his music is delivered in an almost naked grab for the audience's approval. He really got my juices flowing. And in a funny way, he reminded me of Jagger. I know Brown's dancing, singing and sexual presence inspired Mick.

The inspiration definitely worked: years later after playing the song 'Everybody Needs Somebody to Love', Solomon Burke surprised Mick one night onstage and handed his cape to one of the only singers in the world who he thought could wear it.

As for BB King, he was the man. And a man of impeccable rawness. I suddenly felt tough listening to BB, with his voice and guitar – tough, strong, wise, sad and bluesy all at the same time.

Jimi never knew it, but he changed me forever by giving me those two records because they inspired me to play much better. But they weren't the only gifts Jimi gave me. One afternoon he came back to the flat with a basset hound called Loopy. I don't know where or how he got it. He lived with Loopy for a while, but he was travelling and couldn't really take care of him, and because I loved Loopy, he gave the dog to me. I thought that was pretty cool, except that Loopy never got house-trained and was always crapping on the floor and Pat Arnold didn't think that was cool at all, so she threw Loopy and me out.

The thing about Jimi was that he was unique in every way. He was part black, part Cherokee and part Mexican. He was discovered in New York, and after the Isley Brothers he came to the fore. Around the time of the British invasion of the States, when the Beatles and the Stones and all the British groups were going there, Jimi did just the opposite. He invaded England and it didn't take long before he became a worldwide sensation.

I loved his freedom and fluency over the neck of the guitar, even though he liked to keep himself medicated. We all know how Jimi played but to actually see him live was something else. It knocked me out. If Jimi was in the same town as the Jeff Beck Group, which often ended up to be New York, we would jam with him. We did the Staten Island festival together, but my most memorable jam with him was one time when we were playing the Fillmore East the same night Jimi was playing somewhere else in the city. We all met down at the Scene club, Jimi and his boys, me and my boys. Buddy Miles on drums, the Chambers Brothers were there too and we got up and played. Jimi loved my bass playing and would call across the stage, 'Hold off, let the bass have a go.' I would do a solo, then Jimi would come in wizard-like and do a mind-blowing virtuoso solo. Occasionally a musician's musican comes along and there is a unique type of buzz created. Jimi created this buzz big time, as did Stevie Ray Vaughan. Strangely, Jagger took me to see both these legends.

The time I spent with Jimi was always mellow. He loved his spliff and Quaaludes. He was five years older than me, which means he was twenty-seven when he died though he seemed many years older than that. His death was a real shock, a genuine blow. The week before, in mid-September 1970, he was playing at a three-day 'Love and Peace' festival in Europe. A promoter got shot and a few motorcycle gangs went to war. Jimi had to run for cover and once he was off the stage, one of the gangs burnt it to the ground. Jimi came back to London pretty shook up.

The night before he died I was hanging out at Ronnie Scott's in Soho with Jimi and others. It was pretty late when he walked out, without saying goodnight, so I raced after him and found him walking down the ramp of the club with some girl tucked under his right arm.

I called out, 'Hey, Jimi, you forgot to say goodnight.'

He looked over his shoulder, saw it was me and whispered a quiet 'Goodnight.'

I only met Brian Jones once, when he was sitting in the wings of the main studio at the Olympic Studios in Barnes, where the Faces and Stones did a lot of recording. Glyn Johns and Nicky

Hopkins introduced us, I walked up and said, 'Hi,' and he muttered something or other. He was in his own world, and somehow maintained a presence that was clearly outside. In a beaten-up dreamland held closely to his own heart. Lisping his way through scenarios that only he could understand. I felt this kind of exchange between us that is hard to expand upon.

Brian was 'me in a blond wig', as we were later to say, but as a musician he was a functional guitarist. The thing about him was that he'd been a Stone from the beginning, and fit into the push and pull that the band had. But I think towards the end of his life the bottom was falling out, and he just lost the drive. I know that the others saw it coming. He was picking up every instrument but the guitar. Trying to play the sitar, recorder, the pipes and all kinds of things, which is okay as long as you don't lose focus. He was a good guitar player, but he wasn't playing anything else very well. Drugs and rock and roll had consumed him.

The last song he did with the band was 'Honky Tonk Women'. They recorded it sometime in early June 1969, but by then Mick and Keith had already decided that Brian had to go and that someone should replace him. Brian was only twenty-seven when they found him dead in his swimming pool on 3 July 1969.

In a way, maybe Keith was right when he said about Brian, 'Some people aren't meant to live till they're thirty.'

The Stones' famous Hyde Park Concert on 5 July 1969, Mick Taylor's debut, had been on the schedule since before Brian died. But his death had happened just two days before so the event turned into a memorial concert for him. Estimates later put the crowd at between 250,000 and 500,000. Mick opened the concert with a eulogy for Brian, then released thousands of butterflies into the air.

Earlier that Saturday afternoon a fated 'brushing into' happened. As crowds were pouring into the park I was walking along the perimeter road, hoping to find a spot close enough to the bandstand so that I could hear the music. That's when a car pulled up next to me, the window came down and someone shouted, 'Hey, Ronnie . . .' and both Mick Jagger and Charlie Watts jumped out.

This was the first time I'd actually met Charlie. I didn't know him when he played in my brother Art's group, and until that day the closest I'd come to meeting him was one afternoon when I was crossing Oxford Street and he was stopped at a light in his chauffeur-driven Mini. He waved at me and I waved back. Charlie doesn't drive.

He never got a licence because he suffers from some sort of bizarre fear of engines, but that hasn't stopped him from buying cars. He once bought a 1936 Alfa Romeo simply because he loved looking at the dashboard. Charlie also owns a really beautiful burgundy Lagonda. Recently he commissioned a scale model of it from my brother-in-law Vinnie. But when he first bought the Lagonda he also bought himself a burgundy suit to match, so that he could wear it when he sat behind the wheel in his drive, engine ticking over, going nowhere.

The three of us stood there at the perimeter of the park for a few minutes.

I wished them well, 'Have a good gig.'

'Nice to see ya, see you soon,' they replied.

'Yeah, sooner than you think.' I left them and me with that!

In 1971, the most beautiful house in the world came up for sale – the Wick, in Richmond Hill, which was built in 1775, had twenty rooms, a beautiful view of the bend in the Thames, and belonged to the actor Sir John Mills. Its commanding aspect could equal any in Europe, and has been the subject of many an artist's painting. He wanted £100,000 for the house, plus an additional £40,000 for the old three-bedroom cottage at the bottom of the garden that belonged to his wife, Mary Hayley Bell, complete with her gypsy caravan, where she wrote such classics as *Whistle down the Wind*. I wanted to buy the Wick, but didn't have enough for the house and the cottage, so I sold Ravenswood Court, where Krissie and I were living, for £28,000, used that as my deposit on the Wick, and convinced Ronnie Lane to buy the cottage. Like most purchases of mine, I went way beyond my means. I was a young man buying one of London's most beautiful properties. Biting off far more than I could chew. Optimism perservered: I knew I had a tour coming up.

I fell in love with the house because it was so gorgeous, with its Adam's fireplaces, Grinling Gibbons' reliefs and three oval rooms, placed one above the other, but also because John had a wonderful snooker room with a rare old Thurston table. When I admired it, he told me that the table once belonged to the legendary Joe Davis, one of the greatest players in the history of the game and the winner of twenty consecutive snooker world championships. It was a very valuable piece of furniture all on its own, and a genuine treasure for anyone who loves snooker and the history of the game. Nothing was going to stop me from buying that house and the snooker table was part of the deal.

John loved it too and told me, 'Take it with my blessing, it's yours.'

I now owned the most beautiful house in the world and the most beautiful snooker table in the world. Now I could really get into the game. That table has rock history exchanges ingrained in the woodwork.

Also the day we moved in, we found a small handwritten note Sellotaped to the mirror in the hallway. It read, 'I hope you will be as happy as we were at the Wick – John and Mary.'

Krissie and I hoped we would be too, but things don't always work out the way you hope. The house quickly became an annex of Whitethorn Avenue, because my whole family loved it when they came round. My dad was very proud that his son had a house with more rooms than most of our family had, combined, and my mother was there occasionally to cook us breakfast. I even hired Doreen, Art's wife at the time, to be my secretary.

My first major project there was to spend £25,000 building a music studio down in the basement so that I could make a solo album. I put in state-of-the-art equipment incorporating a Neve desk, Studer and Revox tape recorders, a Three M8 track machine with interchangeable four-track heads and another sixteen-track machine. From the first day the studio was ready, the house was throbbing with friends twenty-four hours a day, all coming around to play music. George Harrison would show up with the Monty Python crew and we'd jam, and the actor John Hurt would show up and eventually we'd all wind up in the pub in the hotel just below the house. Day would turn into night and another day, and by then more friends would show up, and before any of us knew it we'd been up for four days drinking, getting stoned and making music.

We'd fall asleep on the studio floor and wake up to find a room full of musicians who hadn't been there when we crashed. Greg Allman, Paul McCartney, Keith Richards and Ringo. We'd play music until we couldn't play any more, go to the pub for a couple of days, then come back to the studio. Whoever came over would bring their instrument or they'd pick up whatever they could find lying around, and we'd play. One night, Keith

Moon – the Robert Newton of rock – Ringo and Andy New-mark all wanted to play drums, but there was only one drum kit, so I ended up teaching them to play the guitar. I taught them the chord of E, and we got stoned and played the chord of E all night. I still have all the original eight-tracks of those months of recordings, tons of tapes, I'm getting them organized real soon, sure there are some serious treasures buried in there.

The Wick had musicians queuing down the stairs day and night to get to the studio. I asked everyone who showed up, 'Please play on my album with me,' and tried not to let them leave until they did. Everyone was pretty supportive of me doing my own album. Clapton, however, accused me of sound-ing too much like him. 'You copied me, you bastard.'

'Yeah, Eric, I know. I really copied you on a song like "My Secretary". I'm using the same effect you use.'

Before long, people like Jagger and Harrison were nagging me to let them go home, claiming, 'I've got my own album to do.' Which is how that became the title of my first solo album.

When I was writing 'I Can Feel the Fire', Mick gave me a hand on the song. I then helped him out on 'It's Only Rock and Roll'. Andy Newmark had gone missing so we woke Kenney Jones up. The session came together with odds and ends, but we got the basic track cut. We recorded in my studio at the Wick, with Mick doing the vocals and both of us on guitar, Willie Weeks on bass and Kenney Jones on drums. David Bowie and I did backup vocals. We're the guys singing, 'I like it, I like it'. Mick then got the Stones to overdub on it. Charlie even kept Kenney's drums for that set. He said he wouldn't have done it any other way.

Then they took it all over to Island Studios, where Keith said, 'I took the precaution of removing your guitar parts.' He did leave my twelve-string part on, though. Mick released the song as a single in November 1974 and it topped the US charts, and then used it again as the title of the Stones' next album. With a song like 'It's Only Rock and Roll', you can't really get into who wrote which note. We were bouncing ideas all over the place. Mick had the chorus already and it was trial and error, like most songs. You shape them up and before you know it, you've got the chorus, the verses, your middle eight, and the solo place. The song moulds itself pretty quickly. It was like that with 'Maggie May' too. It came together real quick. You have no clue how well these songs are going to do.

Mick and I cut a deal. 'You can keep "I Can Feel the Fire" and I'll keep "It's Only Rock and Roll".' I had no bargaining power but, really, it was okay. We were writing songs together and Mick would take some ideas and structures which would become a Jagger/Richards song. I didn't mind going through years of all that. It was my apprenticeship.

It wasn't just top-quality musicians swarming around the house, I had great engineers and studio designers too, including Gary Kellgren, who had launched Record Plant studios, with his partner, Chris Stone, all over America where everyone who was funky would record. Electric Ladyland was his first session and then came Zappa, Stevie Wonder, Lennon, Sly, you name it. Anyway, Gary cancelled everything, came to the Wick and helped on the design of the studio and its set-up and saw the whole project through. Tragically, when Gary went back to L.A. in 1977, his air hostess wife, Marta, found him drowned in his swimming pool with one of his girlfriends. He had been trying to fix his underwater speakers. Gary had pretty much lost the use of his right arm after falling through a glass shower door years earlier and shredded his arm so bad the doctors wanted to amputate it. His girlfriend was trying to help Gary but she couldn't swim properly either so they both drowned.

Even though all of us were jamming all the time at the Wick, *I've Got My Own Album to Do* took the best part of a year to finish and wound up being mostly Andy Newmark on drums and Willie Weeks on bass. Andy was from Sly and the Family Stone and I got Willie from Donny Hathaway and Aretha Franklin. He was funky and soulful and the first night Willie came over to work with me, he walked through the kitchen, noticed that George Harrison was there, kept right on walking until he found me somewhere just out of the room and pulled me aside, 'Hey, man, you've got a Beatle in your kitchen.'

The same year we moved into the Wick, Krissie and I got invited to Mick and Bianca's wedding reception at the Byblos in the South of France.

Bianca Perez Morena De Macias of Nicaragua was an aloof kind of girl who appeared kind of cold, but the ice melted because as soon as she put on airs, I'd tell her, drop the shield, let's have a laugh, and once that happened we actually had some good fun together. She does nice things now and uses her name for a lot of good causes, the environment, refugees throughout the world, AIDS in Africa and human rights. Steam on, girl.

Mick invited Krissie and me, and chartered a commercial jet to fly everyone down to Nice, France. There was Paul McCartney at one end and Ringo Star at the other, because they were speaking to each other at the time, and in between there were Moonie, Clapton, Ronnie Lane, Mac, Kenney Jones, PP Arnold, Stephen Stills, Nicky Hopkins, Krissie, me and Mick's parents, Eva and Basil (who is always called Joe). A whole fleet of cars was waiting to take us from there to the hotel in St Tropez. I didn't know the South of France yet, so this was really something special.

Krissie and I arrived at the hotel and secretary Jo Bergman greeted us with our room key. I asked where Keith was and she said, 'Down the corridor in that bathroom on the left.' I spun down there, banged the door, which swung open, and several arms greeted and dragged me in among much laughter. I was home in a foreign land doing a line with Keith, Bobby Keys and Marshall Chess.

I didn't know Bobby Keys, either, but I knew who he was. Besides being a big old Texan who speaks like one, he's one of the greatest rock sax players ever. He was part of the group and played with Delaney & Bonnie & Friends before he started playing regularly with the Stones. He plays tenor on the original version of 'Brown Sugar', which they recorded before my time. I knew that Keith and Bobby were close, and it was real nice to be in their company and in their bathroom.

The actual wedding consisted of a civil ceremony in the town hall, which got held up for a couple of hours because the local police couldn't cope with all the reporters and photographers. That was followed by the religious service in a nearby church, with thousands of people in the streets waiting to see the bride and groom. Then there was the party at a local restaurant. Finally, Mick and Bianca left on a rented yacht for their honeymoon.

But just because their party was over, that didn't mean our party had to end. I didn't get back to London for at least three days. Keith and Bobby and Marshall and Krissie and I all lay around the pool on cushions, and stayed stoned.

The next time I saw Bobby was at Olympic Studios. He was in the big room, recording with the Stones, while the Faces were in the smaller room next door. I ripped him off the Stones, and got him to play on 'Had Me a Real Good Time' with us. The next thing I knew, the two of us were having a real good time. I invited him for a weekend at the Wick, he moved in with his saxophone, we got stoned and he wound up sleeping on, under and next to my snooker table, although he kept referring to it as a pool table.

He grew up in Lubbock, Texas, a neighbour of Buddy Holly, and is still a lifelong friend of the Crickets. Over the years he's played with everybody, from George Harrison, John Lennon, Clapton and Carly Simon to Joe Cocker, BB King, Sheryl Crow and Etta James to name a few.

But little did I know during that bathroom meeting in the South of France that it would be the start of lifelong friendship, and a very long journey together through freebase, coke, heroin, booze, more freebase and finally sobriety.

1, MAIDS OF HONOUR ROW. RICHMOND.

8

Rainbow

Pete Townshend came to the Wick one night, because he was worried about Eric Clapton.

After Eric's group, Derek and the Dominos, busted up in 1971, he withdrew with his then girlfriend, Alice Ormsby-Gore (Lord Harlech's daughter who, sadly, died of an overdose), and the two of them stayed stoned on heroin for two years. I mean, they became hermits. The only time I can think of during those two years when Eric came out into the real world was in August 1971, when George Harrison invited him to Madison Square Garden in New York to take part in his Concert For Bangladesh. He showed up, played, and after that he and Alice just shut the door again and stayed smacked out.

All their friends wanted to do something and many of them tried, but Eric and Alice didn't want to know. Pete grew so worried that he decided we just couldn't have this any more, and was determined to do whatever he had to in order to get them straight. His answer was to put together a concert and then to convince Steve Winwood and me that it was time to drag Eric out of his reclusion in Surrey and up to London for rehearsals. Which is exactly what we did. We literally dragged Eric out of his house and moved him into mine. We made him spend ten days at the Wick with us, rehearsing. Along with Eric, Pete,

Steve and me were Jimmy Capaldi from Traffic, who played drums and sadly died in January 2005, Jimmy Karstein also on drums, Reebop Kwaku Baah, who was on percussion, and Rick Grech on bass.

The Rainbow Concert was held on 13 January 1973, at the Rainbow Theatre in Finsbury Park, formerly the Astoria, where, back in '57, I first saw Duke Ellington's orchestra with Sam Woodyard on drums and 'Cat' Anderson on trumpet and where I also played my first concert with the Jeff Beck Group. During rehearsals, it was obvious to me that Eric hadn't lost anything over those two years in seclusion. He'd always been my premier guitar inspiration, and when we took the stage at the Rainbow that night everyone else knew it too. The place was packed and went wild when we opened the show with one of rock's definitive love songs, 'Layla'.

George Harrison was in the audience that night with his wife, Pattie Boyd. She was an absolute beauty who had had a bit part in the movie *A Hard Day's Night*, and had met George on the set. He fell for her, married her and wrote the song 'Something' for her. But Eric was in love with Pattie, too, and he'd written 'Layla' for her. From the audience's reaction, everybody must have known that.

We did the Hendrix hit 'Little Wing' and lots of Eric's big songs like 'Let It Rain', 'Badge', 'After Midnight' and 'Bell Bottom Blues'. By the time we reached the end of the set with 'Key to the Highway' and 'Crossroads', no one had any doubts – Eric was back.

That show was a turning point in his career because, as he later said, 'Pete Townshend gave me faith in myself.' It was also a turning point in mine. Eric and Pete had me doing the Duane Allman slides in numbers like 'Layla' and I had to learn all these complicated Clapton songs which I'd never played before. That they wanted me to be their Duane Allman was a big feather in my cap. The fact that they elected me to play the part of Duane suited me fine, as he was my bottleneck hero ever since I heard him play on Aretha's 'The Weight'. All the more so because it was the first time I'd played with the really big boys, boys I respected. I felt like Elmore James.

It might have been a turning point in Pattie's life, too. Eric had been in love with her but now she fell for Eric. George found out about them and when Eric got up the nerve to see George to tell him, 'I'm in love with your wife,' George let her go. But she wasn't going to be taken without me being her loving inter-mediary.

That was around the same time that Krissie had a short fling with George, they holidayed in Portugal. Remember, I'd pinched Krissie from Eric, and later, after Pattie and Eric split up, I had a lovely thing going with Pattie. We loved to go to Paradise Island on many occasions, where Sam Clapp gave us his home and hospitality. So Eric and I have always had this kind of sparring thing about girls we've known, and if you look at it sort of like a jigsaw puzzle you can see how our lives have fit together over the years. Pattie and I still remain friends these days and we will stay in touch through my art and her fantastic photography.

Eric and I have stayed friends and we've teased each other with humour. Around that time I discovered that Eric had the hots for Barbra Streisand. I was at Wendy Stark's party one night in L.A. and Eric was there too, and when Barbra rang the doorbell, I answered it. She was late, and I didn't know her at all so I shouted, 'What fucking time do you call this, Barbra, you're late.' She shouted right back, 'Well I'm sorry the fuckin' traffic was horrendous!' She then gave me a hug.

We sat down on the couch, talked a bit, then I said, 'Wait a minute,' found Eric, dragged him over to the couch, pushed him on to Barbra's lap, adding, 'He loves you,' and left the room. Eric was livid with me, but contented.

9

Cancel Everything

It took me a lotta hard work to get here, and I aint gonna blow it now.

Ronnie Wood

The Wick was becoming a hive of recording activity as well as a thriving debauchery camp. While I was making my album, Krissie had been out on the town with some girlfriends at Tramps nightclub. She found Keith there having a really bad time getting hassled. He asked Krissie, 'Help me get out of here, I've got to get rid of these people.' She said, 'Ronnie's at home in Richmond working on his album, why don't you come over?'

She brought Keith back to the Wick for the evening, and he stayed for four months. It wasn't as if he didn't have any place to live, he had his Redlands estate out in the country and a big house on Cheyne Walk. He did go out every few days to get fresh clothes, but otherwise he was living with us in the main house.

After a couple of months, Keith moved into the cottage at the bottom of the garden where Ronnie Lane had once lived. Ronnie'd long since gone – he was off in the wilderness with his gypsy caravan. So that was now Keith's place, except that he was rarely there because we hardly ever came out of my studio in the basement.

We never thought about asking Keith to leave because we were having too much fun producing great songs with great mixtures of different musicians, and those months just flew by, the two of us lost in our own world. He and I were already working on the interplay between our guitars, calling it 'the ancient form of weaving'.

Those early days with Keith opened the door to the Stones. But they also gave me great confidence musically. We were making fabulous music in a buzzing environment and the Wick had a revolving door populated with the world's top musicans.

I was still close to Robert Stigwood, at least as close as you could get to him, and loved going to his big country house in Berkshire because he threw wonderful parties. One night, late in 1974, I found myself at his place, sitting in between the two Micks, Jagger and Taylor, when MT leant over and told MJ, 'I'm leaving the group.'

That's always been a sort of a cliché among musicians, because we are always saying it to each other, so when Taylor said it to Jagger I just laughed. But Taylor looked at me and said, 'I'm serious,' and just like that, he got up and left the party.

Mick Taylor was one of those musicians who stood still onstage, much like Bill Wyman. He was a fabulous guitarist with great technique, but he wasn't encouraged to write songs because the 'Jagger and Richards Monopoly' wasn't going to let him in. I know that he found the Stones too restricting and thought that if he wasn't progressing in the band then he must be regressing. He worried that he wasn't fully appreciated, never thought he was any good and never realized how great he actually is.

So Jagger looked at me and said, 'I think he is serious.'

I replied, 'Sounds like it.'

Mick thought about that for a few moments and mumbled, 'What am I going to do? Will you join?'

I answered, 'Of course I would, except I'm with the Faces and I can't let them down. I don't want to split them up.'

He said, 'I don't want to split up the Faces either, but if I get desperate can I ring you?'

I said, sure, and we left it like that. We even shook hands on it.

Several months later, when he finally got desperate, I was sick in bed in Los Angeles. The smog in those days was really awful and used to make me feel rotten. Mick rang to say, 'I'm really desperate, can you help us out?' and I said okay, not only because this was a chance to play with the Stones, but also because it would get me out of L.A. He asked me to meet him in Munich, so I flew out a few days later. I was feeling closer and closer to Mick, Keith and Charlie so there were no nerves about performing well enough for them. I just wanted to see my pals. Mick and Keith were already beginning to treat me like the younger brother that I would become. I guess my whole life, right from Number 8 Whitethorn, through Rod and up to Mick and Keith, I have always been playing with the older guys. From Switzerland, the Stones and I moved to Munich, where I found myself in the middle of a crowd of guitar players at the Musicland Studios, including Marriott, Beck, Clapton, Wayne Perkins and Harvey Mandel.

Mick was multitasking. He was auditioning replacements for Mick Taylor, but doing it in his own inimitable style. What none of us realized at the time was that we had come to Germany on the pretext of auditioning but in the meantime, as long as we were there, Mick was getting us to play for free on the Stones album that would become *Black and Blue*.

Despite my friendship with Keith and Mick, it didn't really bother me that the Stones were looking at other people. Life goes on, I was out on the road with the Faces and they needed to find someone quickly. Steve Marriott would have been fine as a Stone, exactly the type of guy who might have got along with them, but Steve wasn't a guitar virtuoso of any kind. He was just a strummer and they needed a lead and rhythm guitar player. On the other hand, Jeff Beck was a great guitar player, but he's choosy where he turns up so he wouldn't have worked out. Clapton said to me in Munich, 'I'm a much better guitarist than you.'

I responded, 'I know that, but you've gotta live with these guys as well as play with them. There's no way you can do that.' Which is true. He could never have survived life with the Stones. Some of the guys hoping to join were American, like Wayne Perkins. Keith told me they loved Wayne's style, but they had doubts about his ability to fit in. They weren't sure he could live with them, or understand their sense of humour. After all, the Stones are a seriously English band and in order to get along with them, you've got to relate to them.

Even for the English guys, they weren't easy. Keith would play with some of these great musicians, then say, 'You're an asshole, fuck off.' Or, 'I can work with you, stay.' But he didn't say it until after these guys recorded and Mick got the take he wanted.

Then it was my turn.

I walked into the studio, took one look at Mick, Keith, Bill and Charlie and announced, 'I've got a song. I've played it to you before. We're gonna do "Hey Negrita". Let's cut it.'

And Charlie said, 'He's only just walked in and he's bossing us around already.'

From the moment the five of us started playing 'Hey Negrita', I'd like to think the job was mine. During the 1960s Muddy Waters and I had a conversation.

Him: 'Hey, Keith my man.'

Me: 'I'm not Keith, I'm Ronnie.'

Him: 'You're my man from the Rolling Stones.'

Me: 'Not yet but I hope to be.'

Him: 'I know you're my man from the Rolling Stones.'

And he left it like that.

The Godfather telling me I was already there. A lot of the black blues legends used to think I was Keith. With the established Stones as they were, Keith was the guitar player. People like Howlin' Wolf, Hubert Sumlin and Buddy Guy took a while to realize that I added my own contribution to the Stones. This meeting with Muddy would also be a precursor for the multitude of times in the future when people get me muddled up for Keith. People have seen us together so much they must just think, if it's not him it's him.

I took on so much in 1975, I was back and forth between the Faces and the Stones and my friendship with Keith was becoming more and more solid. When the Faces had a gig in Kilburn, I insisted that he come along to play 'Sweet Little Rock and Roller'. It seemed to me like a good idea at the time, especially because we were always having guests appear with us, and it was nothing new.

Of course, I cleared it with Rod and the others before I invited Keith. I just assumed that they realized I wasn't doing anything more than showing off my new pal, but I was wrong because my mates in the band misread my friendship with Keith and his appearance sparked off the rumour that I was leaving the Faces.

The trouble started with Elton John, who was driving with Rod to the gig that night. When he heard that Keith was going to play, he told Rod, 'That can only mean one thing. Ronnie's leaving the band.' But Elton had it wrong. So did the papers who picked up on it.

Rod told the other guys what Elton told him and they all decided it was true. I know they did because none of them would speak to me onstage that night. There were so many bad vibes going on that they actually played with their backs to me. And they still weren't talking to me on the way up to Coventry for the next gig.

I couldn't make any of them understand that, just because I was hanging out with Keith and Mick, it didn't automatically mean that I was bailing out on the Faces and joining the Stones. Except, of course, I was about to do just that. The Faces were an ongoing unit and we'd planned two tours of the States for 1975, and I had every intention of being on both. But the Stones also had a summer tour planned, and their dates fit neatly in between our dates, which meant I was available, and I had every intention of playing on that tour, too.

While the Faces tour that spring was fine, it was not as good as it could have been because Rod and the others knew I was going to spend the summer with the Stones. That didn't sit well with our manager, Billy Gaff, either, but then very little I said or did sat well with him.

Gaff was short, stocky and Irish, and learnt the music business while working for Robert Stigwood's company. He'd once been Long John Baldry's manager, and was fabulously theatrical whenever he spoke, emphasizing everything with sweeping arm gestures. Physically he was a mess – he looked as if he'd just survived the *Titanic*, and we used to call him 'Shredded Wheat hair' because he had one of those thin comb-overs and when he got ruffled, his hair would stick straight up.

The five of us in the Faces were always carrying around different gripes and grudges against Gaff, and telling each other, 'Just wait until I see that Billy.' Our resentment would build up until we couldn't take it any more, then we'd storm into his office and explode. Lanie would turn the desks over and throw all the files on to the floor, and Kenney, Mac, Rod and I would throw paper and drinks everywhere. We'd trash his office while he stood there pulling out his hair. It was total, brilliant madness. 'Bill it to Gaff!!' was our cry.

Towards the end of the Faces, and the more famous Rod became, the more of a pain Billy seemed because I got it into my head that he was focussed on Rod and saw him as his meal ticket. Rod's song 'Maggie May' hit Number One on both sides of the Atlantic at the same time. The funny thing about the song was that it was a B-side. For whatever reason, instead of playing the A-side (which was 'Reason to Believe') the DJs flipped the record and took everyone by surprise by going wild for 'Maggie May'. They played the hell out of it and the song topped the charts. I played the bass and the guitars on that.

So instead of worrying about the Faces, it seemed to me that Billy spent his time making sure that Rod was under his wing. When Gaff Management set up Rod's first record label, Smiler, the rest of us started to wonder what was going on. And why is Billy only looking after Rod? The boys felt left out, like also-rans.

That made the first of the Faces tours of 1975 a lot more tense than it might have otherwise been. Instead of just riding it, like I did, Mac got upset, and after a while Lanie got real upset too. I didn't have any angst about Rod's sudden success,

I said well done, and wished him good luck, because he was older than me, and I figured my time would come. The only thing that has really ever bothered me about Rod is that lead vocalists always get the best girls.

None of us knew it at the time but, as that first tour progressed, we were starting to get billed in various towns as 'Rod Stewart and the Faces'. We were never meant to find out, so someone would arrive in a town before we did and take down all the signs that we might see along the road from the airport or the hotel to the gig. But one night in Detroit, a few were missed. We arrived at the gig and there was Rod's name in big bold letters and Mac got so upset that he smacked Gaff and shouted to our driver, 'Keep going.'

The next thing any of us knew was that Lanie was quitting. I figured that he wasn't really quitting, except this time he meant it and he did. He turned it into one of those 'it's Rod or me' things. Lanie said to the rest of us, 'Come with me and we'll all leave Rod before he leaves us.' That wasn't going to happen, so Lanie went home.

We tried to replace him with the Japanese-born Tetsu Yamauchi, who could hold his own with us when it came to playing bass and was no slouch either when it came to drinking. With hindsight, we should have known that as far as the Faces were concerned, Ronnie Lane was irreplaceable. Tetsu is now back in his native Japan.

In April, I sat down with Mick and Keith in the Munich Hilton and we had a little meeting. Keith admitted to me that his first choice to replace Mick Taylor had been Steve Marriott, but the Stones agreed that what they really needed was a lead and rhythm guitar player, and eventually settled on three names – Jeff Beck, Eric Clapton and me. No matter who was up for the job, I fitted the mould.

Keith said to me, 'You're in the band.' I told him, 'Yeah, I know.' Keith added, 'We're not going to tell anyone for years,' and I said, 'That's fine with me.'

My dad never again referred to me simply as Ronnie. I was Archie's son, 'Ronnie Wood of the Rolling Stones'.

He came to the show in Wembley in 1982 – one of the only gigs he ever came to, there he was in his wheelchair. He was the first to arrive and the last to leave. I loved seeing him there. He went down each row of the seating area, shook hands with everyone, kissed all the girls and made them sit on his lap as the show rocked on.

Keith and I were still in Munich when the cops raided the Wick looking for Keith. They'd been staking out the cottage at the bottom of the garden from a hotel room at the top of Richmond Hill for a month. On the night they decided to swoop, nothing happened. Keith hadn't been there for two weeks. Real efficient. Instead they found little traces of coke, and my wife Krissie in bed with her girlfriend, Lorraine. Sleeping. Krissie was alone in this big house and her mate had moved in to keep her company.

The girls got arrested because of the coke.

The papers got hold of the story and I got to read about my wife's lesbian drug sex party.

The story claimed that the Flying Squad (very low-flying) found both girls in the nude. The Stones' secretary, Shirley Arnold, swept into action and the lawyers sprung them.

Krissie explained to me what had happened and I can see why the press went wild. She was let off. I was not surprised in the slightest that the cops had busted the Wick. Every time Keith would leave the Wick he would be in some outlandish outfit and when we all piled into some waiting limo or big Bentley there would be a troop of us. Trooping the colour, leaving the Wick. We were hardly incognito. It would have appeared quite, quite obvious that the inside of the Wick was not the average residential abode.

10
Flatbed

The Stones 1975 tour was forty-six shows in twenty-seven cities across America, and opened at Louisiana State University in Baton Rouge on 1 June. It was my twenty-eighth birthday and it was my debut. We took to the stage to the music of Aaron Copland's *Fanfare for the Common Man*. But the mayhem that follows the Stones wherever we go actually began five weeks before in Manhattan.

On 26 April we all flew to New York, and checked into two hotels with phoney names. Mick and Charlie stayed at the Plaza on Central Park South using the names Michael Benz and Charlie Ford. Me, Keith and Bill checked into the Pierre on 5th Avenue, Keith as Mr Bentley, Bill Austin and Ronnie Morris. Billy Preston was with us too, using the name Billy Hillman. Please note which two people got named after really expensive cars and how the rest of us were named after old bangers.

A few mornings later, at around seven, we gathered at the Plaza, went out the rear door, sneaked into an ice cream van and went downtown to the corner of 12th Street and 5th Avenue. A flatbed truck was waiting for us, all set up with amps and instruments. This was Charlie's doing. He read somewhere that black jazz artists used to roll through Harlem playing on a flatbed, so he nicked the idea for us.

We'd announced a press conference to kick off the tour and told the media to meet us at the Feathers Restaurant, at 9th Street and 5th Avenue. Since then, we've often set up decoys like that when we have to deal with the press, and today it's a lot harder to get away with it because they know us so well. But that one was easy and they were naively expecting a whole bunch of one-on-one interviews at tables in the restaurant.

Instead, we climbed on to the flatbed, which had the tour logo as a backdrop, plugged in, and started playing 'Brown Sugar'. We drove to the restaurant, as crowds gathered along the street and started following us, stopped just long enough to catch everyone's attention inside, then kept right on going down 5th Avenue. Journalists raced after the flatbed, yelling at us, complaining that we'd promised them interviews. And the more they yelled at us, the more we yelled back, 'Fuck you.'

We kept right on playing and right on rolling and more and more people going to work followed us on foot, like we were the Pied Piper, which messed up traffic all over that part of Manhattan. Folks came up from the subway, saw us rolling by and God only knows what some of them thought.

The cops were there, trying to manage crowd control and I recognized one or two of them from a Faces tour. They were pointing at me and shouting, 'Hey Ronnie, you promised me tickets . . . where are my tickets?'

I also spotted Shep Gordon coming around the corner carrying his briefcase on the way to his office. He managed Alice Cooper and Groucho Marx. He spotted me, did a double take and called out, 'What the fuck are you doing?' But I couldn't get into a conversation with him because I was having enough trouble just trying to keep upright and play at the same time.

That afternoon we all moved to a house in Montauk, on the eastern tip of Long Island, to rehearse for the tour. What I didn't realize was that it was Andy Warhol's house. Andy was around a lot, but never said much. He'd watch us and I'd watch him and he always struck me as a piece of art himself, clicking away on his hand-painted Brownie camera.

After a month or so, we were still in Montauk, just about ready to leave on tour, when Mick handed me a contract. I was an employee.

I was handling my own business affairs at the time (I would joke that it was the first time I had a manager I could trust!) and while I was trying to figure out my contract, Bob Ellis, who managed Billy Preston, spotted me and asked me if I needed any help.

I said, 'No, why?'

He said, 'Because you've got it upside down.'

I never had a clue what kind of money I was making with the Faces. My only concern was that I had enough money six months ahead to pay for my flat and maybe have a little bit of money left over to buy a cheap Bentley. I've always had Bentleys through the years.

I asked Bob, 'What do you think? Is everything all right with the contract?' He turned the contract the right way up, looked at it and pointed to one spot. 'That's where you went wrong. There. See? You signed it already.'

The day after we arrived at Andy's house, we had a big party to celebrate Bianca's thirtieth birthday. Then we settled down to work. The combination of genres of music and art only propelled us all, and over the next several weeks I had to learn 200 songs. We went through the entire Stones repertoire. I actually knew more about those songs than they did because I'd grown up with them, but I'd never played them before, so I memorized Mick Taylor's stuff and Brian Jones' stuff, and when the time came, it was no hardship for me to play them.

Even these days, rehearsing for a tour or an album, Mick or Keith will play something and I'll tell them, 'It doesn't go like that, it goes like this.' Or they'll start in the wrong key and I'll have to correct them, 'It's not F, it's G.' I'll remind them, 'Come on guys, you wrote the fucking thing,' and one of them, usually Keith, will shout back, 'Just because I wrote it, that doesn't mean I know it.'

So for me, the music was the easiest part of becoming a Rolling Stone. The steep learning curve was living like a Rolling Stone.

To begin with, we had all these shaven-headed monsters camping out in Warhol's garden, and we needed security everywhere. We had groupies with the Faces, but the Stones had so many. They had male groupies, too, who nearly always seemed to be doctors. People who could write prescriptions.

The Stones were from a whole different planet, a planet of themes, dreams and schemes. Their shows and posters were raunchy and suggestive. When the Faces plugged albums we did it relatively gently. When the Stones plugged albums, they went to town. When *Black and Blue* came out they put up a huge billboard on Sunset Strip with the words 'I'm Black and Blue from the Rolling Stones and I love it.' Parents loved it too.

With the Stones they had two of everything, including stages. When one stage was getting set up, the second stage was on the way to the next gig. It was all so much more professional and planned, and every Stones show was a major production. With the Faces, Rod and I and the rest of the guys would just walk up onstage and play. The only non-musical addition to the set was the onstage bar. Interviews with people like Dave Marsh from *Creem* magazine would be snatched moments, taking place backstage as we were getting changed (or drunk) surrounded by the obligatory mayhem. With the Stones everything was an extravaganza, and over the years, every extravaganza got bigger and better. Mick would be flying on a trapeze somewhere, fireworks would be going off somewhere else and the light show would just add to the spectacle. The main stage featured 3,000 lights and huge lotus petals that hydraulically unfolded as Keith walked on to open the show with 'Honky Tonk Women'. At the end of that tour, Keith Moon bought the stage, all twenty-five tons of it, and put it in his garden.

Joining the Stones meant a certain level of luxury duly turned up. We had a private Boeing 720, dubbed *Starship*, that came complete with a bedroom, a lounge, a library, showers, a bar with an organ and, occasionally, naked girls running up and down the aisles. It was the first time I'd ever travelled in that kind of luxury. We'd get picked up on the tarmac and whizzed off to the hotel in a fleet of cars, police escort in attendance.

The Stones had people like Alan Dunn looking at the logistics backstage, had people worried about infiltration, had seriously big bodyguards, had office managers and secretaries and travel staff and forward-planning staff and everything was written down. They had set lists for everybody which had the songs we were going to play and the order we were going to play them in, the tempos for each song, the guitars we were each going to use, and the key we were supposed to play in. They even had newsletters they'd shove under your hotel room door at night so you knew when to wake up and exactly what we were going to do that day.

Unlike the homesickness that I had to live through with the Faces (I would ring Mum, Art and Ted on a regular basis for a taste of Yiewsley) it didn't happen with the Stones. I wondered why and Keith explained, 'Because you're in a proper rock and roll band now.'

I said, 'Because no one gets homesick?'

He answered, 'No, because we have a public fountain named after us in Nicaragua.'

Eric Clapton did a guest spot with us on that tour, and so did Carlos Santana. So did Elton John, although unlike Eric and Carlos, he overstayed his welcome. We were playing in Fort Collins, Colorado, and Elton was supposed to do one number, 'Honky Tonk Women', but he was having so much fun that he pushed our keyboard player, Billy Preston, into the background and stayed for the rest of the set. That could have pissed off Billy. It could have pissed off the rest of us, too.

Keith kept shouting across the stage, 'Get the fuck off and give it back to Billy,' but Elton wouldn't leave. By the end of the show Mick was referring to Elton as 'Reg from Watford'. He was playing our stuff, not his, but he was good enough to vamp three or four chords and make it sound like he knew our songs.

In Los Angeles we all jammed for Peter Sellers' birthday party. I remember playing with David Bowie, Bill Wyman, Keith Moon and Joe Cocker. What I didn't remember was seeing Peter Sellers there. But I certainly do remember him when we shared a dressing room for one night in 1972 at the Rainbow Theatre in London, doing a special performance of Pete Townshend's rock opera *Tommy*. He sat in our dressing room staring into the mirror, wearing an overcoat and a German helmet, muttering to himself like a German version of Inspector Clouseau. I didn't say anything because there didn't seem much point.

A few weeks later, in Chicago, Bill Wyman invited some very special guests to our gig. He called me and said, 'Come down to my room, there are some people I want you to meet.' I did, and there was Howlin' Wolf, Hubert Sumlin, Muddy Waters and Buddy Guy. He'd sent cars to pick them up and brought them to the show. These were the guys who'd influenced all of us. To have all those inspirations of mine there was something. They appreciated our input and I really appreciated theirs. These were the guys who got me rocking all those years ago.

In the Faces I was used to shouting all the cues. The Faces was musically my band. In the Stones Keith does the shouting. Charlie and Bill were taking their cues from Keith, so I did too. There should have been a feeling that I was stepping down, but it's never been like that with the Stones. There is a formula, it works extremely well, and with Keith I had found a sparring partner, a musical brother, a buddy, a bully and a catalyst.

Onstage, I discovered quickly, there's a lot of talking. Mostly it's someone hitting a bad note and Mick shouting, 'What the fuck was that?' And Keith yelling, 'It wasn't me, it was Woody.' Because Bill used to stand way off to the side, everyone thought he was just watching the crowd, that the crowd was his show, but he was actually playing a game called 'Spot the tits'. He'd come over to me and we'd have a long discussion that always began with, 'Nice pair over there.'

Also onstage with the Stones, I found out that a lot gets said without anyone actually saying anything, and I had to learn how to speak that language. I'd never experienced anything to that same extent with any other group. There's a lot of eye contact and signalling and non-verbal communication, all built in. It's easier now because we've been together so long, but in the beginning I had to learn that if the tempo was dragging a bit, I couldn't just change it all by myself. Everything always has to be approved by the board, so I would look at Keith in a certain way so that he knew immediately what I was thinking and then we would both look at Charlie so that he knew, too, and we would all crank it up a bit.

It was a little different if an idea suddenly popped into my head, or into Keith's head. One of us could go right ahead and play something and the other would pick up on it immediately and react to it. Mick and Charlie would pick up on that, too, right away, because we were all speaking the same musical language. When Bill left and Darryl Jones came into the band to play bass, he also had to learn to hear all this non-verbal speak. He's into it now, and so are all the backup people we use. Chuck Leavell has been our keyboard player for years, he took over from Mac (whose spirit and humour are always very close to me), and Bobby Keys is still there blowing his sax, so of course they speak the language. And so do Bernard Fowler, Lisa Fisher and Blondie Chaplin, our backup singers. Lisa is wonderful, always moving and looking great. She has a troop of fans of her own and her version of 'The Night Time (Is the Right Time)' is one of the show's highlights, and so lately is James Brown's 'I'll Go Crazy'. We've all been together as a group for a long time, and we all know what everyone else is thinking.

As my first tour moved through America, I was learning all this new stuff, gaining a lot of confidence, feeling powerful and starting to believe that the Stones would bring out the best in me.

Keith sensed what was happening on that tour, too, because he was telling people that the band finally had the right chemistry. He was saying, 'Woody is made for two guitars but he hasn't had the chance to do it until now. His strength, like mine, is to play with another guitar player.'

Maybe that's one reason why playing with Keith, especially onstage, has always been such a unique experience for me. The more I got to play with him the more I could see that he and I have the same kind of inner confidence. This confidence leads us into daring realms, places where it could all go dreadfully wrong dreadfully easily. I'm sure that's why I love the lap steel. An instrument that you can drive one way into a cul-de-sac with its fine-tuning. There's a thrill of knowing that the slightest slip will produce the vilest disturbance. Or as Cyrano de Bergerac put it: 'Tonight when I make my sweeping bow at heaven's gate, One thing I shall still possess, at any rate, Unscathed, something outlasting mortal flesh, And that is . . . My panache.'

With the Stones, it's not all about Mick. Whatever limelight Mick gets is great for the band but without Keith there wouldn't be a band. In other groups, they follow the drummer. In the Stones, we follow Keith.

Ian Stewart told me once that in the beginning, when Mick and Brian and Keith were still feeling their way into this, Keith wasn't at all interested in being the leader of the band. Brian and Mick were fighting it out, but Keith was happy to let one of them be out front. He had no problem when Mick won out and began getting all the glory, as long as Keith was the one who could make the Stones sound the way Keith wanted the Stones to sound. As far as he's concerned, we're only onstage with him to serve the band. Maybe that's why Charlie was often telling people that he was Mick and Keith's drummer.

It's easy for me to say, okay Keith's at the helm here, and I know when I've got to do this, come in here, I've got the solo here and he's got the solo there or we'll be weaving the guitars together. There were times when we used to bluff it, get stoned out of our brains and just go for it – 'Eyes down and meet you at the end.' Looking back, how did I ever play that, how did we even get through it, let alone trying to remember the set list or where we were?

What I hadn't realized until I joined the Stones was how musically frustrated I'd become with the Faces. The Stones gave me musical freedom and, I hope, that got reflected back in the music we were playing together. Although Keith didn't say it in as many words, I know he sensed it. He gave an interview to some newspaper during that tour where he spoke about me now being a Stone. He said, 'We can do a lot more with this particular band than any other incarnation of the Rolling Stones. With Ronnie the possibilities are endless.'

It is one of the blessings of old friends that you can afford to be stupid with them.
Ralph Waldo Emerson

We were into our fifth week of my first Rolling Stones tour by the time we got to Memphis. But the flight down from Washington DC, where we'd just done two nights at the Capitol Center Arena in nearby Largo, Maryland, was a nightmare. We got caught in a huge thunderstorm and got hit by lightning several times. The storm lasted an hour and tossed us all over the sky, and the turbulence was so horrible that Bobby Keys nearly went through the roof of the plane. All of us thought our number was up.

So after we landed, Keith and I decided we'd had our fill of planes for a bit, said, 'Fuck this,' and announced that we were going to drive to the next gig. It's only around 400 miles from Memphis to Dallas, where we were playing in the sold-out Cotton Bowl, and we had two days to get there.

Keith's friend Freddie Sessler, the drug pusher to the stars, was hanging out on that tour and said he wanted to come along, too. I'd known Freddie for many years by this point (we met the first time at the Pocono Festival when I was with the Faces), and knew how dangerous he could be, but Keith adored him. Jim Callaghan, the Stones' head security guy at the time, also came along. In fact, I think Jim insisted on joining us and I suspect we probably wouldn't have been allowed to go without Jim because he and Mick and everyone else must have known we'd need help at some point along the way. Jim's not with the Stones any more: he got an honourable discharge and is back with his old boss, Bob Dylan, but to this day I'm glad he was there.

We rented a flash yellow Chevrolet Impala and the four of us set off on what we thought would be a leisurely tour of the South. Keith drove, with Jim in the front seat and Freddie and me in the back. We didn't have a plan, except we knew when we had to be in Dallas, so when I decided to collect miniature bourbon bottles along the way, great brands like Rebel Yell and Maker's Mark, we stopped in just about every town we went through to buy some, and it wasn't long before the car had a back window and a boot full of these bourbon miniatures.

Most of the ride was boring freeway, but we were getting stoned and laughing and thought we were doing just fine, except that Keith was driving very, very slow, slow enough to get arrested for loitering, and swerving a bit too much from lane to lane. Unbeknownst to us, somewhere in the middle of Nowhere, Arkansas on Saturday morning, 5 July, people in other cars driving in the same direction got so nervous about being on the same highway as us that they called the cops. There must have been a lot of complaints because the state police put out a fucking huge 'all points bulletin' for four degenerates in a yellow Chevy Impala.

We stopped for lunch at the 4 Dice Restaurant and Gas Station in a hillbilly town called Fordyce, population 5,200. Until that day, I always thought Arkansas was a cool place, because it had given the world Howlin' Wolf and Robert Johnson. I'm not sure how long we were in the restaurant, but Keith and I must have spent a couple of hours in the bathroom laughing. That really worried the guy who owned the restaurant, as well as the waitresses, and the other customers eating there, because the police got lots more calls, and by the time we got back into our car and Keith pulled out of the parking lot at zero miles an hour, the cops pounced.

A patrol car suddenly appeared next to us, the cops motioned for us to pull over and stop (Keith's driving meant we were pretty much already stopped) and suddenly the two cops from the patrol car were standing in front of us with guns drawn as if we were escaped convicts, armed and dangerous.

One of them was aiming a pistol at us, another a shotgun, and they scared the shit out of us. Making matters worse, the cop with the pistol was twitching real bad. I mean, he had such a terrible flinch that I worried he'd twitch the trigger and we'd all get shot. Riot squads and narcotics cops were nothing new to a Stones tour, we see them all the time, but this was straight out of the film *Deliverance*.

The cops ordered us to keep our hands where they could see them, looked us over, then Officer Twitch spotted Keith's knife on the seat next to him and said he was arresting us for carrying a concealed weapon, even though it wasn't concealed because it was right there in plain sight. But Officer Twitch had a gun and a nervous trigger finger, so if he wanted to confiscate the knife, Keith wasn't going to argue about it.

What Officer Twitch and his partner didn't know was that the door panel was filled with grass and coke.

Backup arrived with sirens blazing and before we knew it we were completely surrounded by more cops with more guns. They ordered us to drive with them to the police station. We worried about what the cops would find in the car, so as we drove, completely surrounded by patrol cars, whatever incriminating evidence we could get our hands on got flung out the window. Obviously, they saw us, because they were driving next to, in front of and behind us. And later they went back to find some of what we'd tossed away. One item was a small hand-tooled leather pouch that just happened to have some hash in it. I'm told the police chief, long retired, still owns that pouch but that could be just an urban myth.

Instead of taking us to the police station, they made us park in the garage at the old City Hall, a dark and dingy place with a big brick wall that looked like it was straight out of the St Valentine's Day Massacre. It was quite unnerving. They impounded the car and did a fast search before taking us to the new City Hall, where they brought us into the office of the police chief. He didn't have a clue who we were, but a few of the younger cops did and they wanted autographs. The chief asked them what this was all about, and that's when it started to dawn on him that maybe this bust was going to be slightly different than anything Fordyce had ever seen before. Years later I found out that the chief then rang the city attorney, a young prosecutor only just out of law school named Tommy Mays, who thought the chief was pulling his leg when he told them who they'd just captured.

Mays and his wife were literally walking out of the door to go to his secretary's daughter's wedding, when the chief told Mays that he needed him at City Hall right away. The rest of their conversation, according to Mays, went like this:

MAYS: 'I'm on my way to Sheila's wedding, what's so urgent?'

CHIEF: 'We've got the Rolling Stones.'

MAYS: 'I don't have time for this. I'm going to be late for the wedding.'

CHIEF: 'It's the Rolling Stones, I'm telling you, they're here. Under arrest.'

MAYS: 'I don't believe you. Tell me one of their names.'

Chief asked Mays to hold on, went away for a moment, then came back and said: 'Keith Richards.'

MAYS: 'I'll be right there.'

They never handcuffed us or put us in a cell, but that's because they really didn't have a clue what to do with us. Word was spreading fast that the Rolling Stones were in town and people were showing up with albums and cameras and babies to take photos of us with their kids. The local paper alerted the Little Rock media, and news crews from there were now racing the 120 miles to Fordyce.

Everybody was very nice to us, except Officer Twitch and his partner. We were told we'd only be allowed to make one phone call each, but it took a lot of calls before we found the Stones' lawyer, Bill Carter. He was originally from Little Rock, which meant that he knew how things worked in two-horse towns like Fordyce. Remember, this is a long time before mobile phones, so we kept ringing his office in Washington DC, but it was Saturday and his office was closed. It took forever until we finally located somebody who found him visiting a friend for the weekend in another small Arkansas town, this one oddly enough named West Memphis.

Bill said he would charter a plane and fly to Fordyce to spring us, then warned us, 'Don't say anything, don't do anything, wait for me.' So we waited there all day for him to arrive, and with nothing to do we got bored pretty quickly. To kill the boredom, we got stoned just as fast. Keith had a jeans hat with little pockets around the side, and all the pockets were filled with stuff. We passed the hat around a lot and went off to the bathroom to get high.

I was in the police station toilet at one point when Freddie came in and spilled Tuinol pills all over the floor. There I was, sitting on the toilet, and here comes Freddie underneath the stall door, his face looking up at me from my feet, to fetch his turquoise, red and orange sleeping pills.

Freddie kept moaning, 'Let me in there, I've got to make the evidence disappear,' which is what he and Keith did. But instead of flushing the evidence down the toilet, they swallowed it.

The municipal judge was a fellow named Thomas Wynne Jr and he came in to speak to the chief while we were still in his office. The judge pulled a bottle of bourbon out of his left boot, poured a drink for the chief, poured one for himself, and then those two started arguing. The more they drank, the more they fought. It turns out that His Honour was on our side because he understood just how volatile a situation this was. He worried that every newspaper in the world was going to write about his town and that they would never live down their reputation as being the place that busted the Rolling Stones. All these years later, they still talk about that day as part of the legend of Fordyce.

As the afternoon wore on, the police chief and the judge got ripped, crowds gathered outside and policemen lined up in the corridor with albums for us to sign. We asked if we could have a look around and just outside the chief's office I found a bicycle, which I started riding up and down the hallway. When we said we wanted to see the courtroom, an officer took us in there. Keith and I climbed up to the judge's bench and sat down in his chair, and before we knew it the courtroom doors flung open and people rushed in asking for autographs. The copper couldn't hold them back and we were still at the judge's bench, so I started banging the judge's gavel and shouting, 'Order in the courtroom!'

We made friends with the entire town, and everyone was really very nice. The judge's wife even made sandwiches for us. Then we started swapping things with the locals like hats and stuff we liked. Although our stay in Fordyce was just as memorable for us as it was for the locals, I can't say it was fun because it was a very long, very tense day. We never knew what was going to happen next. We were being held captive by hill-billies with guns. We didn't know that the judge was trying to get us out of town. We worried that the chief would give in to Officer Twitch, throw the book at us and we'd never see the outside world again.

While this was going on in Fordyce, Mick, Charlie and Bill were comfortably installed in their hotel suites in Dallas, thinking everything was all right with us because Jim Callaghan was with us. What they probably should have thought was, yeah, but Freddie Sessler is there too.

The attorney, Tom Mays, spent the entire day trying to work out what to do with us, and never did get to the wedding. Years later he said that the bride herself wanted to leave her own reception and come to City Hall to meet us, the way most of her guests did, but her family wouldn't let her.

It took the cavalry ages to arrive. By the time Bill Carter pulled into Fordyce, accompanied by the judge he'd been spending the weekend with, it was already night. Bill was well equipped to handle our legal problems, but nobody in Fordyce was ready to deal with what was now happening. Calls were coming in from newspapers all around the world for the police chief, the judge, the prosecutor and anyone who'd answer the phone. Some reporter rang from *The Times* in London (they loved his accent) and another reporter rang from the *Sydney Morning Herald*. We just wanted to get us out of town.

With Bill Carter standing next to us to supervise, the cops escorted us back to our car and gave us each a chance, one by one, to get our belongings out. I crawled in and filled a tissue box with dope and got my coat and bag, and did a quick sleight of hand to make the dope disappear. Freddie was next. He took his briefcase with his drugs in it and locked it. When one of the cops asked him to open it, he said he couldn't because he'd lost the key. So the cop sawed it open. Inside were two vials of pharmaceutical coke. He asked him what it was and he told them, 'Tooth powder.'

He got away with one jar, but they busted him for the second.

They also found stuff stuffed down behind the back seat, but this was a rental car and Mays and Carter agreed that it would be hard to prove those drugs were ours.

It was a long process, but it finally ended when they issued Keith a ticket for reckless driving. They took his knife but never charged him with anything for having it. Keith paid his fine, which was $162.50. Once we were done with the legalities inside the police station, it was time to deal with the mayhem raging outside. There were television crews everywhere, so we went back into the courtroom, let them set up their cameras and lights, and did a press conference before heading to our Cessna. There was a gang of school kids urging us on even as we taxied down the runway, some even trying to hang on to the wings. We were out of there.

When the Stones tour ended, I still had that second Faces tour to do. It was the eleventh time the group played the States and, I know all of us knew, it was going to be the last. We rehearsed in Miami, where we rented a house at 461 Ocean Boulevard. I was coming to this tour with a lot more confidence and was full of life. However, right from the start it was clear that there was too much dissent in the group for us to survive for much longer. Ronnie Lane was gone, so the chemistry was very different. Billy Gaff had his own ideas about what the Faces needed, which I felt was to make us a backing group for Rod. String sections, stupid outfits and another rhythm guitarist were added. Girlfriends got way too involved and the Faces' soul was quite rapidly oozing away. I know we were all aware of it.

Everything was going pear-shaped, and by the time we arrived in California to play the Anaheim Stadium we hit rock bottom. It was the most disastrous show of all. We were following Fleetwood Mac and getting our biggest ever pay cheque.

For us this was a major event. But it was never meant to be. Our truck broke down on the way to Los Angeles so our equipment never arrived. When we realized we weren't going to have our stuff in time, we scurried around to rent equipment. With everything else that was going on within the group, playing other people's instruments only made matters worse. This was the last straw and we produced forty-five minutes of sheer embarrassment.

By the end of the set, we were so frustrated and angry about everything that we trashed the instruments, wrecked the lot, including the new Hammond that Ian was playing. I stomped on it and turned it into splinters, not knowing that this one wasn't rented – it was Mac's.

We still had a month or so left on the tour, including two gigs in Honolulu, Hawaii, where we'd also built in some time off. We checked into the Kuwalah Hilton on Oahu to chill out, and everything seemed to calm down for a while, that is until Helen Reddy showed up with her husband/manager, Jeff Wald.

He complained to the hotel that Rod and Britt Ekland were staying in the suite that he and Helen always used, and the management threw Rod and Britt out. We weren't pleased about that, and as Rod and I had long ago become experts at dismembering hotel rooms, we made sure that Helen and her husband really enjoyed their suite.

The bed was rigged so that it would break the moment they lay down, and the toilet so it wouldn't flush. The microphone was taken out of the telephone mouthpiece so that when they tried to ring the operator, no one could hear them. Mac rearranged some of the hotel's artwork. When he and Wald got into a fight, he grabbed Wald in the scuffle and a reproduction of John Constable's 1821 masterpiece, *The Hay Wain*, ended up hung around

Wald's neck. We got thrown out of yet another hotel. Even at the end of the Faces we behaved deliciously and happily bad. Bollocks to those who say the band was rife with in-fighting. We spilt up because the band had come to a natural end.

The tour finally ended, Rod went his way and I went mine. I knew it hurt him that I'd gone off with the Stones, but he was doing what he wanted, was reaching for a solo career and all I could do was follow my own destiny. Not long after the tour ended, I was hanging with Keith at his place in Switzerland when I read in an English paper, 'Rod Stewart Quits Faces.'

In the article Rod announced to the world, 'I can no longer work in a situation where the band's lead guitarist seems to be permanently on loan to the Rolling Stones.' He sounded angry and resentful, but he knew (and we all knew) that that wasn't the real reason. The Faces had simply reached its natural conclusion and we all had different agendas. Right after that I signed on for the Stones 1976 tour of Europe.

Every now and then there's talk of a Faces reunion. The closest we've ever come was in 1986, on a really rainy night at Wembley Stadium. Kenney, Mac and I, with Bill Wyman on bass, and with Ronnie Lane sitting nearby onstage in a wheelchair, watching us and singing backup when he could, we played 'Stay With Me', 'Twistin' the Night Away', 'I Know I'm Losing You' and 'Sweet Little Rock and Roller'. It was a great night and I'm so glad that Lanie was there.

We came close again in 2004, when Rod, Mac and I played at the Hollywood Bowl with Mac as my special unannounced guest. We did 'I Know I'm Losing You' and 'I'd Rather Go Blind' and six other Faces songs. The audience loved it. I know Jim Keltner and Steve Bing dug it too (I could see them in the crowd). I only wish that Ronnie Lane could have been there with us for that one, too.

Why not a real Faces reunion? I don't know. Maybe some-day we'll put it together because we'll all be feeling hopelessly nostalgic. I hope the time will be right one day. But it's lovely to know that the music we played and the hell we raised all those years ago, and that the group Rod once described as 'five blokes who shared the same haircut but only one hairdryer', are remembered so fondly by other people, not just us.

In February 1976, the Stones officially acknowledged that I existed, and actually issued a press release telling the world that I was a per-manent member of the band. Nobody seemed particularly sur-prised. Two months later we started an eight-week tour of Europe, to support the *Black and Blue* album. We did forty-one shows in nine countries, including the UK. It was the first time the band had played a home game in three years. Earls Court was booked for six nights and we got a million applications for tickets.

On 1 June, exactly one year to the day after I played my first gig with the Stones, we were in Germany playing three concerts in two days. We opened at the Westfalenhalle in Dortmund, and during the band intros Mick sang 'Happy Birthday' to me. I think that's the last time we've ever done two shows in the same day, and the little I remember of them was that I had the flu and was sick as a dog. In Dortmund, it was so bad that they had me propped up onstage with one of those folding golf stools. During 'Midnight Rambler', Mick saw that I was almost gone, took off his belt (it was one of those thick leather things with studs) and whacked me on the back of my legs to bring me back to life. 'Have you heard about the midnight Ram—' Wham!

By the time we got offstage, I couldn't stand up and they took me straight to bed. The next thing I remember is lying there and seeing Keith and Mick unscrewing the door to my room. Screwdrivers in hand, they kept saying, 'Don't worry,

Woody, go back to sleep, feel better, we're just going to relieve you of these,' as they stole all my bottles of birthday booze.

What I liked best about that European tour was how Keith and I were getting deeper and deeper into what we refer to as 'the Ancient Form of Weaving'. A finely balanced exchange of skills mixed with smiles, disturbances and delights is what contributes to Keith's and my weaving. The unspoken-goes-without-saying rapport is a major ingredient. From hotel room to stage we carry on putting into a searing melting pot all the riffs we have learnt through the years.

Right from the Brian Jones days, the Stones always had a very unique style that's built around a kind of delay where Keith plays something on the guitar, Charlie follows on the drums and Bill is slightly behind Charlie with the bass. When Brian was playing with them he'd be somewhere in the middle. It combined to create a kind of chugging effect. The 'human riff' and I were taking that to the next level, and now we do it all the time. It takes a lot of concentration because there's a lot of push and pull, but we can still surprise each other and that's why we love to tour. Our guitar interplay is an ongoing adventure. A lot of that comes out of the necessity to create a picture of the songs as they were built in the studio, and to recreate them in a live setting. Think 'Beast of Burden'.

My first European tour with the Stones finished at the open-air festival at Knebworth. That was truly amazing, standing on a stage in front of 100,000 people. I'd never seen anything like it, a huge sea of heads floating in front of me. Actually, Knebworth almost didn't happen. We did a soundcheck the day before and Keith was going through his bag looking for something and there was a razor blade in there and he sliced a playing finger on the left hand. That's a real problem for a guitar player and we were all worried, so someone found a tube of superglue and we tried to stick the flesh on his finger back together. But it didn't work and the skin came apart again because the cut was exactly in line with the guitar string and his finger kept bleeding. There was blood all over the guitar. He got through the gig, and people yelled, 'Right on, Keef,' because they thought self-mutilation was part of the act.

A stage is not supposed to be a dangerous place. But with the Stones, the stage can sometimes be a fucking deathtrap. Once, in Frankfurt, Keith slipped on a frankfurter.

Krissie and I were living in between London and a beach house in Malibu. We'd been married five years and early in 1976 she got pregnant and in late October, right in the middle of our Halloween party, she went into labour. I'd never done this before and didn't know what to expect, so I said to her, 'I'll be downstairs with our guests, so just yell when it gets really bad.'

She stayed upstairs to deal with the pain, while I kept partying because I didn't want to be rude to a house full of people. David Carradine, who starred in a bunch of karate and martial arts movies, was sitting cross-legged on the floor chanting next to Warren Beatty and Jerry Brown, who was then governor of California. Mick Jagger was there, and so was Jerry Brown's girlfriend, Linda Ronstadt.

I could hear Krissie starting to moan louder and louder upstairs, just as someone knocked on the door. She shouted to me, 'I'm gonna have the baby.' I said, 'Hang on a minute,' and opened the door. Sandy Castle was standing there grinning, 'Hey Ron.' He was Neil Young's roadie and was very proudly pointing to the car he rode around in. 'Anything you need?' Just there, in front of my door, was Sandy's shiny white ambulance. 'Matter of fact,' I said, 'Krissie is having a baby right now so you could take us to the hospital.'

He said, 'Let's go.' I went back inside and announced that Krissie and I had to leave and everybody got all excited about the baby. We got Krissie downstairs, and by this time the contractions were coming on pretty regularly, but she now felt safer. The whole party came out to see Krissie get into Sandy's ambulance, and then Warren asked if we could drop him off at someone's house down the beach. I said sure. Then Jerry and Linda asked if we could drop them off too, and I said fine. So with Krissie safely on board, Sandy turned on the ignition and drove us along Malibu Colony, stopping wherever anyone wanted to jump out. Mick stayed with us.

We got to the hospital. Mick and I sat down to wait. And we did this for the next fifteen hours. Mick stayed with me right till the end, and it's a good thing too. I needed him there with me, especially when the doctors came out and said they had to do a Caesarean and asked me to sign papers giving them permission to operate. I was worried for her but the doctor was very reassuring and explained it all to me. The two of us spent most of that night in Krissie's room, both of us holding her hands. By then a crowd had started to gather. Corinthia West appeared (she was one of the Monty Python girls) and Sandy Castle reappeared. Bob Ellis was there as well – he was then my manager (one of the good ones!) and, at the time, married to Diana Ross.

Krissie and I didn't know if the baby was going to be a boy or a girl, and had no names prepared. The time came, the doctors did whatever they had to do, and after my first child was born I went in to see the baby. The nurses asked me what I was going to call it. I looked at the baby, saw that I had a son, and announced that his name would be 'Boy'. So the delivery nurse wrote 'Boy' in blue on the side of the crib, and that was his name for the first couple of hours.

I needed to call my mum and share our joy. I rushed to the nearest restaurant (in those days, phones were plugged into the tables). David Jansen (*The Fugitive*) was having a Hollywood lunch and I rushed up to his table, 'Give me the phone.' 'No way.' We started wrestling over the phone. 'I've just had a baby.' Eventually he handed it over. Later he apologized and sent a bottle of champagne.

Krissie went to sleep and I went home for a few hours to celebrate with our friends. Back at the house, Diana Ross asked me to show her the baby's room. I took her upstairs to a spare bedroom and said this is it. She looked around at the double bed and all the other regular, normal furniture that bedrooms have and said, 'You can't do that. Where's the bassinet?'

I said, 'What's a bassinet?'

She asked, 'Where's the table to change the baby? Where are all the toys and trinkets that go around the cradle? Where's the cradle?'

I had no idea why we needed all of that stuff, but she insisted we did: 'Get your credit card, we're going shopping,' and drove me to some baby shop where she told the saleswoman, he's going to need this and he's going to need that. She made me buy it all. I kept saying, 'Steady on, Diana, it's only a little baby,' but thousands of dollars later we came back to the house with an entire roomful of stuff.

Pretty soon, the nurses at the hospital were on the warpath for me over the baby's name. Some senior nurse came up to me and insisted, 'You can't call your boy Boy.'

I said, 'Why not?'

She said, 'It's just not right. You have to give him a proper name.'

'Why?' I wanted to know.

'Because you have to,' she said.

So I thought for a second, 'All right, call him Jesse James.'

And that's what we did. I named my firstborn son Jesse James Wood. Years later, I found out something bizarre about the real outlaw, Jesse James. His middle name was Woodson.

I had my firstborn son, but when Krissie and I finally divorced she tried to keep Jesse from seeing me. This wasn't fair on him or my other children that I would have. They couldn't understand why they couldn't see their brother and I couldn't understand why I couldn't see my son. For twelve years or so Jesse was with us as much as he was allowed to be. He would come out on bits of a tour, join us on the occasional family holiday, but he wasn't with us as much as I'd have liked. I didn't enjoy him being held from me. Today we are all together as a family should be. It was difficult at the time he was kept from me, but we all got through it. Jesse is my son and now we are all closer than ever.

In early 1977, the Stones signed a four-record deal for something like $14 million. Nobody else in the music business was getting that kind of money, or had ever seen that kind of money, but part of the deal was that we had to make a live recording.

The trouble with live recordings is that it's sort of a coin toss. If you do the songs well, that's great, but if you don't they're still on the album. You can always try to hone down the mix as much as possible when you get the tapes into the studio, but there's only so much you can do.

We arrived in Canada from different places on 20 February, except Keith and Anita, who didn't get there until four days later. And when they did, they were stopped by customs and had their luggage ransacked. This was the beginning of a nightmare few months for Keith, and turmoil in Toronto for the rest of us.

The band and the crew took over a few floors at the Harbour

Castle Hotel, right on the edge of Lake Ontario. It was swarming with police and press from the moment we arrived. We knew something was up and sure enough, on 27 February, the Royal Canadian Mounted Police swooped. They came up the lifts and stairs, dozens of them in plain clothes, and charged into the part of the hotel where we were all staying. Keith was busted, whacked in jail, put on trial and generally given a tough time. When Keith was going through all those problems, we tried not to look on the dark side. He could have been hassled for a real long time but the combination of good lawyers and Keith's 'blind angel', Rita Bedard, a young girl who melted the judge's heart with her love for the Stones, meant Keith didn't get locked up and the Stones didn't have to break up.

We played the first of our two gigs at El Mocambo Club on Friday night, 4 March 1977. The place could only hold a few hundred people so it was over-jammed for both shows, and really rocking. We played some songs that we don't usually do, 'Route 66', 'Little Red Rooster', 'Crackin' Up', 'Dance Little Sister' and 'Worried About You', and wound up having a great time. Everyone in the crowd was dancing on tables and standing on chairs with wine and beer spilling over everybody. Everyone was lighting up joints even though the whole building was surrounded by cops to keep the peace outside. Keith thought it was exactly like the good old days when the Stones first played the Crawdaddy.

On the Saturday night there was a party for us back at the hotel, given by Margaret Trudeau, the wife of the Canadian Prime Minister, Pierre Elliott Trudeau. He was sort of Canada's John F. Kennedy, a good-looking, rich playboy who dated models and movie stars. John Lennon met Trudeau on a trip to Canada in 1969, at the height of the Vietnam War, and was won over by him, saying 'If all politicians were like him, there would be world peace.' Trudeau married Margaret in 1971, when she was just twenty-two, and he was fifty-one, which made her the world's youngest first lady.

A lovely dark-haired woman, she'd been hanging out with us for a while. The first El Mo date was her sixth wedding anniversary and the fact that she was with us and not her husband raised a lot of Canadian eyebrows. She also had a suite at the Harbour Castle, which led to rumours that she was having a fling with Mick. He denied it but stories leaked to the papers that she was seen running through the hotel corridors in the middle of the night with a Rolling Stone.

I was the one who invited her to the El Mo concerts. She was my pal and from the moment I met her, we spent as much time as possible together. We had a wonderful time and her husband's name never came up. I probably should have guessed she was important because she had Royal Canadian Mounted Police bodyguards following her around. It was a story that could never be told back then. We just hit it off so well, I'm not sure what it was. We'd hang out in Keith's room a lot. No one in the band judged me for what I was doing, but they recommended I be cautious. We both knew it was something that couldn't have a future, but we shared something special for that short time.

The day came for us to leave Toronto. The Prime Minister was forced to make a public statement, something to the effect that his wife's business was nobody else's business.

I told her, 'It's been really lovely to know you, we'll probably never be able to meet again.'

And that was the way it went down.

After Toronto, we moved into the Plaza Hotel in New York, to finish the overdubbing and editing of the El Mocambo recordings and what would become the *Love You Live* album.

It was around that time that we got invited to host and also play on the famous television show *Saturday Night Live*. Apparently, we're one of the few bands ever to host and be the musical guests on the same show. We were on with Ed Koch, who was just about to get elected mayor of New York, and Carrie Fisher, aka Princess Leia from *Star Wars*.

As hosts, we got to do some sketches. All of us except Keith, who opted out of it. Charlie and I did a sketch with Bill Murray, something about a restaurant run by John Belushi, where we were all eating cheeseburgers. Well, just before we went on the air, Charlie and I spiked Bill's cheeseburger. We got a bottle of brandy and soaked it. The director said, 'Action,' and Bill took a bite of his brandy-loaded cheeseburger. Remember, this is live television. Bill tried to keep it together but Charlie and I cracked up.

At one point Mick suddenly came over to me and licked my mouth in the middle of 'Beast of Burden'. When the music is right we celebrate.

Still in New York, I was hanging in my hotel room with Keith and Charlie when there was a knock on the door. I opened it and John Lennon was standing there with Yoko Ono. Both of them were dressed in black, and wearing capes. He babbled in his Scouse drawl, 'Hello, John, I'm Ron. You're John, I'm Ron, this is Yoko, John I'm Ron, Ron I'm John, this is Yoko, hello . . .' I stood at the door taking in this bizarre introduction and let him in.

Yoko was carrying her knitting with her and when we sat down, and she sat down near us, John turned to her and said, 'Bollocks, get on with your knitting,' so she found a chair in the corner and kept on knitting.

John turned to Keith, clapped his hands together in anticipation and asked, 'What's the drug of the day?'

A large devilish grin spread across Keith's face. 'Smack.'

And so the day began.

Charlie had just bought a little wind-up record player with a horn speaker and wanted us to see it, so we moved to his room. He put on an old 78 rpm jazz record, and I guess we must have been making a lot of noise because the hotel manager rang up and said, 'One more peep out of you guys and you're all evicted.' Charlie tried to tell him it's only a little wind-up fucking gramophone, but the manager sent up security and we got flung out of Charlie's room. So we moved the party to Atlantic Records, which was where we were working on the album. Ahmet Ertegun's Atlantic was becoming our recording home. We'd know if he'd like an album because he'd fall asleep during playback. 'Ahmet loves it, he's asleep.' He wasn't there that day. We started jamming, and the jam was taped (it's probably locked in the Atlantic vaults these days). We were going through a songbook of early soul and early Beatles catalogue. We were all singing, playing, harmonizing, sittin', passing the ball around. Anyway, we only got through a few songs before John lay down on the floor and started to sweat. The gauge had kicked in, he mumbled something about going to sleep, and did, right there in the middle of the session. He had to be carried out and Yoko followed him, still knitting. We carried on recording without him.

When John was murdered, it hit me real hard. A man dressed up as a whisky bottle came rushing up to me as I was walking through an airport lounge, his face poking out of his ridiculous costume.

'Ron, have you heard about Lennon?' he said, waving a newspaper.

I sat down, legs shaking. There's a big hole where John use to be.

11

Josephine

I suppose thats two cups of tea now?!
Archie Wood.

Back in England in 1977, my relationship with Krissie was on its last legs. Our relationship had spiralled into a sort of warped rock star wife swap with emotions involved. Prior to meeting Jo, I had had a fiery and heartfelt affair with George Harrison's wife, Pattie Boyd. One night at George's house, Friar Park, in Henley I took George aside and told him quite seriously that when it was time for bed I would be going to Pattie's room. Seemingly unflustered he pointed to the room Krissie and I were staying in and added, 'I shall be sleeping there.' When the time came, the two of us were left on the landing, hands on knobs (doorknobs) of the respective rooms. 'Are we going to do this?' I asked. 'I'll see you in court,' George replied and in we went. Pattie was a little surprised to see me. I told her I thought she was seriously neglected, was going to waste and unleashed that I felt so strongly for her. The following morning we were woken by George, who informed me that he had called his lawyers. He never actually did. Pattie and I headed off to the Bahamas and Krissie and George left for Portugal. Whenever I went to Friar

Park, my man George would always greet me at the door singing with his Yukelele: 'Funny little fellow – wears his sister's clothes – don't know what to call him, but I think he's one of those.' Ringo and I would always laugh with affection.

My relationships were passionate, romantic, even debauched up to this point but the weight of them was nothing to compare to the meaningful direction I was about to be pointed in.

I was invited to David Morris' house. He was married to a woman named Lorraine and she was responsible for me meeting the woman of my life. The party was like any other apart from this gorgeous bubbly blonde who was floating around. The blonde reminded me of a young Goldie Hawn, great bottom and all, and was wearing her grannie's blue dress, a Harris tweed jacket and cool beige boots. I had to meet her, so I got Krissie a Quaalude sandwich. She liked that and fell asleep, then I said goodbye to Pattie and went off to find this woman.

I snuck up behind Jo and was ready to give that bum a good grope but she spotted me in a mirror, spun round and looked me straight in the eye.

'I'm Ronnie Wood.'

'I'm Jo.'

'I'm Ronnie Wood,' I repeated just in case she hadn't clocked it the first time.

I had to pull out a copy of *Black and Blue* to point out who I was but she didn't seem particulary impressed. She'd seen the Stones at the Earls Court gigs, hadn't noticed me and had left early because she was having a shit night with her husband.

I asked her what she did for a living and she said, 'I work at Woolworths on Oxford Street.'

I couldn't see how someone this gorgeous could possibly work at Woolies. 'What are you, the manageress?'

She said, 'No, I work on the broken-biscuit counter.' She

reached into her bag, pulled out her diary and showed me some modelling shots of her taken in America. She explained that the six girls and four guys in the diary all worked at Woolies and had won a competition to represent Woolworths in the States. She even told me the names of the other people, including one guy who was, she explained, Mr Woolworth's son.

I said, 'My, they have good-looking girls working at Woolworths,' and kept nattering to her. But after a while I think she decided she didn't really want to be chatted up any more, shook me off and started mingling. There was absolutely no way I was letting this one go. I hid in the bathroom with the door cracked open just a bit, waiting for her to walk by. When she did, I took my chance: 'Psst, come here.' She looked at me as if I was mad. I said, 'Pssst, come here quick, I've got something really important to tell you.' Baffled by me, she walked in and as soon as she did, I slammed the door, locked it, and said, 'Do you want a line?'

Rejuvenated and recharged, my confidence raised, I presented her with an unmissable offer.

'Give me a kiss.'

For me this was love at first sight, the absolute. The next day I went to Woolies on Oxford Street to find her. I waited in my car all day for her. My driver, Frank, must have thought I was being slightly obsessive. After I saw the last member of staff leaving, I asked him about the gorgeous blonde who worked at the broken-biscuit counter, the one who'd won the modelling competition. He gave me a very odd look, and that's when I knew I'd been had. Jo had created a maze of lies out of nothing – full marks for creativity though.

I raced back to David Morris' flat because I had to find this girl again. There was no way she was getting away that easily. I hung around until at last a little orange VW pulled up and Jo got out. I told her, 'You don't work in Woolworths.' She asked,

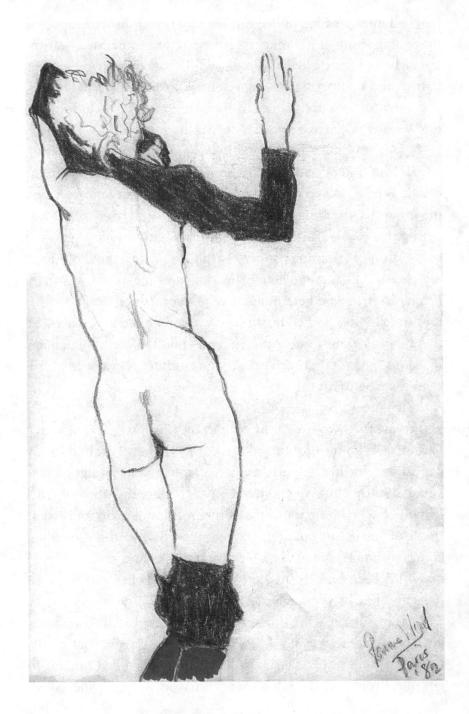

me with mum on the backdoor step.

Fresh out

Getting a lift

with Keith in L.A. Forest Knoll

mum and dad, 8, Whitethorn

Barbarians

At the New York 'Scene' club with Hendrix

Paris, the beginnings

With Marley and Jo, San Francisco

Limo

reflective smokin'

another hat on stage

messed-up painting

Morning

With Jesse in Malibu

With Leah

London

With Leah and Tyrone, Jamaica

Jo and Leah

Fancy dress

With Jo in the St. Maarten 'magic skirt'

Pretty Beat up.

Three generations

'How do you know that?' I said, 'Because I've just spent the entire day waiting on Oxford Street for you.'

Now that I'd found her again, I wasn't going to leave. I hung out with her for the rest of the day at David's house and when it got late, I convinced Lorraine and David that I couldn't drive home because it was too late. They let me stay. But Lorraine and Jo knew what I was thinking (everybody knew what I was thinking) so they put me in the upstairs bedroom, as far away from Jo as possible. I lay in bed waiting for everyone else in the house to fall sleep. When I decided the coast was clear, I crept into Jo's bedroom. She tried to make me leave, but I refused. I crawled into bed with her. She wasn't having any of it and made me leave my overcoat on.

Now that I was appropriately dressed she decided that I could stay. That night she stayed dressed too. Of course I kept trying to get a do, but nothing happened except I got to lay in bed with the fabulous woman who had utterly consumed me.

Work had to continue in the midst of this blossoming romance. The Stones were debuting the *Love You Live* album, so I had to go to New York for a few days. But I knew this was the real thing, and even if Jo thought I was mad, I rang her from the States to say, 'Meet me in two days in Paris.' She had a young son, Jamie, and didn't earn a lot of money. She was pretty reluctant to do this, but I talked her into it and we agreed to meet at L'Hotel, a very chic but very small hotel on the Left Bank. She scraped together enough money to buy a ticket and pay for the taxi from Orly Airport downtown, and arrived at L'Hotel at around eight. She told me later that she got there late on purpose, because she didn't want to appear overanxious.

She went to the front desk and announced that she was there to meet Mr Wood, but the man behind the desk didn't understand. She said, 'I'm here to meet Mr Ronnie Wood.'

He told her, 'Madame, we have no reservation for a Mr Wood.'

She felt stranded, seriously frustrated, and not knowing what to do, asked if she could have a room. The man at the desk explained that they didn't have any rooms because this was fashion week in Paris. In fact, all the hotels in Paris were full.

She nearly burst into tears. She was stranded and skint. I guess he finally felt sorry for her because he let her have a minuscule maid's room on the top floor. Rooms at L'Hotel are tiny anyway, but the maid's room was more like a closet. She went upstairs, feeling like an idiot for getting lured to Paris by some rock musician, and tried to go to sleep in this ridiculously narrow bed. But she couldn't fall asleep because she was feeling so stupid, was so angry at me, and needed to figure out how she could do a runner the next morning.

She woke up every hour and rang the front desk to ask if I'd arrived. They kept telling her no. What she didn't know was that my Concorde flight from New York had blown an engine (when the engine went at Mach 2 my coffee went shooting down the aisle) so we'd made an emergency landing at Shannon Airport, Ireland, and then sat in a holding lounge for quite a while. Freddie Sessler got mistaken for Mick Jagger, which lightened the mood for a while, and once they'd got the engine fixed, we got on our way. As soon as we landed in Paris, I raced over to L'Hotel with Keith in tow. It was around 4:30 a.m.

Just as I arrived I realized that I didn't know her real name. She was modelling under the name Jo Howard, but when I asked at the front desk for Jo Howard, the clerk, who wasn't the same person who'd checked her in and therefore didn't know that she was waiting there for me, looked blank. I tried to describe her, but that didn't do any good. Eventually I managed to convince him to let me go through hotel's guest list. As

I looked at all the names, I spotted 'J. Karslake', and figured that was close because it started with J. I told him to go for it.

The desk clerk pointed to the clock and said he couldn't possibly ring someone at that hour, unless I was sure it was the right person. He must have seen how much I wanted to get hold of this person and rang upstairs. When a woman answered, he asked, 'Are you Miss Karslake? Are you also Miss Howard? Do you know Mr Wood? He's here.'

I heard her scream, 'Send him up.'

She jumped out of bed and quickly dolled herself up, and I knocked on her door. She opened it, I walked in and so did Keith. He went straight past Jo to a tiny table, never said a word, took out a spoon and started cooking up a hit. Jo stood there speechless, with her mouth wide open because she'd never seen anything like this. Keith shot up, then looked at her and said, 'You must be Jo, hello darling,' and gave her a big kiss. Jo glared to me. I simply said, 'You have to excuse my friend, we go everywhere together.' We did then. And for years to come the three of us would hang out constantly, Keith, Jo and I. Patti (Keith's wife) eventually came along, making it four. We would mess about endlessly, invent fictitious countries over long evenings indoors, explore music, travel, and watch out for each other.

Keith stayed there with us for three days. Remember, this room was the size of a phone booth. The management must have wondered what was going on. There was only that single bed, for Jo and me, and Keith took whatever space was left. We were top and toe.

Jo kept asking me, 'When are we going to get rid of Keith?' But we couldn't leave him there alone, in an opiate haze. Plus the three days passed pretty rapidly for Jo and me. On the third day Keith, who was feeling fresher, suggested, 'We've been here three days, why don't we move to my flat?'

'Your flat?' Jo couldn't believe he had his own place in Paris and had stayed in our tiny room with us for three solid days. So we checked out of L'Hotel and went over to the flat. The place was in complete disarray but had more bedrooms than our cupboard abode.

Keith gave us his bed and Jo got busy straightening out the place and we made our nest. We shut the door, leaving Keith alone, got out of our clothes, jumped into bed, and broke it in half.

We were thrown on to the floor and pinned up against the wall and couldn't get up. Keith heard the crash, raced in and found us both naked against the wall. We were all cracking up. That's how our life together began. And although Jo would go home every week or so to see her son, we spent the next five months in Paris, madly in love.

From Keith's place, we moved into a small hotel called Château Frontenac for a couple of months. Jo called it Château Front and Back, and after that we rented an apartment where the downstairs neighbours wouldn't let us walk around with our shoes on. We called that place Complaining Mansions.

The Stones were recording the *Some Girls* album, so the whole gang was there, including Chuch, who was living at the Frontenac, in the room next door to ours. This was all very new to Jo, who asked Chuch, 'What happens?' He said, 'Just stick with me,' and he showed her the ropes of hanging out with the Stones.

Some Girls is one of my favourite Rolling Stones albums. In many ways, the album was a celebration of friends, but I was also enjoying the interplay with Mick. I was having a lot of fun hanging out with him and learning from him. We were building the foundations of our lifelong relationship, through music, wine and song.

There was a small room next to the actual recording studio, which Jo claimed as her own, hung a sign on the door that read

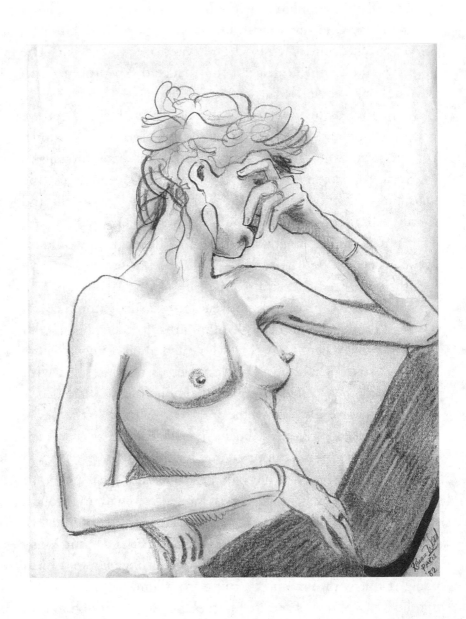

'Jo's Club', decorated it with cushions and candles and spent a lot of time in there reading. I'd sneak in between takes for a quickie. We recorded all night, and never went home before 6 a.m. Jo cooked breakfast for Keith and me, and also looked after Keith's son Marlon whenever he came to visit. Keith would read a bedtime story to Marlon every night regardless of what he was up to.

Jo took to life in Paris as if she was French, and especially liked the fruit and vegetable markets. Although she didn't always get what she bargained for. She went out one day to buy some mushrooms, didn't know the difference between pounds and kilos, and we wound up living on mushroom soup, mushroom omelettes, mushroom everything, for months.

When Christmas came and the Stones took off for the holidays, Jo and I thought about going back to England, but we didn't want to pop the bubble we were in and decided to head for the sun. We needed to find a hot place to fly to and so for holiday advice we turned to the nearest Colombian drug trafficker.

He was a fellow called Victor, which may or may not have been his real name, but that's what everybody called him. He was an erstwhile acquaintance we used to bump into on the road. He was a very flash guy, who dressed sharp, always took the best suites in every hotel, had his own plane and was always telling us, 'Whatever I have is yours.' When we told him we were at loose ends for Christmas and New Year, he invited us to the Bahamas. Or, to put it more accurately, he decided we were going with him to Nassau, and I'm not sure we had much choice in the matter.

It wasn't so much an invitation as an order. He said, 'You are coming with me to my home in Nassau,' and we said okay. He was a very domineering guy and something told us that we had better get on a plane with him. He'd also invited Ringo Starr, so I guess that made it all right with us.

On the flight from Paris, Victor was out of his mind smoking little joints with doojee in them. He had a load of these 'dirty cigarettes', which he intended to take into the Bahamas, and just before landing he handed Jo his stash of DCs and said, 'You're taking this through.'

She told me, 'I'm not going to do that,' and I wasn't going to do it either, but this was a heavy dude and it took a lot of back and forth with Victor before he settled on a way. He took a carton of cigarettes that we'd bought in duty free and rebuilt it, packing the DCs in one box of cigarettes and slipping that box into the back of the carton before resealing.

When we got to customs, and all our stuff got put down on the counter in front of the inspector, there was the carton of cigarettes. The inspector said, 'Whose is this?'

Jo said, 'It's his,' and pointed to Victor.

But Victor said, 'No it's his,' and pointed to me.

I pointed back at Victor. 'It's his.'

And Victor pointed at Jo and said, 'I guess it must be hers.'

It was like a comedy sketch, except that the inspector wasn't laughing, and now turned to Jo and made her empty her bag. He searched all over it and inside it, and then reached for the carton of cigarettes and opened one packet, the wrong one, and we strolled through.

Once we got to the beautiful house, and once Ringo showed up, Victor invited us – actually he ordered us again – to go into the recording studio he had there and start playing music for him. We weren't going to argue with him, so Ringo and I played music for him – I remember I wrote a song called 'Tiger Balm' – and he recorded it. Ringo and I were recently reminiscing about this time we were held hostage by this guy, swapping lines for riffs and drug patters for drum patterns.

As soon as we could, Jo and I raced back to our idyllic existence in Paris. Eventually, we heard, Victor got busted and tossed into prison. It seems his own father hated what he did, couldn't stand the idea that his son was a major drug dealer, and turned him in. It wasn't the last time Jo and I were to holiday with substance entrepreneurs.

At that point in her life Jo hadn't been around the drug scene very much. She had some German sleeping tablets that she'd picked up on some modelling trip, but Keith found them so they disappeared. Those were the good old drug days when you could depend on pharmaceuticals. Downers put you to sleep, except when you drink on them. You counterbalance the downer with the alcohol, or with some pharmaceutical coke, and you're rocking in the middle. There was a pill in those days called Desbutol, it was half turquoise and half orange and it was a half-upper and a half-downer. Freddie Sessler had them in Paris and they were the best Freddie-drug ever. They don't make them anymore.

Jo was scared of the pills, and frightened whenever Keith skin popped. I didn't like watching him do that either because I've always hated needles. But Paris has always been a good place for the Stones, which is why we like recording there. It's much calmer than other places, no constant fan-mania, just druggies and dealers. One of the dealers was a fellow with a French name we couldn't pronounce, so Jo called him Jean-Pierre Le Wanker. He topped himself having sex with some girl – he did an amyl-nitrate popper, blew up and died on the job. That sort of stuff frightened Jo away from any drugs but the most recreational.

Those five months in Paris became a real learning experience for Jo. She'd never seen anything like it. In the meantime, Jo and I were falling gloriously in love, making love at any available opportunity, especially in Jo's Club at the studio. She put scarves up on the windows so nobody could peek in, put a big sign on the door, 'Do Not Enter Without Permission', and we'd spend every fleeting moment together.

Those five months felt like five days and by the time we went back to London, Jo was pregnant with our love child, Leah. She was conceived on a passionate night in Ian McLagan's flat in Battersea.

I first brought Jo home to meet my mum and dad the same night we landed at Heathrow. I didn't know how to explain to them that I'd fallen completely in love with her, because I was still married to Krissie and Jo was still married to her first husband.

We drove to Yiewsley and I showed Jo where I grew up, then brought her inside the house on Whitethorn Avenue and told my parents, 'I just met this girl at the airport and she didn't have a ride, she's stranded, I'm going to drive her home, and isn't she beautiful?'

Jo sat there all coy while my dad gave me an odd look, because he knew a lame excuse when he heard one. So did my mum, who kept mumbling, 'I understand . . . just be careful . . .' and gave me a wink.

My dad always had an eye for the ladies and liked Jo a lot. On a later visit to Yiewsley, once my parents knew the truth, when Jo was putting Archie's beer down on his little table, he pinched her bottom. That startled her. He winked, 'I could give you three yet, girl.'

Jo was becoming my everything, but I wasn't sure how to manage things with Krissie. I had to sort it out with her before I could move in with Jo, and that was going to take me a little bit of time. In the meantime, Jo was taking in the seriousness of the situation. She had a small boy and needed to be sure she was making the right decision by joining forces with me.

Jo was living with her friend Susan. Meanwhile I was met at the door of the Wick by Krissie. The relationship was petering out. I took a barrage of abuse, she was saying she didn't love me and had planned to divorce me anyway. Then she confessed she loved Jimmy Page and had lived with him for months often wearing nothing but a sheet, while I was having my fling with Pattie Boyd. I couldn't handle this any more, and realized that this was my chance.

I decided, it's now or never, and left. I didn't care that it was two o'clock in the morning, I phoned the flat where Jo was staying. When her friend Sue answered I said, 'Wake up Jo. I'm on my way over.' Ten minutes later I got there and told Jo, 'I've left Krissie.'

It's now more than thirty years later and Jo and I are still together. A few days after I left Krissie, Keith Moon phoned me to say, 'I heard you were going out with a new girl. Bring her over. She has to pass my audition.' I said, 'She does?'

He said, 'Damn right she does. We all love Krissie, so I'm only out for your best interests. I mean, hang on, man, you're married.' He was having a sudden rash of morals. 'Bring this new one over, and she better be something because if she's no good, she's out.'

On the pretext that it would be fun if she met one of my mates, I brought Jo to Moonie's place, without telling her that this was an audition. The two of them got on like a house on fire. And as we were leaving, Moonie shook my hand and said, 'You have my seal of approval.'

Sometime towards the beginning of that summer, Krissie got into a road accident. She was in the Mercedes sport that I'd bought for her and went straight through a shop window in Richmond. I went to see her. I walked into Krissie's room and right away she started berating me, 'How could you leave me with my broken back?'

It took a year before all the paperwork was settled and Krissie and I were divorced. By then, Jo and I were in L.A.

Not long after I got my divorce papers, Jo got hers. Their relationship had been cold for over a year. Jo had blossomed independently and I had got her at her most fruitful.

It had all worked out and I'd got my girl. But life with its ups and downs always seems to hand out slaps as well as treasures. By now I'd lost the Wick.

I had been having problems with the Inland Revenue and they'd left me no choice – the demands of £80,000 were simply too much. I never wanted to get rid of my house, never wanted to move out. I'd be inspired by the hot summer days in the garden and take ideas into the Wick studios, where they would multiply and come to life. The house creaks with rock and roll memories and oozed out some of my most accomplished work. Thoughts of Big Don, 'The Oaf', my butler, a sweaty Jeeves who meant well but took the elements of accident to a new level. A man accustomed to beating up the wrong people. And Frank Foy, the chauffeur, a fan of Queen (!), a comforting shoulder for the girls, a reliable, patient man who would always get me home. I still hark back to the treasures of the Wick that come flooding back when I drive past. A wonderful piece of 1775 Georgian architecture, landscaped gardens and a view of the Thames from the top of Richmond Hill that is still one of the envies of European scenery.

I gave Krissie some of the money I'd got from the Wick, then packed up and shipped everything to Los Angeles. I felt like I was starting life over again, this time with Jo, a bun in her oven, and Jo's two-year-old son Jamie. It was 1978.

Pete Townshend eventually bought my house, turned the snooker room into an office and got rid of my table. Apart from this ruinous decision of his, knowing the Wick is in great hands is a big relief. He often reminds me, 'I still have your studio in pristine condition, exactly the way you left it. It's still the same.' Good.

Jo never lived at the Wick. In fact, she only visited there once. I took her by after we'd cleaned it out. We walked through all the empty rooms together, until we got to the oval bedroom, where the only piece of furniture left in the house was a bed. We had a romantic afternoon before moving our love, and our unit, to Los Angeles.

12

L.A. Times

The first place we lived when we moved to L.A. was on Forest Knoll Drive, just above Sunset in West Hollywood, in a very distinct house that had a swimming pool as soon as you walked in and a huge central fireplace in the large open sitting room. People would come to visit us and look around as if it was déjà vu all over again, as if they'd seen the place before (which many of them had). But not everyone admitted that they recognized it because the house was where millions of porno films were shot. I was a great host there, for both business and pleasure. I would lavishly entertain music company executives during work meetings. They got smashed, and their euphoric state helped seal the extensions of my contracts.

We weren't on Forest Knoll very long before we found a bigger place, this one in Mandeville Canyon, not far from Sunset and P.C. Highway. One step away from a log cabin, this historic piece of Americana became a close-knit family home, a little bit of countryside so near to Sunset. The scene of inter-acting and bonding between children and adults alike. This creative atmosphere was somewhat stifled by undesirables. The swimming pool, a voluptuous figure of eight, had once belonged to the synchronized-swimming Hollywood belle Esther Williams. The house also came complete with the wonderful Jaye Carter,

our nanny for many years. Jo and I met her when we first saw
the house and decided, either she comes with the house or we're
not taking it. She helped us raise our children and went off to
help Keith and Mick with their kids for a while, but never really
left the Woods.

Even if being in southern California again meant putting up
with the smog and air pollution (which continued to bother me
and always has) it also meant meeting loads of new people.

At the time Tony Curtis met Cary Grant he was so popular, groupies used to yell, 'Cary Grant is Jesus Christ.' He,
Tony Curtis and I would spend deliciously succulent evenings
together.

Because he paints, Tony and I would spend a lot of time discussing drawing and painting. We'd sit and sketch each other
while sipping precious vintages. He'd scribble away in his minimalist Matisse-like way. He also loved to reminisce about the
old days of Hollywood, but I always liked it best when he talked

about *Some Like It Hot*, and especially when he spoke about Marilyn. I'd chop up coke for myself on top of her photographs and he'd mumble, 'You bitch. You bitch.' He told me that when they were making that movie together, Marilyn was the first one in the studio parking lot and the last one out, 'Because she was fucking everybody.' He shattered my image of her, saying in the early days she'd sleep with anyone to get a part in a movie. And he once gave me a pair of cowboy boots that he wore when he was having sex with her. Keith christened them 'Boots far too big'.

Tony loved talking about England and knew it well. He had a house in London, in Chester Square, and once when we were going back to the UK and he was in London but had to go on some sort of trip, he asked us to house-sit for him. Jo and I said sure, we'd be very happy to. We moved in and he showed us around the house and the tour included the trap door in the floor that led to his wine cellar. He very graciously said, 'You have the freedom of my wine cellar,' which was his first mistake. His second mistake was leaving me there with forty or fifty cases of the finest vintage wines. We had parties at his house every night – and why not, the wine was excellent – and we drank all of his bottles except for one bottle of Château Petrus. When Tony came back a couple of weeks later, he was so angry at me because he'd been collecting that wine for years. I promised to make it up to him, to replace the entire cellar, but he said that would be impossible because some of those bottles were irreplaceable. I said, 'Tony, does that mean we're not friends any more?' He said, 'Ron, I love your company but I can't stand your hours.'

It was at the end of 1978 and we were in New York for a gig. I heard that Muhammad Ali was staying at a hotel over on 8th Avenue – this was just before his rematch with Leon

Spinks – so I went over there. My timing was great because as I walked into the lobby, he was coming down into reception. The place was buzzing. It was mayhem. You have to remember that he was then, probably, the most famous man on earth. There were so many people and there was so much security that I never thought I'd get anywhere near him. But I decided I had to try. I wriggled through a mound of heaving bodyguards, stuck out my hand and was more surprised than anybody else when he stopped and looked at me. I told him, 'My dad would be the proudest man in the world if I could shake the hand of the man.' He shook my hand, and then we just started talking, all the time trying to ignore the hustle and bustle going on around us.

Many years later, I was in New York for an exhibition of my paintings. Ali was in town doing some charity work. I had donated some art to his charity and someone decided it would be fun if we got together. He came to my hotel suite and the first thing I did was remind him of our first meeting. As extraordinary as it sounds, he told me he remembered. Not because he remembered me, but because I'd mentioned my dad. It blew me away that he could recall those few fleeting minutes, especially with the hoopla that surrounded him all those years ago.

But then, even though he was suffering from Parkinson's, his exuberance was still clear. The thing about that nasty illness is that when it gets hold of someone as special as Ali, it might turn him off for a little bit but when Ali fights back, his lightning sharp wit comes bursting through. And he really is one of the funniest people I've ever come across. He reminds me of Jerry Lee and also of my dad, with wit as sharp as a razor.

Ali brought some magic tricks with him that night and started doing them. He showed me magic colouring books and levitating ropes. He said that doing illusions fascinated him and that magic gave him a chance to hold people's attention. This from the man who held the world's attention in the palm of his hand for decades.

He asked me if I wanted to learn a great optical-illusion trick, and I said sure. It's one where you stand at a certain angle and raise one foot and you look like you're floating. It's a great trick that never ceases to freak out my grandkids.

Ali and I have stayed friends and he's always sending me little notes and pictures. He's got the tiniest writing of anybody I've ever met. He writes like a flea. He sent me a little drawing once that was so small I actually took it with me the next time I saw him, showed it to him and had to ask, 'What's that on this piece of paper?' He told me, 'That's a heart that I've drawn with legs on it.'

I've painted him and he owns one of the portraits. In fact, I did an edition of lithographs of him knocking out Franzie, which we double-signed for his charity and they sold out in minutes.

Later that night he decided, 'Let's go out on 5th Avenue and stop the traffic.'

I said, 'What do you want to do?'

'You and me,' he said, 'we'll walk down 5th Avenue and stop the traffic. A Rolling Stone on one side of the street and Muhammad Ali on the other side.'

Unfortunately, we couldn't go because he wasn't moving that well. I wanted to and he wanted to but some people around him said no.

Then his manager asked, 'Hey Ali, who do you think they'd stop first?'

He answered, 'The white boy.'

When I finally said goodnight to him at the door and thought

he'd gone back inside, I turned around to my PA, Donna, and cheered. 'I just hung with Muhammad Ali.'

But Ali was still there, and he called back, 'Hey, I just met a Rolling Stone.'

Billy Connolly — LA.

Pete + Dud — elaborate?

Beltzer?

CHAPTER THIRTEEN

LOSS

It was when we were living in Mandeville that I also got to meet Bob Marley. Keith, Charlie and I had all picked up on reggae in the islands at the same time, pretty early on. Reggae hadn't really hit the rest of the world yet. Keith breathes it and I had the great pleasure of introducing him to Jimmy Cliff. I'd met Jimmy at a party and knew straight away that Keith and had to meet him. They were made for each other. I took Jimmy with me up to Keith's hotel room door and covered the spyhole with my hand.

I knocked "Keith?"

"Fuck off" came the response

I knocked again "There's someone here you should meet."

He opened the door, and his grumpy demenour disappeared. He saw Jimmy, immediately pulled him into his suite, hugged him, sat down, lit a spliff and the two of them have been great friends ever since.

There was something about Reggae that struck a serious chord for us. The fundamental Ital rhythm, a mutual love that weaved into the foundation of our musical creativity, the same

219

Tosh
Stickers — Yellowman — N.Y.C.
Sly Robbie
Earl Chinn — N.Y. Reggae Radio
early MTV
NYC — seminar — Townhall
goat month.
Bbados
Bongo man

13

Loss

It was when we were living in Mandeville that I also got to meet Bob Marley. Keith, Charlie and I had all picked up on reggae in the islands at the same time, pretty early on. Reggae hadn't really hit the rest of the world yet. Keith breathes it and I had the great pleasure of introducing him to Jimmy Cliff. I'd met Jimmy at a party and knew straight away that Keith had to meet him. They were made for each other. I took Jimmy with me up to Keith's hotel room door and covered the spyhole with my hand.

I knocked. 'Keith?'

'Fuck off,' came the response.

I knocked again. 'There's someone here you should meet.'

He opened the door, and his grumpy demeanour disappeared. He saw Jimmy, immediately pulled him into his suite, hugged him, sat down, lit a spliff and the two of them have been great friends ever since.

There was something about reggae that struck a serious chord for us. The fundamental ital rhythm, a mutual love that weaved into the foundation of our musical creativity, the same way blues did. A load of great reggae bands suddenly appeared on the scene, like the Slickers and Heptones and Max Romeo and Pluto Sherrington. In those days Keith and I would take our own reggae records to clubs, tell the disk jockey he had to play them, and if he didn't he risked being on the end of Keith's ratchet. We were only trying to cheer the place up.

In November 1979, Bob Marley and the Wailers were on their Survival world tour, playing at the Oakland Coliseum. One of Bob's guitar players, Al Anderson, had lost his guitar and rang me to ask if he could possibly borrow one of mine. I didn't mind, and even offered to bring it up to him. So I flew up to San Francisco and got a taxi out to the Coliseum several hours before the show, but Marley's security guys wouldn't let me in. I explained that I was there with a guitar for Al, but these were all very large Jamaican guys, they didn't know who I was and all they saw was just some skinny white guy with funny hair trying to get into the show for nothing. I tried everything I could to reason with them, and when that didn't work, I decided that the only way I could prove to them that I was me was by playing.

I had an audition. I stood there outside the artists' entrance to the stadium and played reggae riffs, and they started to groove and after a bit they decided I wasn't messing about. So they let me hang around until Al got there.

He brought me backstage where I hung with the Wailers through a haze of herb smoke. We laughed and joked and jammed a little bit. I told them how much I loved playing reggae with them – and why not, these guys were the reggae kings – and they asked me if I'd come on and play one of their encores with them. I looked at Al, he thanked me for the guitar and brought me back to Bob's dressing room. Bob was standing in the middle of his smoky room, swaying to a slow reggae groove. The customary grefa never stopped burning. His eyes were almost closed when Al introduced me to him. I said hi, and he just nodded. He was a very quiet man and was consciously away from the energy of the rest of his band outside. We shared a couple of spliffs and vibed out to some of his songs. I told him, 'So far you're the only guy in the band who doesn't know that I'm playing with you tonight, is that all right?' He didn't answer. Instead, he gave me a look which said, if you can cut it you're on.

The band put on a fantastic show and when they got called back for an encore, Bob brought me on. We started grooving and while I was playing he gave me another look, this time to say, yeah, okay, you're all right. I figured we'd do one or two numbers, but he and I were having a good time together and he kept me onstage with him for the entire encore, which lasted an hour and a half.

After the concert, the band made us feel right at home. Then Bob and I did some interviews together. Jo and I even had a picture taken with him. I was going to say goodbye when one of the Wailers said, 'You know, Bob really likes you.' That was odd because he was standing right there. It was almost as if he couldn't or wouldn't talk for himself, as long as he had one of the Wailers to talk for him.

'Bob wants you to come play football.' So we played football. He had an indoor pitch backstage where we kicked the ball around and puffed great ganga. So here was an Englishman playing his game in America with a bunch of Rastas and all the time there was Bob really smiling. What a great guy.

Someone else I got to meet in L.A., ironically, was Ian Dury. I say ironically, because he was English too, and our paths had never crossed back home. Without doubt, Ian was one of the most underrated rock legends ever, and a great artist. But I'd never even heard of him until the first time I went to Jo's house to meet her parents.

Jo's brothers Paul and Vinny picked me up in their Mini and they were playing Ian Dury and the Blockheads on the cassette player. I said who's that and they told me. I thought Ian was terrific from that first listen.

I also thought Paul and Vinny were terrific because Jo had warned me that her father wouldn't let anyone drink in the house, and they figured that I might like something so they'd been down to the off-licence and smuggled in a half-bottle of vodka. We went up to their room to have a drink, and Paul rolled a joint before playing more Ian for me.

When we met Ian in L.A., just at the point where his career was really taking off, Jo and I insisted that he come home with us for baked beans on toast. He asked where Jo was from and when she told him that she was born in Billericay, which is in Essex, he said that's where he was from and started calling her (like the song) Billericay Dickie. Ian turned out to be one of the greatest guys who ever walked the earth, and is another guy I miss a lot. He was secretive about his talent as an artist and painter. One night at his apartment in Hammersmith he took me through his planchest. It was very impressive work he'd kept since his art school days.

One night when Rod was in L.A., we heard that Ian and the Blockheads were playing at the Roxy, so we went to see him. But it was really sad because he was unknown in the States and there were only about fifteen people in the house. Lou Reed was on the bill that night. Rod and I went backstage and detuned all Lou's guitars so that when he went on, nothing worked. He never forgave us, but Rod and Ian and I thought it was hysterical.

Graham Chapman and Eric Idle, of Monty Python fame, were also living in L.A. in those days. Eric was putting together a spoof on the Beatles called The Rutles, and invited all of his friends to work cheap. He cast Paul Simon, Michael Palin, Bill Murray, Mick and Bianca, Dan Aykroyd and John Belushi. He dressed me up as a punk Hell's Angel. Actually, we filmed most of it back in the UK, where Eric used some of the same locations that the Beatles did in *A Hard Day's Night*. Our version was called *All You*

Need Is Cash, and all these years later it's still funny. If you look quickly you can spot Jo in it somewhere, and George Harrison makes a fast appearance, too. Lorne Michaels, the man who invented *Saturday Night Live*, is in it, and so are Al Franken and Gilda Radner. The show was the precursor to *Spamalot*, the Monty lot just having a laugh in the post-Python era. Everything was so wonderfully disorganized. It was my sort of day at work. You know, laugh, laugh, laugh and . . . oh, the job's done?

Hanging out back in L.A. with Eric, he and I managed to get thrown out of Graham Chapman's house for laughing too hard. Graham had invited us around to see the rushes of *Life of Brian*, the funniest movie ever made. Keith was there, too, hanging out with a girl called Lil. She was a real mad chick, who liked the bottle and who had a huge laugh that could mow down the wall. Graham had his mum staying at the house and she kept complaining that she couldn't sleep because we were all laughing so loudly. Graham kept saying, 'Please keep it down, my mum . . .'

Keith kept trying to cover Lil's mouth with his hand, but she kept pulling away and yelling at him, 'Fuck off,' then started laughing again. It got so bad that Graham's mum got out of bed and spoke to her son, and he had to escort us to the door. 'I'm so sorry but my mum wants you to leave.'

Another Brit I kept bumping into in those years, and still do, is David Bowie. He's a real down-to-earth creature, a gentle, lovely, incredibly creative man. I took Jo to see him at Madison Square Garden and we were hanging out backstage waiting for him when Tina Turner came up, planted a big kiss on me and said, 'Keith, I love you.' She's always getting me and Keith muddled up in the early days, so I had to tell her, 'I'm Ronnie.' She grinned, 'Well, I enjoyed it all the same.'

When Bowie came offstage, I rushed up to him and announced,

totally out of the blue, 'Oi, Dave, where's that fiver you owe me?' Surrounded by the panic of his entourage, he replied, cool as you like, 'It's in my other trousers, Ron, I'll have to get it to you later.' That's Bowie. Even in the madness of his world, he still has time for the simple honest comfort of his friends. When living in New York David rang me up and asked me to do a show with him at the China Club with Steve Winwood and Carmine Rojas. I turned up thinking we'd have time for rehearsals. We went straight on. Impromptu bliss.

L.A. at the time was rammed with stars of the moment. A buffet of talent. Mick and I went to see Marvin Gaye one night, but forgot to get tickets. We did manage to talk our way back-stage, and spent the whole show watching the man himself from the side of the stage. After the show, we ended up in Marvin's hotel room, waiting for an audience.

There were a lot of people hanging out, and when we didn't see Marvin we went looking for him. We opened the bedroom door and saw him sitting there with his hat on. Mick dived straight in, giving Marvin his advice about which songs he should have sung, and which songs he should probably forget about doing in the show. Mick went on and on, until the poor guy butted in, 'Hey, man, that's all very well, but I'm Marvin's brother. He'll be back soon.'

When we were off travelling, Jo would get her brother Paul to house-sit for us. And one night while Paul was looking after Mandeville Canyon and the kids, a limo pulled up and the buzzer went on the gate. Paul answered it and a voice said, 'Hey Ronnie, man, it's John, man, I've got to see you.'

Paul replied, 'Sorry, Ronnie's not here.'

John said, 'Who's this?' When Paul said he was Jo's brother, John said, 'Hey, man, I've got to talk to you.'

Paul kept saying, 'I don't know who you are,' but now this fellow went into a real sob story about how his ex-wife had left him, and Paul felt really sorry for him so he let him in.

The big fat hulk of a guy falls down on the couch and starts crying his heart out about his ex-wife. Paul didn't have a clue who he was, except that he seemed to know Jo and me. The two of them spent the whole night drinking while John cried on Paul's shoulder. John left at around 5 a.m. and Paul decided it was just a typical night at the Woods' family home.

Jo and I came back at the weekend and Paul told Jo that this large guy, a really nice guy, had come around to the house and spent the night telling Paul about all his problems. Paul said he tried to help the guy sort his ex-wife out, but by now couldn't even remember the bloke's name. She went inside to cook dinner and Paul and I were standing in front of the telly when *Saturday Night Live* came on and Paul shouted, 'There he is.'

It was John Belushi.

We'd befriended him in New York, doing the show with him, and he was always coming by whenever he was in L.A. A few days later, a fabulous Hamer guitar arrived at the house, addressed to Paul. It was accompanied with a note inscribed 'To the Reverend Paul Karslake, thanks for everything, John Belushi.' Unfortunately for Paul, a few weeks later Chuch came by the house to pick up some guitars, didn't know this one wasn't mine and put it with the others for the next Stones tour. It got sent somewhere in a light case, not a hard case, and wound up broken. John also made matching ZZ Top guitars for Jamie and me, Jamie's being a kid-sized replica of mine with Jamie's name inscribed on it.

Jamie had seen John so many times on *Saturday Night Live* and loved the way he did that backflip in his Joe Cocker routine. It must have been the first night that John came by, Jamie asked him if he really did it on the telly or if there was some sort of stuntman. John assured Jamie that he did it on his own and, to prove it, he did it right there in the middle of our sitting room.

He was our real friend and a total loose cannon. Dan Aykroyd use to deliver John to our house because he knew he'd be safe with us. And the three of us would goon out. He was a lovely man and had the hots for Jo. Loads of my friends have the hots for her – Don Johnson use to flirt outrageously with her. He'd take us on his boat (which on one occasion refused to start, much to the amusement of the crowds looking on from the jetty), joke with our kids and make Jo go all giddy. I suppose I just have to accept if you have a beautiful wife, men will flock. John actually loved Jo though and although he was my great pal, Jo was my wife and I'd worked hard enough to get her. One night when I wasn't home, he came by and took Jo to Hugh Hefner's Playboy mansion. When she told me where she'd been, I didn't like that. In fact, I was furious. But it didn't stop John. I'd go off to the studio and he'd ring her and they'd laugh on the phone for hours. It wasn't really a problem, because we loved John and he was our friend, although one night I fell asleep on the couch and they had this conversation:

John said, 'Jo, run away with me.'

Jo was stunned. 'Huh?'

He said it again: 'Run away with me.'

Jo tried to make him understand, 'Come on, John, my boyfriend is asleep on the couch right next to us and you're asking me to run away with you?'

He said he was serious. 'I love you.'

Jo reminded John that they always had a great time together, but as friends, and that she loved him, but as a friend.

That's when I woke up and found John on his knees, proposing to her: 'Marry me.' I announced, 'John, if you weren't so fat and ugly I'd take that as a threat.'

Several months before that incident, we'd met a couple of strung-out dealers who would hang around with the Band (Robbie Robertson and his boys – Richard Manuel, Rick Danko, Levon Helm and Garth Hudson). They were doing some dealing, which is why we befriended them. One of them in particular, Cathy, left a bad taste and smell. She was always offering Keith 'Downtown', but he couldn't stand her. She seems to have worked for us for a while, although I can't remember what she was doing. Whatever it was, she was always hanging at the house. We decided we wanted to get rid of her but she wouldn't go, and at one point actually threatened to blackmail us. That's when Keith reached for his gun, clamped her head in a door and said, 'Here are forty-five reasons to get out of this house.'

She was a girl about town in those days and we heard that John would get his fix from her. He wasn't a real druggie, but he would binge. When we were around, John was hanging with us, laughing, talking rubbish and trying to marry Jo. But in early March 1982, he'd spent most of the night in a bungalow at the famous hotel above Sunset Strip, the Chateau Marmont, shooting up with Cathy. She left him that night and drove away in John's Mercedes. The next morning, John's personal trainer found him there, dead. Cathy was eventually convicted of his involuntary manslaughter. The night he died John had called our house. Jo's brother picked up the phone. We were asleep. John wanted to speak to us. The conversation never took place.

Los Angeles was where I made my Hollywood movie debut. Ringo Starr and I bumped into the director Martin Scorsese through Bill Graham (the toughest, hard workingest promoter), and he invited us to come watch him make *The Last Waltz*, which was about the Band's final concert. A lot of our mates were in it – Clapton, Dylan, Neil Young and Muddy Waters. When Muddy was told there was someone he should meet he whispered to his paino player, Pintop Perkins, 'Come over here, there's someone we should meet, apparently he's famous.' It was Bob Dylan.

While Ringo and I were sitting there watching them shoot, from the audience, Bill Graham came up to us and said, 'You're on.' We said, 'We are?' And he told us, 'Marty says you are,' so we were bundled onstage and into the anchor, which meant the movie, too.

Ringo plays Ringo and I play Ronnie, and if you look fast you can spot us in the final scene.

Another accidental movie appearance happened in New York, in Adrian Lyne's film *9 ½ Weeks*. The movie stars Kim Basinger and Mickey Rourke. I was pulled into the art gallery scene.

Jo and I are friends with the director Adrian Lyne and his wife, Samantha, and Adrian said to Jo, 'Come have a laugh on the set,' and hired her as an extra. I went along, not because I was going to oversee Jo's film career but because I wanted to meet Kim Basinger. I wound up spending half the afternoon talking to her in her trailer, having a great time. She's gorgeous and great company, and I probably would have spent the rest of the afternoon talking to her but I got thrown out by her chaperone.

With nothing else to do, I wandered on to the set. It was supposed to be an art gallery, so I sat down on the stairs to talk to some people and suddenly someone yelled, 'Action.'

Poor Jo didn't make it into the film at all. She should have though, because the dress she was in rocked. Adrian Lyne's loss. It was all happening in L.A., I was hanging one afternoon with Elliot Gould and record producer Ahmet Ertegun – the man who pioneered Atlantic Records, and the man who was with Mick the night he sliced his hand open twenty-stitches wide on a restaurant door – and we were talking about the Marx Brothers and I said, 'I love them, shame we've only got Groucho left.'

So Ahmet said, 'You know, Groucho is a friend of mine. I could phone him. If he's home we can go visit him.'

I couldn't get Ahmet to the phone fast enough.

He rang, interrupting Groucho in the middle of some family party, but Groucho said, 'Sure, come over.'

When we got to his house, I rang the bell and Groucho answered the door himself. He took one look at me and said, 'That's the silliest haircut I've ever seen. What are you, a man or a chicken?'

Ahmet said, 'Groucho, I want you to meet Ron Wood.'

Groucho replied, 'I know, I've seen all his films.'

'But he's not an actor,' Ahmet wanted Groucho to understand. 'He's a musician.'

Without hesitating, Groucho replied, 'I know, I have all his albums. What group's he in?' and proceeded to hum some unrecognizable song.

He brought us inside – it turned out to be some Jewish holiday and there were kids running around everywhere – and Groucho was sitting at the head of a U-shaped table, wearing a party hat. One by one, the kids would jump up on Groucho's lap, and he would say to them, 'You're a lovely little girl. Who are you?'

But the lovely little girl that he really wanted to sit on his lap was his nurse. He leant over and whispered, 'What do you think of my nurse?'

I said, 'She's beautiful.'

Groucho nodded, 'I'd give away all of my money for just one erection.'

14

Contribute

The year after I made *I've Got My Own Album to Do*, I did my second solo album, *Now Look*. On it I did a song I really like a lot called 'I Got Lost When I Found You', which was written by my friend Bobby Womack.

Bobby and his four brothers formed a gospel group while they were all still kids, calling themselves the Womack Brothers. Then Sam Cooke discovered them and renamed them the Valentinos. They toured with James Brown and got into the charts with 'Lookin' For a Love'. But when Sam got killed, the Valentinos' careers didn't last much longer. Although Bobby was married for a time to Sam's widow, Barbara, his brother Cecil eventually married Sam's daughter Linda, and Cecil and Linda formed a really good songwriting and singing partnership called Womack and Womack.

The Womack family was huge. Bobby once told me that his father had something like fifteen brothers and sisters. What's more, they all had really weird names. One brother was named West and another was named East. Another brother was named Friendly. But Bobby has also had so much sadness in his life – so many people in his family have died tragic deaths, including his brother Harry, who was shot by a jealous girlfriend. After the Valentinos broke up, Bobby went off on his

own, writing and playing guitar for Wilson Pickett, Aretha Franklin and the Stones. He also wrote some big hits like 'Across 110th Street', 'That's the Way I Feel About Cha' and 'Woman's Gotta Have It'. But one song he wrote with Shirley Womack, 'It's All Over Now', was not only covered by Sam Cooke, the Valentinos and the Faces, it was the Rolling Stones' first Number One.

I'd met Bobby in Detroit on a Faces tour in 1975 when he and David Ruffin, the lead singer from the Temptations, came up and did two Temptations songs with us, 'Losing You' and 'I Wish It Would Rain'. So when I asked Bobby for help with my second album, he was right there and when he asked me to play on his *Resurrection* album, I was right there, too, alongside Rod, Keith and Stevie Wonder.

My third solo album had been *Mahoney's Last Stand*, which was Ronnie Lane and me doing instrumentals for a film sound-track. Now in Los Angeles, I wanted to do my fourth album, *Gimme Some Neck*, and put together a pick-up band that included Charlie, Mick and Keith, plus Mick Fleetwood, Ian McLagan, Bobby Keys and Mick Taylor on various tracks. But the biggest surprise of all was Bob Dylan's contribution.

Eric Clapton was working on his album *No Reason to Cry* at Shangri-La, which was the Band's studio in Zuma Beach, north of L.A., and I was going out there to help Eric with some songs. Well, one night, I was hanging out with some friends on Sunset Strip, at the Roxy or the Whiskey or somewhere like that, and Eric got hold of me by phone to say, 'You'll never guess who's in the studio tonight.'

He continued, 'Dylan. He's down here playing bass on one of your songs.' I said, 'Fuck, I'm coming out.'

I'd first met Bob at a Faces party in New York just after I did my first solo album in 1974. I really wanted people to appreciate my album, especially musicians like Bob, but never imagined that he'd know it.

No one at the party recognized him. He just blended into the scene. And I know that some of the people there thought he was a photographer. Well, he wriggled his way through the crowd and suddenly there he was, standing in front of me, and the first thing he said was, 'I love your album.'

That blew me away. It made me think that I must be doing something right. We spoke for five minutes or so, until Peter Grant came up to us and announced, 'Hi, I manage Led Zeppelin.'

Bob looked at him and shot back, 'Hey, I don't come to you with my problems.'

The next time I saw him was that night in L.A. I dashed down to Shangri-La and ended up spending two days there, hanging out with Bob. We played music all night, and all through the next day too. Whenever we took a break, Bob would disappear with some girl who had a broken leg.

Shangri-La was a bordello back in its heyday. A hazy maze of winding corridors converted into a recording studio, strange smells and little bedrooms where you could crash. Someone showed me which room I could have, and when I finally got to bed all my blankets were gone. With my best detective instincts, I scoured the room. The window was open and curtains were blowing in the breeze. It was easy to conclude that someone had nicked my blankets and escaped through the window.

When I looked out the window, I could see way off in the distance a little tent pitched in a field. On further investigation, I discovered that's where Bob was giving the girl with the broken leg some gypsy loving. But, not only had he made off with the wounded bird, he'd made off with my blankets.

I love Bob but whenever it was time to play, we'd have to

drag him out of the bushes and start all over again. He was writing a song at the time called 'Seven Days', and I know he liked me because, out of the blue, he just gave it to me. He said, 'You can have this one, Woody,' and so I recorded it on my album *Gimme Some Neck*.

Over the years I've done a lot of guest work with him, both on his albums and onstage. I had a great time playing with him and Tom Petty for three nights at Madison Square Garden in the summer of 1986. Around the same time, we were on location in Bristol shooting some scenes for a movie, where we witnessed some magic moments with the west-country, classically wrong, persona of Reg Presley from The Troggs. Mr 'Wild Thing' was on set in a scene where we had to audition for bass player in Bob's band.

When it came to my time to walk on they shouted: 'Action'. I got into character, when Reg immediately shouted: 'Fuck me. It smokes and it walks!'

'Cut!'

A little later, during a break, I asked Bob to walk over with me to observe the strange phenomenon of Reg (who was really a lead vocalist). He was casually sitting, fingering a Fender four-string, and I said: 'Hey Reg, I didn't know you played bass. How long have you been doing that?' He said: 'All fucking afternoon.'

Bob is, and will remain, a constant inspiration, a true friend.

15

Barbarian

When the Stones announced that we would not tour in 1979, which sort of broke from tradition because the summer after a US tour we usually came to Europe, Charlie Watts formed a group called Rocket 88 with Ian Stewart, Alexis Korner and Dick Morrissey. It was a boogie-woogie band that got together because the guys playing in it just loved playing. Charlie said they were having a great time, so I decided it would be fun to do something like that, and as long as I had time off from touring with the Stones, I'd get some of my mates together and go on tour with them. It was an extracurricular activity, but then touring has always been in my blood. I did those three tours in 1975 because I could, because in those days the energy level was really high and because it was part of my thing to keep working, not to stop.

So I rang around and deliberately put together some risky pairings with musicians who had never played together before, or since, for that matter. I got Keith, and this was the first time he'd ever done a tour with my own outfit. I got Bobby Keys on sax and Ian McLagan on keyboards. Then I got Joseph Modeliste, otherwise known as Zigaboo. He was one of the original Meters, played with the Neville Brothers and is known for having invented the drumming style called 'second-line funk'.

Then I got Stanley Clark, who is the best jazz bass player ever and who, I found out much later, was influenced by me. He told me that I was the reason he took up bass, after hearing me play it with the Jeff Beck Group.

We were two guitars, a keyboard, a bass, a drum and a sax and we called ourselves the New Barbarians. Just like that we headed off on the craziest tour ever, managed by Jason Cooper, whom I met through Tony Curtis and who was the world's maddest, ex-football playing, huge manager. Making things even more interesting, Jason was one of many people Keith can't stand. In fact, Keith hated Jason so much that at one point he chased Jason through a field with a gun offering him forty-five reasons to 'leave Ronnie alone'.

Because Keith owed the court in Toronto a charity concert for the Canadian National Institute for the Blind and his blind angel, Rita Bedard, we opened at the Civic Auditorium in Oshawa, Ontario, on 22 April 1979.

John Belushi introduced us with the line, 'Go nuts, go nuts.' Keith's blind angel was right there with us. When our gig was finished, everyone left the stage except for Keith and me, and that's when Mick Jagger walked on. The three of us played 'Prodigal Son', and everybody in the audience must have thought that was some kind of encore, until Charlie and Bill also walked on and the Stones played the rest of the show. When the Stones were done, Mac, Bobby and Zigaboo came back and we did 'Jumpin' Jack Flash'. That night, I got to lead my band and Keith, and then be led by the Stones and Keith.

I planned the rest of the New Barbarians tour. There was a bit of the Stones organization, you know, set lists and stuff, but also a lot of the Faces looseness. We had our own plane, and we were always jamming or partying. We never had a hit record

because we never even had a record, which means we got bookings strictly on our names. And that makes us the only band in
history, without a record, to sell out both Madison Square
Garden and the L.A. Forum. We also sold out fifteen cities in
between. We went all over the place, but I don't remember
where the hell we went because we were so battered.

Not that the New Barbarians was a heavy drug tour. But
there was more than enough to go around, so we started zipping
through the world without a structured itinerary, so wherever
we went, we went. I booked the whole tour, I was paying for it
and I wanted to take my friends around in style. Mr Generous
here. I got us a Boeing 727, took care of everybody luxuriously,
and wound up £200,000 in debt. I'm not a businessman, but I
made sure that all my mates got paid. As I remember, Jason
Cooper worked it out with CBS Records that they would put
up whatever I owed for the tour, and then they'd get it back
from me through my share of *Gimme Some Neck*.

I wanted to do the whole thing proper, but after Bo Diddley
said to me, 'Are you kidding? I steal the fucking place mats out
of the hotel,' that's when I started to think, did I really shell out
for a jet? Bo kept saying, 'Man, you gotta be crazy.' And maybe
I was. Maybe that's why I lost £200,000 on that tour. But you
know what, in the name of great music, I'd do it again and
wouldn't change a thing.

There were no official recordings from the New Barbarians
tour, but on a search through my archives I uncovered a master
tape, which I plan to release under my record label, Wooden
Records. The rest was just me experimenting for a new album.
Keith had a great time, because all he had to do was sing and
play the guitar and I even let him play the piano. But I worked
myself like a slave, trying to do everything – not just running the
tour, but also singing and playing guitar, harp and pedal steel.

We played Stones songs like 'Honky Tonk Women' and 'Jumpin' Jack Flash', and because I could get my own songs into the show, being in charge this time, we did a whole bunch, especially some from the new album, like 'Buried Alive', 'Come to Realize', 'Infekshun' and 'F.U.C. Her'. We did 'Sweet Little Rock and Roller' and, of course, Bob Dylan's 'Seven Days'. It was everything from reggae, soul, country to rock, and we used to rip the place up. I even got to play the saxophone with Bobby on 'Let's Go Steady', which Keith sang.

I suppose this goes back to my days in Yiewsley. I would spend every moment I could picking up instruments that were laying around the house. I pick stuff up very fast, so if you leave me alone with an instrument for a day or two, I'll figure out how to play something on it. I did it with the drums. When the Stones were recording 'You'd Better Get Some Sleep Tonight', I thought to myself why not, went over to Charlie's drums and had a go. It was only a bit of fun but when I was finished I stood up to give the drums back to Charlie and he said no, carry on, so I did.

It was a two-week deal with the sax. I picked it up, learnt the scales and started to get the feel of it. I didn't know what the hell I was doing, except the sounds were coming out. So I rang up Bobby Keys and said, 'Listen to this.' I didn't know it at the time but when I was done, Jo and him got together and bought me Plas Johnson's tenor sax, the one Plas used to play the Pink Panther theme.

I brought a sax into the studio once when the Stones were recording the *Undercover* album, and everyone just looked at me weirdly. I said, 'Let me give it a go.'

Well, you can imagine Keith's reaction. 'What the fuck are you doing with that?' I said, 'I'll show you,' and started blowing on it. Ian Stewart came to my rescue, 'Give him a chance, he's all right,' and sure enough they did. The song was 'I Think I'm Going Mad'. I played tenor in the brass section with Bobby, Jim Horn and Steve Madeo. This was not only the Stones brass section, but Stevie Wonder's brass section, too. The best brass section in the world. They helped me on my *1234* album on songs like 'Fountain of Love', where I joined them in the brass section and taught them guitar lines to be played on the horn.

Our New Barbarians tour unit was small, just about twenty-five in all, because we didn't put on an event in the way the Stones do. The event was us. Whatever the stage was, we took it. Most of the time the audience was great, but in a few cities, the audience turned a bit hostile. We didn't know it but false posters were being put up saying 'The New Barbarians – Ronnie Wood and Friends – Tonight's Guests Bob Dylan and Mick Jagger.'

We'd be up there rocking and the crowds would be shouting, 'Where's Bob? Where's Mick?' I'd shout back, 'What?' They'd shout, 'Where's Jagger?' I'd shout back, 'What the fuck are you talking about?' They'd shout, 'Where's Dylan?' I'd be up there trying to play music and talk to 20,000 people who thought they were going to see Mick and Bob. 'What you see is what you get.' And they'd be shouting back, 'It's on the fucking poster.'

In Chicago we played the International Amphitheater, and the audience got so cranky when Mick, Bob and Rod Stewart didn't show that they ripped the place apart. I mean, they tore all the seats out. I had to go back and do another concert there for free just to pay for the damage.

After eighteen gigs in Canada and the States, the New Barbarians played one last time, back in England, at the Knebworth Festival in November 1979. We supported Led Zeppelin in their last ever UK gig. The crowd was 200,000 people, twice what it had been when I first played there with the Stones. And by this time, we were smart enough to avoid pissing off a crowd that size, so the official programme notes actually warned 'Don't expect surprise guest appearances from Bob Dylan, Neil Young, Mick Jagger or any other named celebrities being bandied about.'

The New Barbarians disbanded, rock stars who never had a record, although we did have a T-shirt, which Jo designed, but for a little bit of time six of us got lost in the music and it didn't matter about losing all that money. I didn't care about the business side, this was just the boys having a great time, and I'm still like that today. The music comes first.

16

Malingering

We'd only just moved into Mandeville Canyon, in 1979, when Bobby Keys arrived one night, all lit up. 'Hey man, I have made the greatest discovery. It's this thing called freebase. It saves your nose. You don't have to use your nose any more. You smoke it instead.' He showed us how to make it up and that was it for me for the next five years.

What you do is use baking soda or ether to free the cocaine base from the regular cocaine. It takes a lot of time but it gives you a very pure form of coke, which you then put into a pipe and smoke. One problem with it is that it's dangerous to make. Ether can explode and people can get really hurt, or even killed, cooking this stuff. Back at the time Bobby and I were doing it, a freebase explosion blew the face off poor Richard Pryor and nearly killed him.

But that's only one problem with freebase. There are plenty of others. Like the fact that it is not free and really should be called expensive base.

Freebasing also makes you paranoid. You wind up on your hands and knees looking for little crumbs that might have fallen out of the pipe. I banned my children eating meringues in the house after I ended up smoking sugar for the umpteenth time. Jo was walking through the house one day, found the bathroom door locked, knew that Bobby and I had been in there for two days, and started banging on it. 'Come on, you've got to get out of there, you've got to have something to eat.' A few minutes later she looked out the window and spotted Bobby and me crawling through the bushes. She went outside and demanded to know, 'What the hell are you doing?' I told her, 'We know you've got a stash out here and a pipe hidden in the bushes, we know you have, and we're trying to find it.'

Over time, if you do it enough, you start seeing 'them' out there. Dark figures in the bushes. Shadows just around the side of the house. People sneaking around inside your house. They're out there. And they're trying to kill you.

Sometimes someone really was out there. The actor Seymour Cassel, who lived in Lenny Bruce's old house above Sunset Strip, used to come over to my place and he knew how paranoid everyone was, so he would deliberately freak us out by hiding in the bushes. One night Bobby and I were freebasing with Alan Pariser, the man who invented the Monterey Pop Festival and managed Ringo and Crosby, Stills and Nash, among others. We were smoking and Alan looked out the window and saw someone crawling through the garden. He yelled at us, 'Help, someone's there, honestly, I saw someone,' and got really upset. We looked and didn't see anyone, but when Alan looked again he swore that whoever was out there was still out there. The next day Seymour came by to tell us it was him, on purpose, to freak out Alan. He had driven there, freaked us out, and then driven home to answer our paranoid phone call.

Speaking of the group Crosby, Stills, Nash and sometimes Young, I used to bump into those guys all the time. Graham Nash was a harmless kind of guy, who was always very polite. Neil Young was a good guy who had named the New Barbarians for me. He told me that there was a band up in Canada, where he came from, called the Barbarians, and suggested I call my group the New Barbarians, which is what I did.

Every time I think about Stephen Stills, I can't seem to forget that Keith really disliked him, couldn't stand him, and there was nothing Stephen could do to change that. We were sharing a studio once in New York, at Atlantic Records, and Stephen wanted to play one of Keith's guitars. But Keith said no, and actually locked all of his guitars away to keep Stephen from playing them. Then Keith put a sign up on the door that read 'No Stephen Stills Allowed'. I'm not sure that Keith knows why he didn't like Stephen, except that he used to say, 'Stills doesn't know how to do drugs properly.' It was an odd reason, especially as I don't think any of us knew whether Stills did drugs at all!

David Crosby definitely didn't know how to use drugs properly either. He used to mix coke with smack. I saw him do it one night in Alan Pariser's kitchen, and within a few seconds he tumbled on to the floor. I thought, he's never going to come around again. I thought he died five times that night. But he always came around eventually.

Bobby Womack was also a regular at my house, and whenever he'd come to have a hit on the pipe, he'd go straight into the wardrobe, shut the door and stand there in the dark. Hey, where's Bobby? Oh, he's in the wardrobe with the clothes.

One night Bobby went over to Johnny 'Guitar' Watson's house to score, and saw that Johnny had both the outside and inside of his house iron-barred. So he asked, 'Hey, brother, why do you have the inside of your windows iron-barred?' Johnny said, ''Cos there are people out there after us.' Bobby looked out the window and said, 'I don't see anyone.' That's when Johnny grabbed a gun, put it to Bobby's head and said, 'Look again.'

Now Bobby said, 'Shit, they're everywhere.' I once watched Bobby sit in a car for two days as he worked out how to get out of it to go pay a dealer.

Of course, while you're doing it, you think it's fun. We used to have a whole bunch of pipes, and Jo used to colour the water in the water pipe, and put little plastic things in there as well so that they all jumped up and down when we smoked. Also, you never realize the amount of time you spend doing it. Bobby and I would wind up locked in the bathroom freebasing, and not come out for days. He was spending so much time at our house with me that Jo actually asked him once, 'Don't you live somewhere? Don't you have a home to go to?'

Charlie Watts would come over and sit around for hours watching Bobby Keys and me in the bathroom. Keith told me once that he came into the bathroom while we were basing up, sat down on the toilet to have a shit, and we were so busy doing all our rituals that we didn't even notice him. Pathetic. But then, we never noticed all the other people who used to show up either. Once Jo came home and found a queue of people, mostly total strangers but also one of our nannies, queuing up outside our bathroom for a hit on the pipe.

One of my neighbours in Mandeville Canyon was Sly Stone. It wasn't easy for us to connect because he was never awake at the same time I was. But when he heard that there was a pipe at my place, he'd walk into my house with fifteen people, all of them in single file behind him. They'd go into the bathroom, have a hit on the base pipe, and stay there for hours. Then the door would open and Sly and his fifteen friends, still in single file behind him, would leave.

When you're into this shit, you're always making friends with freaks or gangs of vipers. Whatever it took to get a hit. I made friends with a guy named Harry Later, not because we

had anything in common or because he was particularly interesting, but because he was a dealer who delivered to your door.
When word got out that you were looking for stuff, guys like
Harry would show up and give you a present. Once you thought
they were your friends, you'd ring them up at any hour of the
day or night and they'd deliver your stuff. Harry was like the
local pizzeria and there were dozens of guys just like him.

It got so bad that we actually had people letting themselves
into the house in the middle of the night with stash and pipes.
Jo and I would be asleep, but that wouldn't stop us from receiv-
ing a hit right from bedside, as they lit the pipe for us and then
started the whole cycle over again.

While I was high, I didn't care about anything else. There
was a huge fire one night in Mandeville Canyon, and luckily it
took a U-turn on my block and missed us. But the whole canyon
was on fire and my chauffeur got into the house to wake us. He
warned us we had to get out of there, to get out of the canyon,
but we'd been up for five days. He shouted at us, 'The fucking
canyon's on fire,' and all we could do was say, 'Yeah, yeah,
okay,' and go back to sleep. Eventually he yanked us out of bed
and told us we could only take what we could carry. I took some
paintings and a few guitars. Outside, the sky was black with
thick smoke and there was fire everywhere. A few days later I
read that the fire, which was fanned by the famous Santa Ana
winds, caused $70 million worth of damage, destroyed some-
thing gigantic like 38,000 acres, burnt down 200 houses,
injured fifty people and killed three. For some reason, we were
the lucky ones. Our house was the only one on the block that
made it. All that survived of Neil Young's beach house, he told
me, were his fire irons. Meanwhile, manager Jason Cooper
saved everything from his house except his 'beloved' parrot.

While you're doing freebase, you don't know how bad it is for you or how it really messes you up. The first hit is totally euphoric, but you never get back there, so you're always chasing that first time. It's a mad drug. It's not addictive like heroin, because you can stop and sleep and not do it again for days or weeks if you don't want to. There's no physical craving. You just become totally obsessed with finding that first high again, and that obsession drags you into the depths. Some get paranoid. I never really experience regular paranoia. I'm just not made up that way.

We were on tour in the States in the early 1980s, for example, when Keith decided he was going to kill me. I was doing the base pipe a lot and Keith turned into Mr Drug Enforcement Administration. Jo and I had an argument and she rang Keith crying and he went on the fucking warpath. He thought I was shacked up in my room with a woman. I wasn't, I was shacked up smoking pipes. The problem with Keith is that once he gets an idea into his head, it doesn't matter if it's right or wrong, it's in his head and nothing can get it out of there. He caught me, yelled at me, 'Nobody does freebase, it's a waste of time.'

I said, 'Yeah, okay, sure Keith,' and disregarded him by going downstairs to the front desk and renting a second room in the hotel so that I couldn't be found.

Well, Keith got wind of it and formed a posse to come after me. I thought I'd covered my tracks pretty well but it didn't take long for Keith to find me. He barged in, broke the bowl and came straight at my face with it. I turned around and smacked him first in the face, then in the balls, and then in the belly, he was nearly knocked out of the window and we were up real high. He was serious about hurting me and I was serious about hurting him, he smashed a bottle and cut me with it. I stormed out of the room and down the corridor to see Mick and Charlie, who were a couple of doors away. I stood there panting and covered in blood.

But they were working on a song together and, while I stood there bleeding all over the carpet, Mick looked at me and wondered, 'Have you got any ideas for the middle eight?'

I left, quivering with adrenaline and went back to the room where Keith was, back to the madness. I walked in, expecting the worst. He pulled out his ratchet knife, a huge Jamaican blade, and put it to my throat and warned, 'I'm going to kill you.'

I stood right there and glared at him, 'All right, then, go ahead.'

He looked at me for a long time, all the time pressing the knife against me, before he said, 'I'd fucking cut your throat but your girlfriend would never forgive me for all the mess it'd make.'

Keith just looked at me and I just looked at him, and that was the end of that. A stareout. We haven't fought since, unless you include the obligatory knife-to-the-throat biannual greetings. Or we would end up having a few puffs of muta together to bring about a 'ceasefire'.

In those days Keith and his guns and his knives were inseparable. Not so much today because of airport security, but he always had weapons with him then. He used to threaten people with his piece, which was pretty scary, but he rarely fired it. Although we were in a hotel in New York once when Keith was terrorizing Freddie Sessler with a gun, and he squeezed the trigger and shot through the floor. There were a bunch of old age pensioners playing cards in the room just below, and Keith's bullet broke up their party.

I also had a gun, a .44 Magnum. This was a present from Don Johnson from the set of *Miami Vice*, but I didn't have any bullets for it. We were discussing something and Keith stormed off to get his gun. I warned everyone, 'Clear the decks.' Keith came back with his Derringer, pointed it at me and yelled, 'You fucking bastard, Woody.' I calmly pulled out my .44 Magnum. And that was the last time Keith ever drew his gun on me, until the next time.

Everyone I knew was getting pissed off with me. When Bobby Keys and I were freebasing, we were the worst company to be around. Things got so bad for Bobby that he once found himself in the hock shop with his saxophone, begging to get some money to live. And it got so bad for me that I convinced my insurance company to let us have a $70,000 home improvement loan on our house so I could buy more shit. When they sent us a cheque, I put tarmac down on a new driveway, painted the kitchen green, and spent the rest on dope. The insurance guy came out to see the home improvements, saw the driveway and the kitchen and said, 'This is hardly $70,000 worth.' But by then, the money was gone. It disappeared in six weeks.

We were in L.A. for five years, so do the maths and you'll see the kind of money I was spending on this.

Our friends all saw the sense, but we didn't because we were in the middle of it. I always said that when I saw the men hiding in the bushes, snipers, it would be time to quit. I did, and it took five years.

17

Anticipation

Keith stayed with us on Forest Knoll Drive and stayed with us at Mandeville Canyon, which was fine with us.

Jamie had a budgerigar that sang a very regular song and Keith wasn't turned on to the fact that the bird wasn't an alarm clock. He staggered down one morning/afternoon wearing his favourite leather trousers. He took one look at the chirping budgerigar, opened the window and tossed the bird and the cage out. We screamed, 'What are you doing, that was Jamie's pet budgerigar.' Keith thought about it for a moment, then mumbled, 'Nobody told me it was a fucking real budgerigar.'

Then at Mandeville Canyon one afternoon Keith and I were sitting on the diving board, with our backs to the hill, when he turned to me and asked, 'Did you just fart?' I said no. He said, 'You smelly bastard, you stink.' I looked at him and thought to myself, it must have been him, and then we both turned to look at the hill behind us and saw, to our absolute shock and horror, a huge sliding mass of shit, human poo, pouring down on us.

The septic tank up on the hill had broken. This wasn't just a little trickle, it was a gigantic wall of shit and it was on the move. I ran for my wellington boots and a shovel and did what I could to keep it back because I didn't want it to get into the house. Jo's mum, Rachel, was there, and she kept yelling, 'You're going to get diseases, don't touch it, you'll get ill.' We put masks on to keep from breathing the stench and kept shovelling away, but it was too much. It overran us. Luckily the pool stopped it, otherwise the house would have been engulfed with excrement.

Around this time, while Jo was pregnant with Leah and just about ready to drop, she, Rachel, Keith and I were lounging around the pool when Keith rolled a joint. Rachel couldn't believe what she'd just seen, was against drugs and demanded that Keith explain himself, 'What's that you got there?' He answered, 'It's a joint.' He held it out to her. 'You want some?' Rachel got up, grabbed the joint and tossed it straight into the pool.

Keith was shouting, 'You crazy bitch,' and Jo was saying, 'Mum what the hell are you doing?' It took us a long time to calm Keith down and explain to Rachel why doing that to Keith was a really bad idea. Finally she sat down again next to Jo, and Keith moved over to the diving board where he sat down, prepared the grefa and rolled two joints. Rachel never took her eyes off him. When he was done, Keith offered one to Rachel. 'There's one for me to smoke and this one is for you to throw in the pool.'

Later that afternoon, Jo went to Keith and said, 'Do me a favour, my mum's never seen cocaine before, please, please be really cool.' He said, 'Don't worry, darling, I'll break her in gently.' Jo cooked us all a really nice dinner and while we were sitting around the table afterwards, Keith announced, 'And now for dessert.' He pulled out a stash of coke and put it on the table. I jumped up with Jo and started clearing the table, the first time I'd ever done that. She and I went into the kitchen, I guess to decide what we were going to do about Keith, when Rachel came in. She said, 'Do you realize what he's doing?'

Jo explained gently, 'Yes, Mum, but he's been doing it for years and you have to understand . . .' She looked at me, but asked Jo, 'Does Ronnie do cocaine?' Jo assured her, 'No, no, he doesn't do it.' It was three days later, after Keith and I had been up for seventy-two hours, when Rachel went to Jo to say, ' Now I know Ronnie does cocaine.' Again, Jo tried to assure her mum that I didn't. But Rachel said, 'Not much. For the past three days he's been walking around with a straw behind his ear!'

When it was time for Leah's birth, there was a party going on, just like there'd been a party at the Malibu house when Jesse was born. I was busy timing Jo's contractions, and also trying to be a good host to loads of people, many of whom I didn't know (except that a lot of them were dealers). Jo went to the bathroom, her waters broke, and I decided I wanted to sketch her while I was timing her contractions. She got angry at me and yelled, 'Just leave me alone,' and went nice and quiet.

The party was in full swing, but I was worried about her and decided it would be best to ring the doctor and get rid of our guests. He came over and was standing at her bedside, staring down at her when she woke up. Again, for some unknown reason, she got furious at me. Jo had had a baby before and was well versed in the art of birth.

By now her contractions were two and a half minutes apart and the doctor said we had to go to the hospital so I drove her to Cedars-Sinai. To get her mind off the pain, I started to sketch her and my muse did her best performance yet. Within half an hour or so, Leah was born. We had our love child. I was so elated because it was the first girl to come along in the Wood family for many generations. The nurse showed me the afterbirth. I found it mesmerizing, almost interplanetary. I was lifted to that indescribable place that comes with the birth of your child. A little bundle of purple fun. I was in the room with Jo, all dressed up like a doctor wearing an apron, gloves, boot covers and a mask, making a home movie of the whole thing.

The nurse kept saying to me, 'Get out of the way,' and I kept saying to her, 'Get out of the way yourself, I'm filming this.'

A few hours later, Keith showed up and said he had to see Jo. I told him the only way he was going to get in to see her was to dress the part. So the two of us donned our operating-room gear. I said, 'Come with me,' and we were heading into the recovery room to find Jo when the nurses stopped us.

The nurse in charge barked out, 'Hang on, who's the father?' Keith and I answered, at exactly the same time, 'We both are.' And she let us both in.

18

Shackles

At the end of February 1980, Jo and I decided we wanted to get a little sunshine away from the L.A. madness.

The place we chose, St Maarten, a small island not far from Barbados, is like a watery black Vegas. Split in two halves, the Dutch and French island is designed for the rich shopper.

On landing on the tropical jewel, a wary officer's eyes watched as I checked into his domain and country. Upon my arrival he immediately questioned my Sharp boom box. It weighed and sounded a ton, and I'm sure he wondered what I was going to do with it. Play it or sell it. This guy took an instant dislike to me. I knew I'd see him again.

Four days into our hot break we decided to see the town at night and ended up in a casino. A friendly croupier introduced us to some good-time boys and their girlfriends. Luigi and Mohammed were the party boys' names. We asked if they could find us some puff as they didn't have any, so we left the casino and thought nothing more of it.

Unknown to us Luigi and Mohammed tracked us down to our new holiday house after spotting the nanny, Jaye, at the local market. Fitting in with their plan to stalk us, the following evening they knocked on our door bearing gifts. The envelopes contained the puff we wanted but also cocaine, the very substance we thought we were getting safely away from. This opened a major can of worms, cascading into the very situation we longed to avoid, namely trouble with the law, mitigating circumstances and incarceration.

The boys and their girlfriends partied with us. Within twenty-four hours we were locked up. Why we were locked up was a total mystery to both Jo and me, until we realized just how serious about their drugs these guys were. It unfolded that a security guard on our home estate spotted the boys hanging twenty-two kilos of coke up a tree outside our house. They had been followed by police after digging up the container from the nearby hillside. They had transported the stuff in my rented car, which I had lent to them when they said one of their girlfriends was sick and could they borrow it to take her home. They came back into our house and carried on partying as though nothing out of the ordinary had happened.

These boys were later found to be members of a major international drug cartel. When the police arrived with all this knowledge, I was alone on the top floor of my luxury, song-writing four-storey beach haven. I was strumming away in a very Bobby Womack, reggae combined way, fishing out some new guitar riffs on my precious Silver Dobro.

Jaye the nanny called loudly to me in her New York Ella Fitzgerald voice.

'Woody, the police are here!'

I thought, 'That's funny, I didn't think I invited them to my songwriting session.' Jo saw police hovering around the house from the bathroom window, which was on the floor below. She called up too. 'Ronnie, come down here now – the police want to see you.' I stopped the rich strain of musical creativity I was into and grudgingly went down the stairs, guitar in hand, to see what this needless fuss was all about. I saw Jaye, three officers at her side, and I stumbled on the last marble step, dropping my Silver Dobro.

'Are you Ronald Wood?'

SMASH.

'Shit, I've just dropped my Dobro, I can't believe it, officer, can you?' I asked heartbroken as I held the broken baby.

'Sure looks like a fine guitar. Are you the owner of this vehicle?' he said pointing to my ride parked outside.

'No, I rented it.'

'It has been involved in a crime.'

'I fail to see what that has to do with me.'

'Your signature is on the rental document which holds you responsible for everything it's involved in. May we search the premises?'

Looking at my sturdily surviving guitar, I didn't really care for this intrusion.

'Where do you want to start?'

'Why don't we go from the top of the house down?' said the officer.

I thought this was the best idea he'd had so far.

'Great, I'm dying to see how the place is laid out. Still haven't had a good snoop round yet. I've been waiting for my wife to finish unpacking so I've been staying out of her way at the top of the house. It's the songwriting place.' I led the gaggle of officers up the mass of stairs.

'I know it's a long hike but look at this cool attic!' We arrived exhausted after the long trek.

'Where else have you been using these drugs?' said a man with a threatening twitch who stood there holding a bag with evidence of some white stuff.

'Nowhere, now look at the view – stop sodding about,' I said quite civilly.

The other policeman, who looked like he'd stepped out of *Deliverance*, said, 'Every drug we find on these premises will be considered in your possession.'

I said, 'I haven't got any. Chance would be a fine thing.'

Pushing me downstairs into the first room on the left he said, 'Is that your jacket?' revealing an awful garment.

I said, 'It's not, I'm on holiday, and I wouldn't wear that.'

'Well then you have a lot of explaining to do. These Quaaludes are class A drugs,' pulling out pills from the pockets.

They started prodding and poking about, finding more articles of clothing, all containing empty vials. As we went down through the house each room revealed some sort of paraphernalia – mainly empty Ziplocks with traces of coke and the odd illegal pill thrown in.

'I don't suppose you own this jacket?' said a weird officer. As the incriminating bundles piled up, I looked at the arresting officer and said, 'I know this sounds corny but I don't own that jacket.'

He said, 'I think you had better ride with me down to the station.'

They turned to Jo and told her she was coming too. She replied, 'I can't possibly go with you dressed like this.' In her moment of clarity she had realized that she needed somewhere to hide the twelve-gram rock she had stashed in the folds of her skirt, that Mohammed and Luigi had given her.

Whilst changing she fumbled about in the presence of a female police officer. Her sleight of hand meant she had tossed the stash into a pile of kids' swimming-pool toys. She looked at the nanny, 'Throw those water wings away, they're broken. They're not safe for the kids.' Jaye got the message and the rock was history. We were driven to the station separately. This was the last I saw of Jo for six days and nights.

I checked in. They took the laces from my sneakers and looked suspiciously at me as they led me into the dark. A right turn. A push. A crash. I shouted, 'I'm in the slammer.' I thought of Jamie and Leah out in the holding room, and Jesse back in England.

Unravelled to me over the course of the next day or two I discovered, through our mutual messenger and fellow convict Malcolm, that Jo was behind the wall and just across the courtyard. Risking solitary himself, he would on a few occasions pass notes, containing important messages from Jo to me on the end of a broom handle through the bars on my cage. He always said to eat or destroy the note after reading it. I did, and he always got caught. He claimed to Jo to have partied backstage with Keith and Charlie in 1975. He also discovered a band holed up inside my prison, calling themselves the Rolling Stones of St Maarten.

The jailers were not impressed by who I was, nor were the animals that stared up at me from their freedom corridors during tropical rainstorms. There were mice, lizards, frogs and cockroaches looking into my human zoo.

At mealtimes I would climb up the bars to a hole in the wall and shout across the courtyard to Jo, 'Don't eat the meat.' Then mention to my jailers that the people who ate this meal before me must have really enjoyed it.

As a cigarette, a few matches and a tear of strike paper were fed through a well-fingered hole, I realized that this was at least my third day inside with no word from any legal eagles on the outside as to my release. I would thank the faceless neighbours on the left for the smokes as I was escorted to the roach-ridden toilet and washbasin.

Fearing total neglect and oblivion, I'd lie on the concrete shelf that was my bed and rest my head by arranging my sneakers in a special way so I could take my rest at ten o'clock lights out each night.

They said the bucket in my cell was for pee only. Oops. The mistake I made on the first day would not be repeated. As each day stretched out with still no word, magazines would be shoved under my door once in a while. 'Look, that's me!' I pointed out to a guard when I saw a Rolling Stone mention in a tabloid, 'I'm in that band.' Didn't make the slightest difference.

All this time Jo was locked in a single cell surrounded by local male prisoners. She seized the situation and ended up making good friends and telling them stories to pass the time. They would crowd round and listen to the stories of glamorous rock and rainy England. You really can put her in any type of situation and she'll sort it out. From our cells Jo and I would often hear Mohammed maundering on about things that would really piss off the other inmates. 'Hey you guys, tune in to channel four – there's a great programme on.' 'Shut the fuck up!!'

When a full carton of Marlboro was shoved through my bars, I heard familiar legal voices floating down the alley from the prison entrance room. I knew hope was on the horizon. After identifying the culprits face to face in an interrogation room, both Jo and I were led at separate intervals across the street to the main courthouse, where, in a private hearing, we were severely reprimanded by the judge as to the company we should not keep and warned not to do it again. We were informed that we could go home, arrangements permitting, the following day.

When the time came, we went straight from jail to the airport in the chief of police's car. 'Looks like I'll have to see you play guitar on the mainland 'cos you won't be allowed back on St Maarten,' he said.

As me, Jo and the reunited children took off in the private jet the lawyers had meticulously arranged, I looked back in amazement at what we had just survived and took a glass of the only nourishment that I had craved whilst locked up. A glass of cognac.

It wasn't just strange people in casinos who I'd associate with drugs. With the Stones there are some of the world's foremost suppliers. The most famous of these characters was Freddie Sessler, the same Freddie Sessler who was with Keith and me on the trip through Fordyce, Arkansas.

Mick, Bill and Charlie tried to keep Freddie away, but Keith liked having Freddie around, so Freddie was allowed to hang with us. Sometimes I liked him and sometimes I didn't, but I wound up spending a lot of time with him, and maybe I would have been better off if I hadn't. He was one of those larger-than-life eccentrics who bragged that he was on a first-name basis with everybody in show business – and probably was – from Billie Holiday and Billy Eckstine to Frank Sinatra. He liked me, but he really loved Keith.

Freddie adored being called 'the ultimate Rolling Stones fan', which is the way he was always described right up to the day he died in December 2000. Because he was, by then, into his seventies, he also loved being called 'the world's oldest rock and roll groupie', which is how he described himself. But Freddie's real claim to fame was that he'd spent decades providing pharmaceuticals for everybody who was anybody in rock. I'm talking about a man who showed up with milk bottles full of high quality Mallencrodt and Merck. He was a sex-fuelled, vodka-charged, coke mountain.

When we were in Woodstock, New York, rehearsing for the

1978 tour, Freddie had so much coke for Keith and me that, suddenly, it was three days later. We sniffed five grams up each nostril and set off through our blissful high. I thought at the time it was the funniest three days of my life, and it was the birth of two incredible dances invented by Keith and me. We named them the Inlet Outlet (standing) and the Horrendous (laying down). Freddie was especially good at passing around a barbiturate called Tuanol. One of those pills would send you into next month, but Freddie always wanted everyone to take a handful of them at the same time. Keith always trusted the dosage Freddie gave him. Whenever Freddie tried to force a bunch of pills into my mouth, I'd hide them under my tongue and when he wasn't looking I'd spit them out. I would take one or maybe two, but I could never bring myself to take as much as Keith and Freddie.

Keith's door was always wide open for Freddie and, even today, Keith misses his friendship. Freddie was funny, but he also had an evil side and could do really nasty things. If you had a new girlfriend, he'd show up somewhere with your old girl-friends just to put the cat amongst the pigeons. He loved to present them to Jo, but her tactic was to make friends with them, rather than take the bait. Oddly, though, towards the end of his life he began showing a lot of genuine kindness to my family. He'd write long letters to my children, confessing his nicer side. Maybe it was his way of trying to make up to me for the horrible things he used to do.

Then there was Dr Steve, such a big Keith fan that his tongue would hang out every time he was in Keith's presence. Dr Steve's claim to fame, which made him particularly useful, was that he was a neurologist. This meant he could write prescriptions, which meant he got the best stuff straight from the factory.

Those were only a couple, but over the years there were thousands of these types trying hard to befriend us. Bill and Charlie were never interested and steered clear of them because drugs really weren't their thing. Bill preferred 'hunting' girls, and at least in the beginning Charlie would drink, although he hasn't had any booze since the mid-1980s.

So Bill and Charlie refused to get involved with these guys and so did Mick. He's got a sixth sense when it comes to people.

Mick has always been a lot more particular than Keith and me about who he got stoned with. One night in the mid-1980s in New York, he was at my house and we got particularly drunk and coked and he said, 'Ronnie, walk me home.' He had red wine stains all around his lips. So I walked him home from my place on 78th and Riverside to his place over on 81st. When Jerry Hall opened the door, he looked at her and said, 'Who are you?'

She screamed, 'You've been out with Woody again!' Mick just winked at me and went inside while Jerry went ballistic.

Keith has been famously quoted as saying, 'We have never had a problem with drugs, only with policemen.' But then Keith is the luckiest man in the universe because he had the constitution of an ox.

I suppose that Keith did heroin solid for ten years and most people don't live through that. Rock and roll is littered with people who never made it. Add Janis Joplin to the list of Brian Jones, Jim Morrison and Jimi Hendrix, for starters. Keith claims that the only reason he's still alive is because he promised himself that if he was going to do anything, it would only be top-quality junk and he insists that he never compromises. But that's not easy because the really good stuff was sometimes very tough to find, and there was always plenty of other stuff being dangled in front of his face. People looking for an in with the Stones would track Keith down and offer

With Bernard Fowler, Keith and Isaac Hayes

At 'laughing waters' the morning after my proposal.

With two best men

Wedding shots.

such a gathering

Jesse and Jamie

Jo singing 'And then he Kissed me' at wedding.

Jesse, Leah with big sister Lisa Fisher

Jamie, Ty, Leah

Wimbledon with the family

Live Aid

the cage is open, Rio

with Hubert Sumlin

'92

Ron, My dear,
So they've
got you back in
the zoo.!! Where
you belong.!
Quite right.
All for it. Know
where you are, eh what?
Stop malingering.
Wire brush & Dettol.
Best thing for you.
Twice a day.!
Good luck.!

Any idiot
can face a crisis—

It's this
day to day living
that wears you out.

Anton Chekhov
1860–1904

him whatever they had, which wasn't always the best, and sometimes he took it.

The fact that Keith has survived is down to a bit of know-how, sure, but also a lot of really good luck, a few miracles and some understanding high court judges. True, the media has romanticized it out of all proportion, but Keith is partially responsible for that because he caters to the press and has always been aware enough of his image to give reporters what they want to hear.

His best line was when he told some reporter that the way he stayed alive was by regularly checking into a Swiss clinic and having a complete blood transfusion, the way you take your motor into the garage for an oil change. The media loved that one and flocks of reporters went in search of Swiss clinics where that sort of thing supposedly happened. Over the years, if Keith disappeared for a week for whatever reason, they'd write that he was back in embalming detox.

One detox method that Keith has used, and I know because I did too when I found out that no needles were involved, was the electric shock box. This was a contraption invented back in the 1970s by a doctor named Meg Patterson, where you put a little clip on to each of your ears, adjust the amount of electricity that the box generates, then go to sleep. You do it when you're coming off heroin because it takes away the withdrawal. Keith nicked one of the boxes from somebody and had it converted so that he could detox whenever he wanted to.

19

Misguidance

The Stones released *Emotional Rescue* in 1980. I remember that while recording in Paris, Keith was very adamant about working above and beyond the call of duty. At about four in the morning, just when everyone was getting really tired, after we'd really done well and cut a couple of basic tracks. Keith would say, 'Right, now we're going to do this,' and we'd all go 'Ahhh . . .!' while Bill would be hovering in the doorway. Keith's catchphrase at the time was 'Nobody sleeps while I'm awake.' There was one night when I'd actually managed to get out of the studio for some well-earned rest. It didn't last. Keith climbed over the fence outside, jumped into my garden and broke into the house. In my sleep I could hear the door bursting open, boom, boom, crash, bang. Keith burst in, 'Nobody sleeps while I'm awake,' and I was dragged back into the studio. So they were a slave-driving bundle of sessions, but we did get an amazing amount of work done. We didn't tour the album, though, probably because we were all so tired.

However, we did an extensive stadium tour the following year to promote *Tattoo You*, which was filmed to make the movie *Let's Spend the Night Together*.

Mick and Keith had been writing a song that we originally intended to use on the *Some Girls* album. We recorded it the first time in 1978, but didn't finish it until a year later, so we used it on *Tattoo You* instead. That song, 'Start Me Up', is the reason why *Tattoo You* spent nine weeks in the charts at Number One.

While we were in Nassau recording *Tattoo You*, Alan 'Logs' Dunn (long-time assistant to Mick and logistics boss) decided to take a trip out to sea with his girlfriend in a small boat with a put-put engine. After several attempts to start the failing outboard, they realized they were adrift at sea with no food, no water and no protection. They began an epic 800-mile drifting odyssey. At one with the elements, Alan starts to hallucinate, seeing towering cities rising from the sea, the coast of Cuba (even though Cuba was nowhere near), mechanical fish, plus the inner workings of his watch. He had to be knocked out by his girlfriend a couple of times to stop him walking in the three feet of water he imagined to be out there.

Concern and disbelief broke out at base camp. Keith and I hid our concern by recording non-stop for three days in the safety of the studio. The elements had torn Alan to pieces and three days later, upon his return, we gasped a huge sigh of relief that he was back. Where did he think he was, on his father's yacht?

After the US leg of Tattoo You we toured Europe, recorded the studio album *Undercover*, then went home. None of us knew that we wouldn't get together again for three years. None of us knew that we wouldn't tour again for seven years. None of us had a clue just how close the Stones could come to splitting up.

Just because I tried to clean up for that tour didn't mean I was going to stop altogether. I knew it was dope and drink messing me up and clouding my judgement, and I knew I was hanging out with too many weird people and doing too many dangerous things, but I couldn't stop and I'm not sure at that point I even wanted to stop.

One guy I hung with in those days was a dealer named Gary, which I'm sure wasn't his real name. We used to let him stay with us at the house because he always showed up with great coke, which he carried in a bank bag which he kept inside a locked case. One night Gary went upstairs to bed, and I was downstairs in the rat room with Jo's brother Paul, and I decided to get into Gary's case and help myself to some of his stash. Paul and I worked out a whole plan. I sneaked upstairs on my belly, just like a commando, and got into the room and picked the lock on his case, took loads of Gary's stash and crawled out without him ever waking up.

Back downstairs I told Paul, 'We got away with it, we did it,' then realized, shit, I'd left the bank bag outside the case. If Gary saw that he would know what had happened, so I had to do my commando crawl again, upstairs and into his room to put the bank bag back inside the case.

While I was fumbling with it, trying to pick the lock again, Gary woke up. I crawled fast into the next room, jumped on the bed there and pretended to be asleep. Gary got up, saw his stash on the floor, knew right away what was going on and found me. He was furious with rage, and jumped up and down on the bed shouting, 'You've been in my stash.'

I pretended like I didn't have a clue what he was talking about, and held on to that line long enough to convince him that he'd been so stoned when he went to bed that he'd left the case open by accident.

After a while he calmed down and decided that maybe he

did leave it there himself but he was soon accusing me all over again. He said, 'I saw it with my own eyes.' I asked him, 'Who are you going to believe, me or your own eyes?' Eventually he gave up, 'Oh yeah, you're right,' and never brought it up again, which is just as well because it's not a good idea to steal dope from a dealer.

The drugs and the money I spent on them drove me from one manager to another, until I eventually wound up with some of the dodgiest in the business. Jason Cooper and I parted company and I met an English bloke living in L.A. named 'Mr Vulture'. He was a guy in his late forties who turned out to be involved in all sorts of shady show-business deals, except I didn't know that at the time. What I did know is that he had great coke and tons of it. Mr Vulture and his wife used to invite Jo and me over to their house. We'd bring our little pipes, sit down on the floor, he'd cook up gallons of base and the four of us would get high together. I'm not sure now if I liked him or if I just liked his coke, but his wife was scary. She was a big bulky woman with ridiculous hair and freckles who was always talking about sex.

At the end of the evening, or the next day, or two days later, he'd go up to a special stash room that he had built in the house that was filled floor to ceiling with cocaine. The door to his stash room was electronically controlled, with a computer-coded lock and hidden behind a wall. He'd open it and I'd look inside (this really was Aladdin's Cave) and he would shovel some coke into a bag for me. Honestly, he had so much that he actually used a small shovel. Then he'd give me the bag and we'd go home and stay stoned for another three days, or five days, or a week.

Mr Vulture was always giving us gifts, asking how much do

you want, do you want more, here, have some more. Every day was like Christmas. What I didn't know until much later was that he had a laboratory in the basement to make the stuff, and a cupboard filled with guns. I never saw his laboratory and I never saw his guns because he would only let us into certain rooms of his house. But I saw the secret room and one day I said to him, 'You'd make a great manager,' or maybe he said to me, 'I want to be your manager,' and because we were in the middle of getting high, I said, 'All right then,' and that's how Mr Vulture became my manager. He was a crook from day one. Among other things, Mr Vulture took one of my paintings, made some terrible prints of it and sold them without asking me. He also bossed me around, which I didn't like.

Jo suspected that Mr Vulture was up to no good and that having him as my manager was a really bad idea, and she kept asking me, 'Why did you say yes? Why would you let someone like that be your manager? He's giving us thousands and thousands of dollars' worth of coke and has never asked us for money. Does that sound right? Mr Vulture's dodgy.'

I tried to listen to her because she's always been a good judge of character, just as my mum was. But I can be stubborn.

I'm not sure how I met the next sleazy businessman in the chain of events. Let's just say he's 'Harry'. Harry was a skinny bloke with unusual features, a pointy nose and wavy hair and, I guess, at the time, in his late thirties. He was the sort of man who could slip into a room, then slip out of the room, and no one would notice. He was very quiet and was always watching you, which made me nervous. I don't really know what Harry did for a living, but he had a house in Malibu and he told me once that after being away doing whatever it was he did, he arrived home just as someone was blowing it up. He said that he was driving up to the house, there was an explosion and the windows blew out and the roof blew off.

I asked, 'What did you do?'

He answered, 'Drove straight on past it.'

Jo and I wanted to find out what we could about Harry, but we never got more than bits and pieces, and the bits and pieces we got worried us. He was also throwing a lot of money around, at a time when we were struggling on $200 a week. Harry was saying to us, 'That's all you're going to get,' but there he was splashing out $50,000 here and $50,000 there. We wanted to ask about that money, and where was our money, but there was nobody to ask.

We were also starting to get worried about the blokes hanging around Harry. One of them was called 'Dick', although we always thought he was a really nice guy. But Dick got stopped in Miami one day as part of a routine traffic check, and the cops found some grass in the back of his car and what we heard was that when the cops started questioning him, he told them, 'I know plenty of things you would like to know.'

They wanted to know, 'Like what?'

So Dick told them everything he knew about Harry.

Whether Harry got arrested and then fled the country, or he fled the country first and was arrested somewhere else, I don't know, and frankly I don't care. Dick apparently testified against Harry, changed his name and now lives somewhere in the universe under witness protection.

Before his arrest, Harry introduced us to a British solicitor living in L.A. named Nick Cowan. One day I told Nick about Mr Vulture. Nick offered to look into it and before I realized what was happening, Mr Vulture was out and Nick eased his way in and took over as my manager. I didn't think it could get any worse but in some ways it certainly did. I really have had fuck-all luck when it comes to picking some of my managers.

The Stones weren't touring and I was running out of money.

Letters arrived at the house every morning, but I never paid attention to any of them. When Jo discovered a large box of unopened envelopes, she decided it was time to take the bull by the horns.

She said, 'I can't stand this, Ronnie, we need to open these.' I think I just shrugged. She insisted, 'We have to, there are bills in there and you really need to pay them.'

'Okay,' I said, 'fine.' She started going through the letters, which she now does all the time. One of the more interesting things she found was a statement from one of my advisors, showing that money had come in but that it went right out again. There were all sorts of deductions, like $150,000 here and $300,000 there. She wanted me to tell her what they were, and wanted to know why so much money was being taken, and I answered, 'I think it's some kind of tax scheme,' but I really had no idea.

Obviously I should have paid more attention but I've never been good at money. I can earn it, and I have earned piles of it, but my problem comes with holding on to it. As it happened, I'd let too much money slip through my fingers and we were broke. Jo and I sold the house on Mandeville Canyon and moved to New York. We weren't sad about leaving southern California. New York felt much more real than California and lacked the sometimes plastic feel that L.A. has. It was time to go.

We took a place in Greenwich Village in 1981, on Bedford Street. The madness that we'd known in L.A. had followed us to New York and Miami; we couldn't shake ourselves loose from it. Part of that is my fault because I have trouble saying no to people. We weren't there too long when a rough character showed up saying that he was a debt collector and demanded money we owed to Mr Vulture.

I said, 'What are you talking about?'

He said, 'Mr Vulture's in jail right now, you owe him $150,000, he needs the money and I'm here to see that he gets it.'

This came as a total shock to me. I didn't know Mr Vulture was in jail, didn't particularly care, and there was no way we owed him anything. I later learnt that he'd been under police surveillance for two months, suspected of manufacturing and packaging cocaine for use in freebasing, and when they finally raided his home, they found $250,000-worth of coke, thirty-four guns and two pipe bombs. As far as I was concerned, this was his problem and had nothing to do with me.

I told Nick Cowan about it and he grew concerned for our safety and suggested we get out of the country, at least until everything with Mr Vulture and his debt collector mate cooled down. So Jo and I went to Mexico and laid low for six weeks. Jo kept asking, 'Why can't we just go to the police?' She wanted to be absolutely up front and honest and tell the cops everything we knew about Mr Vulture, and in fact, about all these people. She didn't understand why we had to lay low in Mexico, or why we should allow ourselves to be threatened by some debt collector. I didn't know either, except it seemed safer than anything else I could think of. Then just like that, one day Nick rang to say that the coast was clear, that we could come back. I have no idea what he did, but whatever it was, the Mr Vulture problem went away.

For the next twenty years or so, Nick Cowan was my manager.

We came back to the Big Apple and bought a brownstone house on West 78th Street and I had a studio installed in the basement. Then Nick saw the state of our finances and, with Harry as his sidekick, kept us on a budget of $200 a week. We were struggling and didn't know how we were going to live on that, so I looked for ways to earn money. The best thing seemed to go back to painting. I told myself, this is how I'm going to pay for groceries.

Painting and drawing had been on the backburner for all those years, so I was going to get back into art. I went to San Francisco and borrowed a studio and started doing woodcuts, monotypes, silk screens. Nick took all the work I produced and sold each piece for a few hundred bucks. Little by little the cash started coming in.

Bizarrely, there were people then (and there are still some people today) who can't quite get it into their heads that's what I do – play music and paint. And breed.

On 21 August 1983 my son Tyrone was born. Jo and I were blessed with another bundle of joy, a boy with an extraordinary nature who is calm, beautiful, a great judge of character, a shining light in the Wood clan. I remember staring out of the window of the Mount Sinai hospital in New York while I waited for the news. I had another son. After his birth, while Jo was still in the hospital, I offered her a line of coke to celebrate. But she was now in a different place, a maternal, breastfeeding place with our son in her arms. She told me to stop being ridiculous and get it together. Our family was expanding and it was clear to me that as a father I had been blessed again. When naming him, we asked Leah (who was five at the time) what we should call him and her suggestion was Trumpet Head. In hindsight, it was probably not best to get advice from the little girl who thought the Lear jet and leotard were named after her. Mind you, we were going to call her Holly – just for a laugh.

My years in New York were filled with jams of the finest nature. The studio I had built in the basement was like an earthing ground. There was a code that you'd have to tap in at the top of the stairs to get beneath the surface. Once I had tapped that code in and closed the door I could enter my own subterranean world, which often was not a very good thing because I'd get trapped down there with all sorts of unearthly people. Most of the time, though, I was playing with the best. Steve Jordon and Charlie Drayton were my in house play-mates.

Keith rang me in 1986 to come to Detroit where he was producing and playing on Aretha Franklin's remake of 'Jumpin' Jack Flash'. He wanted me to play on it too. I had grown up listening to this woman and seeing her there in the studio was absolutely inspiring for me. At one point I hid behind the organ speaker and just watched her sing, just her and that fantastic control she had over the piano. Never forgot it.

She was belting out the song in that familiar awesome voice, wailing and chain-smoking Kools Menthol at the same time with a gold medallion hanging around her neck, swaying in time to the music. She'd brought all her sisters and a huge portion of her (pretty rotund) family into the studio control room that day. Keith and I could hardly get in there because of all the people and all that flesh.

After that gig, I went back to New York to play two gigs at the Ritz with Chuck Berry – what a gas. First he apologized about giving me a black eye and then I said, 'It wasn't me, it was Keith.' He said, 'What the hell, I love you anyway.' Running around like that, playing with these guys was a great blast. As were the couple of gigs I did at Madison Square Garden with Bob Dylan and Tom Petty that we put together in 1986. A winning example of ingenious lyrics and remarkable riffs.

Living and breathing music twenty-four hours a day is a trait shared by most great musicians, and early on Charlie spotted one of these types and recognized his great potential.

In October 1981, a then unknown soul phenomenon opened for the Stones at the L.A. Coliseum. Charlie said, 'You have to listen to this guy before he becomes famous.' And when Charlie says that, the rest of us take notice. Even though most people think Charlie's strictly a jazz man, he's right up to date with the new bands. He's the one who is always finding the new guys, and to prove it he's the one who introduced us to Oasis, Christina Aguilera and Jack White among others.

On Charlie's say-so, we gave this little rocker his first break. When he stepped out onstage we were all – especially Keith – a bit surprised because he was wearing a raincoat and stockings. 'That's the trouble of conferring a title on yourself before you've proved it,' said Keith. The crowd was a bit surprised too and started lobbing fruit and vegetables at the guy. But it quickly became clear that this guy had something special. He brought so much vavavoom to the stage. That's how TAFKAP, the artist formerly known as Prince, became a star.

Five years later, Sting and I were with Prince – playing 'Miss You' – at Wembley Arena. By then, Prince had a massive entourage and was completely surrounded by a lot of huge black bodyguards. If you wanted to talk to him, you had to dig through this mound of muscle. What you found when you got to the middle was this very polite little guy. A real gentleman. But the thing that always struck me about him is his love for music. He breathes it and sleeps it.

One of the characteristics of musicians who ooze music is that they have a top-notch band and Prince was no exception. Because this gig was organized so fast, we had no time to rehearse, so when it came to the night, the pint-size pop Prince asked, 'What you gonna do when the middle eight comes up?'

I suggested we leave it out. He understood and the band understood – they were real tight – and I got on with them as if we'd been playing together for years.

Backstage, I found a little girl who looked totally lost and asked her if she was all right. She said she was. I said, 'Do you need help finding your parents?' She said she was fine. Turns out it was Kylie Minogue.

After that, Prince and I would meet every now and then in social circumstances. But it's always the same old problem. We'd bump into each other in a club or at a bar where the music was so loud that normal talking was virtually impossible. We found the only way to defeat this was to sing our conversations to each other.

For both Jo and me, those years in New York were like one very long party, with lots of alcohol and lots of pills and lots to smoke. We had also done a little bit of downtown together back with Keith in Paris. I don't do needles, so we were smoking it. We still called them DCs, dirty cigarettes. Jo would only take a puff or two and never thought it was becoming a problem until one morning when she woke up and had a craving for a DC, but I didn't have any and she burst into tears. That was the first time either one of us saw how this was affecting her. She said to me, 'Oh my God, I've got to stop,' and she did, right there and then. She's very lucky like that because she has the ability to say this has gone too far, I don't want to do this any more, I quit. I wish I could do that but I can't.

When Jo stopped doing DCs, she had no come down, and after Paris she never did lady again, at least not deliberately. After we moved from Greenwich Village uptown to that great brownstone on West 78th, we got to know the queen bee of dealers, a woman who called herself Betsy.

We had no idea at the time how major she was, or that she was Public Enemy Number One and the most wanted woman in the city of New York. We just got on great with her, she had terrific coke and all this cash lying around and she used to take pity on us. She knew we didn't have any money so she would give us plastic bags that were left over from some of her deals to scrape. It was the day when we thought we were scraping together bits of coke to do a line and it turned out to be downtown that Jo got sick as a dog, and that was the last day she did heroin. It was also one of the last times we had anything to do with Betsy.

She was living on West 79th Street, and we didn't know that the cops were photographing everybody who came in or went out. I'd walk over there to score. It was winter and so I had a big fur coat on with the coat's big fur hood over my head. When the cops showed up and ordered us to testify in front of a grand jury about Betsy, we went into a panic. They brought out pictures of me that the police surveillance team had taken and asked if I recognized this man dressed like a fashionable Eskimo. I didn't want any part in this so I kept saying, 'I have no idea who that is, nice coat though . . .' We weren't much of a help to them, but the cops didn't need our help, they had everything they needed on Betsy and they put her away for a long time.

With the drug scene happening all around them, our children couldn't help but notice. Jamie used to come downstairs in the morning and if there were joint ends in an ashtray, he'd nick them. He and Leah also often found people crashed out in our living room. Once Jamie noticed someone on the sofa, thought the man looked familiar and stared until he recognized Christopher Reeve, who was out of his brain. He came running back to us, crying, 'You destroyed Superman.' Our houses had so many parties that there were bound to be little accidents. When one landlady tried to sue us for cigarette burns at the top of the curtains, we needed to find a way out of it. Jo found a roll of film, thinking it was ours, only to find out it was the landlady naked with a teddy bear between her legs. She immediately dropped the lawsuit when we handed back the film.

As a family we have always laughed a lot, and that's probably because our children can be very funny. Their parents can be too. Jo would dress up as the Easter bunny and hide eggs in the garden. We'd sing and dance for them and I would film them at every party. But Jamie and Leah could be especially mischievous. Jamie put a banger in one of Keith's cigarettes, it exploded in his face, and Keith chased Jamie round the garden waving a knife and screaming blue murder. One morning, Leah and Jamie came into our bedroom to wake Jo and me, found us sleeping nude, fetched their paint brushes, painted my willy green and called it my pickle.

20

Hitched

People around us knew that we were a strong, happy family. Both Jo and I come from secure loving backgrounds and we installed that in our own kin. Good family is pretty much all you need, and those around us, including Keith, saw this. While Keith was still young, his mum Doris ousted his father Bert and although I don't know the full story, eventually Keith lost contact with his dad. He was about eighteen when that happened, around the same time he left art college, and Bert stayed out of his life for the next twenty-one years. Then, one day, almost out of the blue in 1982, the two of them got back in contact and Keith arranged to meet his dad at Redlands.

I was in the UK at the time recording and was at Keith's beautiful house (where the Richards and Woods families had gathered) the day that he told me his dad was coming. I knew that he would probably want to be alone with him because after all those years they had a lot of catching up to do. So I said I had to leave, but Keith asked me to stay.

I said, 'I don't think I should.'

But Keith insisted. 'I can't meet my dad on my own,' he said, 'because I don't know him.'

So I stayed there with him, and he and I leant on a windowsill together, watching the drive until a car pulled up.

Keith said, 'You go meet him.'

I said, 'I can't do that . . .'

Keith was all nervous and that surprised me because I'd never seen him nervous before. 'Go ahead,' he started shoving me towards the front door, 'you bring him inside.'

'Okay,' I said and went out to meet his dad.

The back door of the car opened and this real old nautical type got out, smoking a pipe and with bandy legs. Keith shouted down to me from the window, 'You didn't know I was the son of Popeye.'

I looked at his dad and extended my hand. 'Hello, I'm Ronnie, what's your name?'

He shook my hand. 'My name is Bert.'

I could see that he was nervous too, so I said, 'Come on then, Bert, you don't seem too bad to me.' I gave him my arm.

He took it, said, 'All right, let's go in,' and Keith met us at the door.

I was the one who introduced them, 'Bert, this is your son.'

Bert was a wonderful guy and I got along really good with him and so did my mum and dad. Keith thought it would be fun if one night we all stayed down at Redlands with him and Bert, and after a time we left our parents alone to get better acquainted. We found my ma, pa and Bert fast asleep on some Afghan cushions in the main sitting room. Keith and I looked down on them from the gallery, and watched them for a few minutes, all crashed out, until Keith said, 'Look at this house full of hippies.'

What I loved about Bert was how he would be smoking his pipe and fall asleep in his chair, sitting upright, then wake up again, look at his pipe and say, 'Hello, my beauty,' pick it up and relight it.

Keith and Bert stuck together, like glue, for the rest of Bert's life.

If I'd helped Keith with his relationship with his dad, he certainly repaid the favour with my relationship with Jo.

On 9 September 1984, Jo and I were at Keith's place in Ocho Rios, Jamaica. We'd decided we wanted some sunshine and he said come stay with me. Jo mentioned to him that this was our anniversary, that we'd met exactly seven years before, so he decided that she and I had been together long enough and that it was time we got married. He didn't just say it to me once, he said it to me several times. 'When are you going to get married?'

The truth is that I had been proposing to her for years, but that Jo kept turning me down. I'd say, 'Let's get married,' and she'd say, 'We're very happy the way we are,' so I started thinking maybe we don't need to get married and had pretty much given up asking her.

On the afternoon of the 9th, Keith pulled me aside. 'It's about time you proposed to Jo.' He was determined to make me do it so he booked a secluded table for the two of us, right next to a waterfall, in the most romantic restaurant on the island. 'Come on, ask her.'

Jo didn't know anything about it, so that night she and I went out to dinner to celebrate our anniversary alone and when the waiter came by with the menus, I sat there with a long face, trying to figure out how I was going to propose, all the time convinced that I was going to get turned down yet again.

After a while Jo wanted to know, 'What's the matter with you?'

My answer was, 'Will you marry me?'

She looked at me from over the top of her menu, shrugged,

'Oh, all right then. Now, what are you having for the main course?'

Back at Keith's, I got on the phone to announce to Jo's mum, my mum and to everybody else we knew that we were getting married. They were all thrilled for us, but I think Keith was probably the happiest of all.

We returned to New York, then went home to England for Christmas like we usually did, and as soon as we got there Jo threw a wedding together in under three weeks. She designed her own dress, which was beautiful, had it made for £300, and organized everything except picking up my brothers. That was down to me and I forgot.

Our original plan was to be married in church – a real old-fashioned family wedding – but there was no way any church would allow us to do that. I was Church of England and Jo was Roman Catholic, and my church wasn't going to let me marry her, and her church wasn't going to let her marry me, or anyone else, because she was divorced (which is why I didn't take it personally). So we opted for 'a church blessing', which meant we needed to find a vicar who'd agree to it. We didn't know one, so we asked around and the vicar who came recommended said he would only bless our marriage if we would meet regularly with him for a few weeks before – and then promise to visit him annually, you know, to top up our spiritual guidance. This was so he could counsel a couple who had been living together for seven years and already had two children, about the sanctity of marriage. Part of his spiel was why it was so important that we come back to the church, and how he was looking forward to seeing us in church regularly. Jo and I just sat there and nodded a lot.

On the night before the wedding, Jo went to see a play and then for dinner with a bunch of girlfriends, then spent the night at Lorraine Kirk's house. I went out for a New Year's Day stag night with Jeff Beck, Peter Cook, my brother-in-law Paul (whose hangover the following morning became a thing of legends), Uncle Fred and Gordy MacGregor, who was the long-term partner and childhood sweetheart of my cousin Rita. We hit Soho with a vengeance. We hit bar after bar, most of them grubby, cheap and stuffed full of vagrants, winding up knee-deep in piss and rum. As was required on the night before one's wedding, we decided to wind up the night in a famous strip joint called the Raymond Revuebar. At least we thought we'd wind up the night there viewing Mr Raymond's ladies. But we were spotted the moment we got inside by suspicious security – it would have been difficult for them not to notice our raucous behaviour, being the noisy, pickled gaggle that we were – and found ourselves quickly escorted out to the pavement. We kept telling the security blokes to let us be, but they weren't having it, especially when Peter Cook suggested he knew a place one of the ladies could put a bottle of champagne.

As it was the night after New Year's Eve, most places in London were shut. I still think this was a clever ploy of Jo's to make sure her husband-to-be didn't have many debauched options. As we walked past the Ritz Hotel on Piccadilly I announced, 'I know a bloke here, they might let us in.'

The others were all for it – at that point in the evening they were all for anything – so we stepped inside this remarkably decadent and extraordinary place, and I explained the situation to the night staff. 'It's my stag night. I need a drink with my mates. Can we get a room?'

Unfortunately no rooms were available, but the staff were very hospitable and offered us the lobby. There was a piano, we ordered massive amounts of champagne and everyone in the hotel had a great time, except most of the guests. We sang long into the night, in that fabulous opulent room. At dawn as the guests were sleepily walking to breakfast, our troupe got up and left.

Ten years later, on another night strolling round London with a different group of revellers, I tried my trick again – 'I need a drink with my mates. Can we get a room?' – and the same thing happened. The same staff were there and greeted us with, 'Ronnie, we haven't seen you in ten years, come in, come in.'

When I got up (two hours later) on the morning of my wedding, I was convinced that everything was arranged, that my and Jo's parents would be picked up on time, except in the excitement of getting ready I'd forgotten about my brothers Art and Ted. We were high and rocking all the time, right up to our wedding, and I honestly thought I'd ordered a car for them. But if I did, it never showed. So they missed our wedding, which was for family in the Buckinghamshire registry office, and only just made it to the church by the skin of their teeth.

Our blessing was held in a tiny church in a Buckinghamshire village called Denham, not far from Pinewood Studios. My sons, Jesse, Jamie and Ty, were our pageboys and wore little red bow ties. So did I. Our beautiful darling daughter, Leah, was our bridesmaid along with Jo's sister Lizzie and Domino Kirke.

The church was filled with celebrities. Keith and Charlie were my best men. Rod Stewart, Peter Cook, Bill Wyman (with Mandy Smith on her 'debut' public appearance), Jeff Beck and Peter Frampton were all there. However, there were a few noticeable absentees. Keith's wife Patti and Mick's wife Jerry didn't come as one was about to give birth and the other just had.

Anyway, the vicar took one look at the audience, saw a room filled with famous faces, and he started babbling in his sermon. 'There are many stars in the sky, but some of them only give off little light, and there are so many stars in the congregation today, but never forget that stars can dwindle and fade . . .' And so began his preaching.

Oh my God, it was awful. Peter Cook was sitting right near the front, couldn't believe what the vicar was saying, and started preaching back at him. 'The triangle . . . God . . . self . . . Holy Grail . . .' Suddenly the whole congregation started whispering and sniggering. The louder the vicar spoke, the deeper he dug himself into a hole. He went on and on about bright stars and dim lights, and our friends in the audience started repeating whatever he said, only louder.

This wasn't a church service as you'd know it. This was Rock and Roll meets God. It was perfect. We were married. We got up from our knees and greeted our friends and the press outside the church. Jo and I jumped into the white Roller limo that was waiting to take us to the Bull, a hotel down the road, where we were having a wedding party and had rented rooms for the family. Just as we were about to drive off, Keith grabbed his fish and chips that he'd brought with him and jumped into the car with us. He pulled out his blow and gave us a hit each. The watching congregation saw our three heads dip out of view as we 'toasted' our wedding.

The church service put everyone in a party mood and this mood spilled into the obligatory wedding photos. The first photo was Jo, me and family and by the end of the session it seemed that the whole congregation had piled in and were squeezed into the shot.

The Bull was rocking and dinner looked nice. Peter Cook decided we were 'the dancing act of the 1990s'. But the life and soul of the party – the real star of the wedding – was my dad. He played his harmonica, sang, told jokes and held court in his wheelchair. The Dirty Strangers got up and they played, and then Keith and I got up and played with them. And while we were playing, Jo decided this was her wedding and she could do anything she wanted to, so she got up on the stage with us and sang 'And Then He Kissed Me'.

She was very happy that the guy who shot the wedding video also got her singing. She cherished that video, reminding me all the time how precious it was. Unfortunately, a few days after the wedding the snooker was on. The World Championships were in full swing and I was rooting for my mate Jimmy White. I had to run out and didn't have any spare tapes to record it. But I knew there was a bit at the end of the wedding tape where I could record the match. A couple of days after that, Jo decided to show the wedding video to her mum, got to the part where Keith and I were playing, and said, 'Watch, Mum, this is my bit . . .' and there was Jimmy potting a black. There was nearly an early divorce.

Jo and I spent our wedding night in the Bull, a night of hot passion, and the next day when we came down for breakfast and saw the papers, we were in shock. There we were on the front page of every national newspaper in England. It blew our minds, not only because we didn't have a PR person handling the wedding, but because there were lovely headlines and so many lovely pictures, and all the stories about us were so sweet.

After breakfast with my dad, we went back to the house we were renting in Chiswick. I was recording around then and didn't have time for a honeymoon until later. Keith came along with his dad and so did Peter Cook. They all camped out and we rocked for a few more days.

Jo and I had our honeymoon the following November. We went to Bora Bora, somewhere Jo had always wanted to go, to hang out in the South Pacific. It was the most beautiful atoll either of us had seen and great to have some time for just the two of us. I bought Jo a beautiful black pearl and learnt how to get rid of hiccups by standing on my head. One afternoon, the bartender started to make a rum punch for us, but I insisted he use vodka instead, and today that drink at that bar is still called a Woody's Number 3.

Nothing changed when we got married. We'd just rubber-stamped our relationship. Before our wedding we didn't mind not being hitched, there was something kinda cool in us two just dating with our kids scampering about. I often feel like that with Jo, right like I did in the early days of our relationship. In fact I kept asking Jo to marry me years after and I'll keep asking her forever.

21
Overcast

The Stones met in Amsterdam in October 1984 to discuss recording a new album that would be called *Dirty Work*, and there was obvious real tension in the air between Mick and Keith because Mick was in the middle of doing his first solo album, *She's the Boss*.

He'd been in Mustique, where he was working on the album with a bunch of great musicians like Herbie Hancock, Jeff Beck and Pete Townshend. Keith didn't approve of this and was very vocal about it, telling Mick that none of us should go outside the Stones. I think Keith's thinking is that when any of us go and do our own thing it weakens the Stones. He just didn't like seeing his sparring partner shadow-boxing. Looking back, I suppose this feud had been brewing for five years, from about the time we made *Emotional Rescue*. While we were in Amsterdam Keith took Mick out for a drink. By five that morning they were back in Keith's room and Mick decided to call Charlie, who was fast asleep. 'Is that my drummer? Why don't you get your arse down here?' Charlie in his Gemini serenity got dressed in a beautiful Savile Row suit, tie, shoes, had a shave, came down, grabbed Mick and punched him into a plate of smoked salmon. He pulled him up and nearly punched him out the window. Keith grabbed Mick's leg and saved him from going out the window, down twenty storeys and into the canal. 'Don't ever call me "your drummer" again. You're my fucking singer.' That was Charlie's way of saying don't disrespect me, I am my own man.

This moral strength is not out of Charlie's character but the violence is. When Charlie told me he'd been drinking, it made more sense to me. Charlie had been going through a bad patch for the past couple of years, doing some speed and some heroin but mostly drinking. He decided it was his midlife crisis, but whatever it was, he was a different person and it almost cost him his marriage. He and Shirley are the longest-running marriage I know, a remarkably strong pair. Within a year of his fight with Mick, Charlie fell down the stairs at home. The shock of that made him realize where his life was going and he stopped drinking, smoking and drugs, all in one go. Nobody knows better than me how hard that is. Charlie is a noble example to me, a formidable rock and a true inspiration.

We were scheduled to take a break before we started recording *Dirty Work* in Paris. I think we all needed it as the Stones had been sliding over thin ice in Amsterdam. We were getting better at family holidays, in fact they were becoming our forte. Our family was growing and we were becoming more responsible, loving parents. This holiday was certainly not like the time Jo and I went to Miami back in 1981.

We always have too much luggage with us when we travel, although most of the time we manage to remember all of it. This time we left one of Jo's suitcases on the carousel at Miami Airport and only later realized it was filled with some great clothes. But we never went back to the airport to find it because both of us were too high to bother.

I can't remember how long we were at Ruze's house, but sometime during the first few days, a big limousine pulled up the drive and a bunch of older guys in well-cut suits got out. The guy who was clearly in charge was in his fifties, Italian and bald. Let's call him Tony. When Ruze came out of the house to greet him it was *Goodfellas* frightening.

After Ruze introduced us to him, Tony said to me, 'What's the biggest amount you've ever freebased in twenty-four hours?'

I had no idea but I came up with, 'An eighth?' That's three and a half grams.

The boss guy said, 'What do you do, sleep all day?'

I guess they were trying to impress me, because one of Tony's henchmen went into the kitchen and put a great big Pyrex jug on the stove and started cooking up coke by the pound. I'm talking about more coke at one time than most people have ever seen.

They wanted to test it. Tony pointed at Jo, 'Hey you, come here,' took a big hit off his pipe, and blew it into her mouth. She breathed it in and it must have tasted awful because she made a face and said, 'Ewww. What did you have for breakfast?'

Brilliant. Jo had just insulted some big player. We were all silent, unsure of what was gonna happen next. Jo just laughed and sat down.

There was a long awkward moment, until Tony declared, 'I like that girl.'

We sobered up fast when Tony pulled me aside one afternoon and said, 'We want you to do something for us. When you go back to France, we want you to steal the master tapes and the album artwork of the Stones recording sessions and get them to us so we can bootleg them.'

He wasn't asking me, he was telling me, and that really frightened me. There was no way I was going to steal those tapes, for him or for anybody, so I went to find Jo and told her what he wanted us to do, and we agreed that it was time to get out of Miami. We thanked Ruze and his friends for their hospitality and announced, 'We have to leave, now.'

Tony decided, 'You're not going anywhere until we settle our little business.'

I said, 'We've really got to be somewhere,' but he and his mates weren't interested in our travel plans.

I worried that they were going to hurt us, but Jo decided, 'They're not going to do anything to us while we're here, because they need us.' That's when we agreed that the way out of there was to make them think we were giving in.

I went to the boss and said, 'Okay, I'll see what I can do.' And we bullshitted our way out. Jumped on a plane, got back to recording and reality with absolutely no intention of flogging our work. Never holiday with a dealer, or the mafia.

22
Welding

When the Stones met in Paris early in 1985, Jo and I relocated the family for a few months and sent the kids to an Anglo-American school so that I could get on with rehearsing and recording. The tension was still very much there between Mick and Keith. I found it really difficult as these two are the spine and organs of the band. We tried to get down to work but it takes time to settle into a new album because there are songs to learn and musical avenues to explore.

Mick left pretty early on in the rehearsals to concentrate on some solo stuff, and while he was away, the mood changed. Keith took over the recording sessions, which opened the door for me to get some of my music on to the album. He and I wrote 'You Can't Cut the Mustard' which he sang, also mumbling under his breath, 'Mick doesn't work other bands.'

Those two have had this love-hate thing since they were growing up in Dartford. Like any 'marriage' made up of strong-willed people, Mick and Keith were going through the standard bad patch. We all reunited back in Paris and the studio time was organized so that Mick and Keith wouldn't be in the studio at the same time.

Right after his album came out, Mick and David Bowie did

245

a video, covering 'Dancing In the Street', which had been a huge hit for Martha and the Vandellas twenty years before.

Then our album came out. Mick announced that he wouldn't tour to support *Dirty Work* and that's when things got really bad between him and Keith. Instead of going out with us, Mick went ahead with his second solo album, *Primitive Cool*, and launched himself into a solo tour. Tensions in the Stones were now so bad that when a reporter asked Charlie about our new album, he answered, 'Is it out yet? Is it any good?'

Dirty Work was the most troubled period of our entire journey. You can tell that because I've got four songs on the record – which is a clear sign the Mick and Keith songwriting engine was in need of an overhaul.

I honestly believe that none of us is as strong individually as we are collectively. It's something that's hard to define. We need each other and when one of us is alone, there's something missing.

Keith and Mick stopped talking. They'd never had a fight like this before. It was like a bizarre competition about which one could say the nastiest thing about the other.

They were saying it was the end of the band but I never believed it. Mick and Keith grew up from the sandpit. They went to primary school together and stayed mates until Mick was eleven when he went to a different school and eventually Keith's family moved away. But they met again when they were like sixteen and seventeen, when Keith spotted Mick at the train station going to London, carrying two albums. One was Chuck Berry's *Rockin' at the Hops* and the other was *The Best of Muddy Waters*. Keith said he knew all of Chuck Berry's licks and Mick said he had a band, and they have been so tight ever since that Mick is right when he says that they were born brothers by accident to different parents.

The way Charlie sees it, Mick and Keith are not just brothers, they're 'brothers who always disagree', and he says that the thing with them is, if anyone gets in between them they will suddenly agree with each other and squeeze the guy in the middle.

Sometime back in the late 1960s or early 1970s, before I joined the band, Mick and Keith were in the States together and decided that, instead of flying home, they'd come back to England on a ship. They found themselves trapped on-board for five or six days, with no place to hide from the other passengers. A few people on-board must have recognized them. But there was one little old lady in particular who sensed that they were famous and was really determined to find out who they were. She stalked them for days. Finally, she gathered up enough nerve to corner them and asked, 'Who are you? Just give us a glimmer.'

Ever since, Mick and Keith have referred to themselves as 'the Glimmer Twins'. Keith has often admitted to me, 'Mick is my wife, whether I like it or not. We can't get a divorce.'

Keith and Mick are sealed tight and have been mates for more than fifty years. And it doesn't take me to remind them, as I sometimes do, 'You better sit down soon and start writing together because you owe the world a few more songs.'

During the grudge in the 1980s someone needed to tell them that they were being missed. Even though they weren't talking to each other, they were both still talking to me. I was the middleman, passing messages between the two.

It was the same thing in 1978 after Keith and Bill had stopped talking for years. Bill was angry at Keith because of all the drugs and Keith was angry at Bill because he didn't want anyone telling him that he had a drug problem. I thought, this is crazy, and as long as they were both talking to me, I made them both come to my room and have it out. Keith said to Bill, 'You never liked me,' and Bill told Keith, 'I never disliked you,' and that was the end of their feud.

I was resolute. One afternoon in 1988 while I was on the phone with Keith, I got my chance. He was in the islands and we were talking about him, Mick and the band and just then the other line rang. It was Mick ringing from New York to tell me that he had been phoning Keith but Keith wouldn't take his calls.

He said, 'I can't get through at all.'

I said, 'I've just spoken to him.'

Mick said, 'He doesn't want to talk to me.'

I said, 'I'll make sure he takes your call. I'll ring you right back.' I hung up with Mick and phoned Keith to say, 'You guys have got to sort this out, Mick really wants to talk to you.'

Keith said, 'I thought he didn't.'

I said, 'But he does, and he's going to ring you right now.'

So I hung up with Keith and rang Mick back to say, 'He's ready. Call him now. And when you're finished, call me back.'

Half an hour later Mick was on the line again to tell me, 'We're talking, it was nothing at all, just some exaggerations in the press.' And then Keith rang, 'We're talking.'

I was seriously relieved, not just because it meant the band wouldn't have to suffer any more, but also because I know how important those two are for each other and for everyone else. Plus I was sick of being middleman, a job that had taken too long.

23
Pride

Mid-feud, towards the middle of 1985 and back in New York, Dylan rang me up to ask if I wanted to do a charity gig with him. I said sure, because I was always happy to do anything with Bob, and not long after that he showed up at my house on West 78th Street to talk about what songs we might do. I knew all of his songs but hadn't ever played any on a stage. He was showing me chords when I wondered, 'How about if I get Keith in here, too?'

Dylan said, 'Yeah, okay,' so I rang Keith and started to explain, 'I'm here with Bob Dylan,' when Keith blurted out, 'Bob who? Fuck you.'

I said, 'Dylan's invited me to play some charity gig, and I'm inviting you along, too, and right now he's downstairs in my studio,' but Keith was in one of his moods, and when he is it helps if you're living in a different country.

I said to Bob, 'I'm not so sure that Keith can make it, so if you're happy to do it with just me . . .'

He was cool with that and went back to teaching me the chords and running his songs. Two hours later the doorbell rang. I opened it and there was Keith saying, 'So what the fuck do you want?' Knock me out.

I said, 'Bob is downstairs, be nice to him.'

'Yeah well,' Keith wanted to know, 'what the fuck is he doing messing around with my mate?'

I begged, 'Keith, please, just come downstairs and say hello.'

He followed me down, walked into the studio and threw open his arms, 'Bob . . . so great to see you!'

The three of us started rehearsing and got through pretty much the whole Dylan catalogue. Keith and I would play all these riffs and Dylan kept asking, 'How'd you know all that?'

And Keith would tell him, 'You wrote it, you schmuck.'

We ended up teaching him what he taught us.

On the day of the gig, a limo came to pick up Keith and me at my place. Keith and I weren't too sure what this was all about, and were only tagging along to help Bob out. A truck pulled up driven by Bob's daughter, and Bob hopped in, 'You coming?' he asked, 'We're on in Philadelphia, man.'

'Philadelphia?' That was ninety miles away and would take us at least an hour and a half, not counting time to get out of Manhattan.

Bob said, 'Follow us.'

So Keith and I got into the limo and told the driver, 'Follow that truck.'

Keith looked at me and said, 'This better be fucking good.'

It was better than good, it was Live Aid. There were 72,000 people at Wembley Stadium in London, and 92,000 where we played at JFK Stadium in Philadelphia, plus 1.5 billion people watching on live television in a hundred countries, all to help raise funds for famine relief in Ethiopia.

The show closed with Bob Dylan, backed by Keith and me. On the stairs up to the stage, Bob turned to us and said, 'Let's do "Blowin' in the Wind".'

I said, 'What?' He repeated, 'We'll do "Blowin' in the Wind",' and by then it was too late to argue with him because we were onstage.

I couldn't believe it because that was the only song of his we hadn't rehearsed.

Right in the middle of the song, one of Bob's guitar strings broke. I saw it, thought fast and took off my guitar and handed it to him, leaving me there in front of all those people, playing air guitar. I reached behind and was handed the broken-down remains of an axe that I could busk with a slide on. When we finished our last song we turned around to find to our surprise the entire cast gathered behind us, breathing down our necks.

In December 1985, Mick, Keith, Bill, Charlie and I suffered what could be the most emotional loss that we as a group had ever gone through, when Ian Stewart died at just forty-seven years old. I'm not saying that Brian's death didn't affect them, but Brian was out of the band when he died, and Stu was always very much the heart of the Stones.

When Andrew Loog Oldham took over as the Stones manager and demoted him, Stu took it in his usual stride, and with his Scots humour, and got on with life. He loved his music, especially boogie-woogie, and never really liked the rock and roll life. When we needed him to play on a song, he would only play if he approved of the music. You could tell what he really liked because in those early days, when he was in charge of the band's tours, he would book them into hotels much too far from the gig for the guys to chase girls, but suspiciously close to a golf course. Over the years we all moved into big houses, and Stu made money, too, but stayed in the same house where he'd always lived.

He was a lovely guy with a big chin, who used to call Jo 'Petal', and say, 'Marianne Faithfull should be put to sleep.' He called me and Keith 'my little three-chord wonders' and the band 'my little showers of shit', and any complicated middle eights were 'Chinese chord sequences'. He called the shots for the shows and no one went onstage until Stu came back and said it was all right. In fact, no one did anything until Stu gave them permission.

Stu was absolutely irreplaceable. His death was very sobering, especially since he led a real clean lifestyle, though what he ate was not the choicest. That was the irony, that he always warned us not to burn the candle at both ends.

As a keyboard player, he could really play boogie-woogie. He also thought he could play the drums but he was careful enough not to play them too much while Charlie was around. He'd lower the snare drum and move the cymbal and Charlie would come back and know that Stu had been at his kit. But when you ask him these days, Charlie tells us that he misses Stu for that.

The month before Stu died, Charlie had taken a 35-piece jazz orchestra into Ronnie Scott's. It was madness because there was no room for seven trumpets, four trombones, nine sax players, two basses, three drummers and so forth. It's tough enough to get a four-piece combo in there. But Charlie loved that gig and so did Stu.

Very few people know this, but the reason Charlie brought his orchestra into Scott's was because the club was suffering and he wanted to keep it open. He personally paid the band (thirty-five musicians don't come cheap) and gave all the takings to Ronnie Scott's, which I'm sure saved the club. Being the lovely guy that he is, on the first day of rehearsal Charlie had a table set up with booze, and because the musicians he hired weren't used to that kind of hospitality, within a couple of hours they were all legless. Anyway, when the gig finished, Charlie decided it had been a lost opportunity because it hadn't been recorded, so Charlie and Bill financed the filming of *The Charlie Watts Orchestra Live at Fulham Town Hall*, which also became Charlie's first 'solo' album.

The concert at Fulham Town Hall was on a Monday night. Stu wasn't that well, but he adored this band and insisted on being there. Charlie sensed something was wrong and forbid Stu from picking up anything heavy. Two days later, Stu phoned Sherry Daly, who ran the Stones office and still does, just to say hello. Sherry was amazed that Stu was on the phone because he never just rang people out of the blue like that, and she even asked if he was okay. He said he was. Stu then went off to do a gig with his own boogie-woogie band, Rocket 88, that night, and on the way back stopped on the motorway at 3 a.m. for a fry-up. He had a doctors appointment the next morning and while waiting in the surgery he had a massive heart attack.

Keith was supposed to meet Stu later that day and when he heard the news, he locked himself in a room for three days and wouldn't come out.

Eric Clapton, who joined us onstage a few months after Stu died for the memorial concert we held at the 100 Club, always said that Stu was the Stones' beacon to stay straight to the integrity of the music. He always had these critical comments about the band, opinions that would've earned anyone else a slap in the face, but Stu was always right and always had constructive criticism. Even today, every once in a while, someone will ask, 'What would Stu think of this?' For Keith, that's always been a criterion.

Funnily enough – going back to helping out the early Faces, he always had time and encouragement for me through the Stones, too. When we all gathered to see him off at his funeral, Charlie said 'Who's gonna tell us off now?'

We played him out to *Boogie-Woogie Blues* and then, because he died before the *Dirty Work* album came out, we added a little boogie-woogie piano fadeout at the very end, just for him.

24
Gunslingers

Not touring with the Stones for all those years meant that Jo and I could do all the things that parents always love to do – go to school shows, make home movies, have birthday parties, play games with the kids, laugh all the time and try to help them with their homework. That was great and Jo and I look back on those years as being very special. Not touring meant that we could be home to watch our kids grow up. And they could watch us grow up too. But I needed to work, so whenever friends rang and asked me to play, I went to wherever they were and brought my guitar. Straight after my birthday in 1986, I joined Fats Domino, Jerry Lee Lewis and Ray Charles in New Orleans for a concert taped at Storyville Hall for an HBO special. Fats, Jerry Lee and Ray each played their biggest hits and then, at the end, everyone joined in and we jammed together.

Here were three of the greatest piano players ever, and I had the best seat in the house, right there next to them, just watching them play, and they'd shout for me to take a solo once in a while. The great harp player Sugar Blue, Paul Shaffer from the *David Letterman Show*, Kenny Lovelace and Roy Gaines were with us.

After the gig, we all went back to Fats' house, where he had Creole Gumbo cooking in a huge pot with chicken feet and bones sticking out. Jerry Lee took one look at those bones and told me, 'That's Fats' brass section.'

When Ray arrived, Jerry Lee nudged me, 'You know that Ray can see?'

I said, 'Really?'

He insisted, 'He can see.'

I couldn't believe it. 'But he's blind.'

'Let me tell you something,' he waved me off. 'I'm doing the awards with him, the Rock and Roll Hall of Fame, and Don and Phil Everly walk in and right away, Ray says, "Hi Don, hi Phil." Nobody said their names, but he knows. So I say to him, "How the fuck can you know which one is which unless you can see?" I'm telling you, that motherfucker can see!' Later that night, Fats was showing me around the house and I spotted a grey and maroon Dansette record player on a table in his bedroom. It was so old it had cobwebs coming off it.

I told him, 'That's the same little record player we had in our house when I was growing up, listening to your first record, "I'm Walking".' He liked that a lot. In fact, I learnt all my first Chuck Berry licks on it too.

At that point, two opportunities came my way. One was to tour with Bo Diddley, the other was to open a club in Miami. I jumped at both, but would have been much better off if I just picked one.

Bo Diddley has been a music legend since my childhood. He was born Ellas Bates in Mississippi in 1928. He dropped out of school at the age of ten, took violin lessons and taught himself how to play the guitar. He was the lead singer in a washboard trio before going out on his own in 1951 (funny, I started with washboard). Four years later he had his first hit song 'I'm a Man', named himself Bo Diddley after a one-stringed African guitar, and hasn't looked back since.

When I first heard of him, in the early 1960s, it was a time when everybody who could play the guitar wanted to play like him, and all the bands touring England covered his songs, including the Stones, who he played on the bill with in 1963.

Bo had invited me to play with him in 1985, when he did a Celebrate with Bo and Friends concert at the Meadows Amphitheater in Irvine, California. We played with Mick Fleetwood, The Beach Boys, Denis and Carl Wilson and Mitch Mitchell, who'd been with Jimi Hendrix. It was a great experience to be playing again with Bo, one of my all-time heroes, and sometime after that gig he and I talked about going on tour together. We were going to call ourselves the Gunslingers and the plan was to spend eighteen months in 1987 and 1988 playing the States, Japan and Europe. Bo was all for it and so was I.

When I met up with Bo and his band to rehearse in New York in 1986, I walked into the rehearsal room with a long list of Bo Diddley songs that I wanted us to play: 'Diddley Daddy', 'Road Runner', 'You Can't Judge a Book by Its Cover', 'I'm a Man', 'Mona', 'Crackin Up' and 'Hey Bo Diddley'.

But Bo didn't want to play any of them unless I did it clean. I put down my guitar and told him, 'I guess I'm in the wrong place then.'

He said, 'You sure you ain't drinkin'?'

I said, 'Sure I ain't.'

'What's that bottle of vodka doing under your chair?' he asked.

'What's that bottle of Baileys doing under yours?!' I laughed

We slapped hands and embarked on being gunslingers. We were joking but Bo's manager got worried. Her name was Margo Lewis, an old friend of mine from the 1960s, and I hadn't seen her in years. I met Margo before I met Bo, when she was the keyboard player with Goldie and the Gingerbreads, the first all-girl American rock band. There were plenty of girl groups around, like Diana Ross and the Supremes, and Martha and the Vandellas, the Ronettes, but the Gingerbreads were different. They were four white girls who sounded like black girls and didn't just sing, they also played their own music. And they really rocked. In 1964, when Brian, Mick, Keith, Charlie and Bill went to New York for their first American tour, someone threw a big welcoming party for them and the Gingerbreads were the house band. I think the Gingerbreads got discovered by the Animals, but what I remember about them most is that they were the first group I ever saw who used a B-3, a furniture-sized Hammond organ. (Here's to you Booker, Mac and Chuck.)

Margo talked Bo into the finer points of touring with me. Bless her. She knew the score real good. The way we laid out the show was Bo opened with four or five numbers, working with his four-piece band led by his bass player, Debby Hastings, and the group guitarist christened the 'Prince of Darkness'. Then I came on and did a few songs, with my stamp on them, with Debby and the band, and then Bo came back and he and I did four or five numbers together.

Of course Bo's got an ego, but that's all right with me because he is the man who put rock in rock and roll. He's even in *The Guinness Book of Records* for being the composer with the most songs written about himself (sure Jerry Lee must be up there with him). On that tour he even wrote one song for me, a slow twelve-bar blues called 'Money to Ronnie', which really surprised me when, quite out of the blue, he laid it on me in public.

So once he understood that I was cool with Bo being Bo, we recorded our *Live at the Ritz* album onstage in New York, and when I listen to it now it's obvious why I have always loved playing with him. He's the man, and in his uniquely Bo Diddley way, he does whatever he wants to do and doesn't give a shit about anything else. The difference between Bo and me is that I think of myself as a pretty conscientious guitar player, but Bo just wants to get on that horse and ride, and he doesn't worry about whether or not there's a saddle.

With one guitar at his side and practically no backup, if one failed he was fucked. He's always been pretty good at breaking strings too. Debby told me, whilst she was tuning his axe up for him, that he used to break them on purpose in the middle of a show whenever he wanted to settle back and just tell jokes. He carried a big old fat wallet full of strings and that was his backup. He'd merrily change strings, in his own time, during a performance.

The guitar he was probably most famous for was handmade, rectangular, and heavy as hell, packed with stuff inside. He has the vibratone in there and an envelope filter, and all the things you would normally find in a stomp box. His guitar has tree-trunk size strings, which don't bend, and they're so high off the neck that the action is very severe. He's also in open tuning. No easy feat, believe me.

I didn't play his guitar onstage because I didn't want to offend him. Nowadays he'd sometimes use a Gretch, which is much lighter, and a weird Australian-built guitar with lights and gadgets that go off in the back of it. He's sitting down these days when he plays because he's dealing with diabetes, he's getting on in years and has a bad back. See, in those days, he'd lug that big square monster all over the stage, as well as his own equipment into the gig, so no wonder he has a back problem.

Being the absolute master of rhythm guitar, Bo lays down a monstrous locomotive rhythm: a San Francisco reviewer once said his sound is like 'the devil moving his furniture'. Whenever he took a solo, I moved into the rhythm part that Bo had just laid down. It's a natural thing.

Unnaturally one night in San Francisco in the 1980s when John Lee Hooker sat in with us, ego and noise collided. Between Bo and John Lee each doing their own thing, the music got so loud it was like playing in pea soup. You couldn't hear anything properly. I kept looking at Debby and she kept looking at me, then Debby finally went over to John Lee's side of the stage to find out what was going on, and John Lee didn't know either. He asked her, 'Where the fuck are we?' She didn't know, so she shouted back to him, 'Where the fuck is the one beat?' You need this beat, otherwise you're playing on luck.

We were in trouble. Debby tried to lead everyone around with the bass line, but Bo doesn't follow other people. John Lee is doing his own thing. We had a twelve-bar blues, well, John Lee doesn't do twelve-bar. Maybe he does thirteen-bar, maybe he does nine-bar. So he's off and Bo is somewhere else doing his own thing, and in the middle of all this lovely confusion, Debby and I are just laughing because what else could we do? The funniest thing of all is that the next morning, the San Francisco reviewer decided that the Bo Diddley, John Lee Hooker, Ronnie Wood jam was the most awesome ever.

We travelled long distances by road. I had a Winnebago so that Jo and the kids could come along, and Chuch was always there, plus my then manager, Phil Carson (another of the decent ones), sometimes came along too. Phil was at Atlantic Records in the UK before forming his own management company. We were in Japan when Bo asked me to design the album cover for the *Live at the Ritz* album. There were a lot of people partying in my room at the time, but that's nothing new to me (I did most of my important oil paintings in that kind of situation) and it didn't stop me from getting some ink and brushes and doing the drawing of Bo and me. He has one of my drawings from a long time back when he had a tooth missing.

Bo was wonderful to tour with and you were guaranteed to have a laugh, especially with him and his girlfriend, Marilyn. He would make her film his every movement in every song during every show. He would invent gadgets to help with the filming, cameras taped to fantastic devices so that not a shot was missed.

He also told me a lovely story about starting out in Chicago. He said that when he first got there from the Deep South with nothing but his guitar, he walked into Chess Studios and the great Mississippi blues musician Willie Dixon was there.

Willie stared at Bo for a minute, then said, 'You look like you might need some help, young man.'

Bo said, 'Oh man, I'm totally lost.'

So Willie took the young Bo under his wings, showed him the ropes, and helped him present his music and his career. I sat for hours listening to this man, and played the George Bush Sr. inauguration with him at the White House. I loved hearing early stories of him, Jerome ('Bring it to Jerome'), his percussionist, and the Duchess, the first lady bass player I had ever heard of. Once you get him going, you can't shut the legend up.

25
Shift

It was during the Bo Diddley tour that I took up the offer on the club in Florida. I should have passed. Yet with its impressive appearance and untouched Miami location I felt sure it would be a hit. Woody's On The Beach was the first big nightclub in the art deco surroundings of South Beach, and at a time when the area was yet to boom. I should have known it would end badly when Keith christened it 'Weedy's on the beach'.

Before we got there, South Beach still had crack dealers all over the place and the palm trees were just being planted along the streets. Now you can't move down there. When Jo and I went to see it we found ourselves as guests of honour at a groundbreaking ceremony with the mayor, who handed me the key to the city for starting this new venture. Jerry Lee Lewis cut the tape.

The club was designed by Barbara Hulanicki (of Biba fame) with input from Jo. It was very *Miami Vice*, very cool and absolutely throbbing. There was a private bar inside the club, and then inside the private section of the club there was an inner sanctum, and inside the inner sanctum there was an inner-inner sanctum which was reserved for Jerry Lee, me, Bo, Ray Charles, Toots, Fats; the boys.

It was wonderfully designed with a guitar-shaped swimming

pool which encouraged photographers and young models to shoot there.

When we began Woody's, we watched the deco hotels get renovated and the palm trees sprout in a place that would become familiar to so many. We were the first decent club in that part of Miami. Bo and I officially opened Woody's as part of our Gunslinger tour. Unfortunately, two years later the fire department closed us down. For noise apparently – well what did they expect? It was a live music club!

With Ray Charles, Fats Domino, Jerry Lee Lewis, the Crickets, Buddy Guy and a whole bunch of blues people we had some huge nights there. Thursday night was reggae night and we had a house band called Woody's Orphans. I hired my mate Bobby Keys to be the musical director, so I knew the music would be rocking. And I was right about that. Woody's holds happy memories for me but it was really pricey. Although we had a great time in Miami, flying back and forth from our home in New York was taking its toll. Jo and I were beginning to get homesick and beginning to get skint again. We were thinking about moving back to England when we were confronted with the seedy, non-glamorous side of New York. We saw, up close, the violent side.

We went out to dinner one night, to a terrific Indian restaurant in midtown Manhattan called Nirvana. Jamie and Leah were with us. So was Jo's friend Melissa. She excused herself to go to the toilet, and was gone such a long time that Jo started to worry. That's when Melissa came back to the table, trembling and covered with blood. She told us a man had been hiding in the women's loo, accosted her, robbed her and then beat her up. She had stood in the elevator covered in blood to get back to the table and no one batted an eyelid. New York was ruthless in those days. Melissa just shouted, 'Woody, Woody! Look what they've done!'

Jo rushed Melissa to hospital and I took Jamie and Leah home. Both of them were pretty shaken up. Once I'd got them home, I had to leave for the studio because we were recording that night. I didn't know it until I got back, but just after Jo got home, she heard some kids out on the street breaking into a car. She leant out the window and shouted at them. They looked up and just waved their knives at her.

The attack on Melissa and those kids with knives was the straw that broke the camel's back. I got home at dawn, and by then Jo had already made up her mind that we were leaving New York.

'All our family and friends are in London. I want my kids to be safe. We're going home.'

I wasn't going to argue with her, in fact I agreed, so we packed up the house in record time and flew back to the UK. We stayed with our long-time friends Lorraine and Simon Kirke until we found a house in Wimbledon, arranged a mortgage and moved in at the end of 1986.

26
Brakes

The house in Wimbledon was smaller than anything we'd ever lived in, but there was a studio at the end of the garden. That was my hang-out and I spent most of my time there. It was lovely being home. My kids were swamped by family and friends, Jo and I rekindled old friendships and rolled back into London life. Life was sweet and we were welcomed back into open arms.

One morning after a big party I found my friend, snooker champ Jimmy White, passed out in my studio at the bottom of the garden. His wife at the time, Maureen, had been looking for him all morning. When she found him, she grabbed his collar and dragged him all the way up the lawn. Halfway back to the house he woke up. She was still yelling at him. All he could say to her was, 'What's for breakfast, love?' Jo and I watched the whole thing from the window in hysterics.

One of our local haunts was a pub called the Hand in Hand, which due to past scuffles Jimmy affectionately calls the Hands Round Throat. We became inseparable. In fact he helped me judge the pub of the year competition along with Denis Compton (who played MCC cricket and also won the cup with Arsenal), Willie Rushden, Sophie Dahl and Tim Rice. An appropriate gaggle for a serious competition. Denis was getting on a bit by the time we were judging, so one pub in Putney lost points with him after we were led up numerous corridors and stairs before finally reaching our table. 'Don't like this pub, Ron, too many steps,' he'd say.

The house in Wimbledon was great at first but the shape of the building began to stifle me. It was lovely but when you have the amount of guests we did it began to feel like a sweatshop. I felt as if I was permanently edging past friends and acquaintances to get somewhere comfy.

The jewels in the house's crown were my music and art studios. I did lots of my first really big oil paintings in that studio at the bottom of the garden. During parties I would sneak off to this sanctuary and paint in peace, often accompanied by the Dirty Strangers or Terence Trent D'Arby, Johnny Marr, Bobby Womack or Jerry Williams. I was writing a song called 'Goodbye' with him when I recived the news my father had passed away. I started doing large oils of the Stones, and then taking silk screens from these. I was really getting into it again and I went to San Francisco to work on some woodcuts and monotypes. It was decided that I should approach Christie's Contemporary Art and negotiate a deal to produce a series of prints.

The result was a series called 'Decades', an edition of black and white portraits of stars from different eras. The 1930s was Louis Armstrong, Bix Beiderbecke and Bunk Johnson. The 1940s was a triptych of Charlie Parker. The 1950s was James Dean, Marlon Brando and Elvis. The 1960s was the Beatles and the Stones, but I left Brian Jones out and put myself in. That's artistic licence. The 1970s was Rod Stewart, David Bowie and Johnny Rotten. The 1980s was Madonna, Annie Lennox and Kim Wilde.

To help me be more productive with my work, Cowan organized some arsehole with funny hair to get me out of bed and 'be creative'. This didn't work and the guy just pissed me off. It wasn't until I was introduced to a professional art printer named Bernard Pratt that I formed the necessary artistic partnership that I needed. He has a studio in Kent and we hit it off immediately. I felt so inspired down at his studio, where he enlightened me to new techniques, let me jump on any of the machines and print away. Bernard has been an inspiration and a friend to me for twenty years. Some people you can just work with – we're creative together and respect each other.

Bernard and his wife said I could stay whenever the inspiration took me, and I started going down there for two or three days in a row. I would work through the night, come down at about three in the afternoon, have something to eat and work through the night again. On one night a hurricane swept through Kent and to my horror the ancient, historic town of Sevenoaks was reduced to one oak.

I really took to this and worked hard at it. We were producing beautiful screen prints, etchings and new originals for a series of exhibitions around Europe.

At one of the gallery shows in Sweden the deal with them was rather odd. Instead of money, they gave me a mauve Volvo. I drive Bentleys. Months later, I heard strange noises outside the house and went to see what it was. We were surrounded by police. A police helicopter was floating over the house, having tracked the car. Of course, the bloody mauve Volvo turned out to be stolen. The art gallery didn't buy the motor; they'd rented it in Stockholm, delivered it to me in London and said it was mine to keep. So the police took my Volvo away, which meant I never got paid for the art show. Such is life – next!

This wasn't the only time I had trouble with the police over cars. Years later I went to the premier of a film my great friend Vinny Jones was starring in. After the film I pinched a life-size cardboard cut-out of my mate, threw it in the back of my Bentley and drove off to a party. Later that evening some wary neighbour looked down from their window at my parked car and saw a 'dead body in the back of a Bentley'. In no time at all, much to the amusement of me and the other revellers, armed police surrounded my car, popped the back door and found Vinny in all his cardboard glory.

The parties at Wimbledon all got to be too much, so I'd disappear for days on end with my snooker player mates, Jimmy White and Ronnie O'Sullivan, and we'd get ripped. The three of us would return when the house had quietened down a bit. Jo would spot us, know we were up to no good, notice strange smells and then Jimmy would own up. 'Oh sorry, love, that smell is my fault. I just threw up in your dustbin.' Behind closed doors, Jimmy, Ronnie and I have forged affinities with the many characters of England. The three of us remain firmly locked in friendship.

Jimmy and I shared a lot of ups and downs. Once, we'd been up all night playing snooker and partying, and by morning had moved into the sitting room with a few other people. Jo had taken the kids to school and gone back to bed. Her dad, Michael, happened to be staying with us at the time. He was a wonderful man who looked like Peter Ustinov, made architectural models including the Thames Flood Barrier, brought Lambrettas to the UK and had a Lambretta museum down in Devon. He came down one morning and found us all, still up. He cooked us breakfast but none of us were hungry. Jimmy and I were joking around in the living room. He joined in on the joke, had one last laugh and then he died in front of us.

On the way home from his funeral, with Leah and Tyrone in the rear seat, we had a car crash. It was a rainy night, Jo was driving and we could see there was oil on this stretch of motorway. Both of us felt drained by the funeral. I was munching on little white sweets to try and stay awake. Next thing I knew the car spun, we were on to the gravel and then we were broadside in the fast lane.

Other cars were speeding past us, and I was terrified someone would smash into us. I did the unbelievably stupid thing of getting out of the car and standing in the fast lane to alert oncoming cars that we were in trouble. That's when a car came at us from the side, headlights came screaming at me and I jumped over the bonnet of our car. That car swerved, knocked into another car, bounced back into ours and caught my ankles. The kids had some cuts and Jo was okay, but I was tossed into the gutter and didn't dare look down, thinking, 'That's it. I've lost my legs.'

The police arrived, plus a load of bystanders – and when I spat out the white sweets someone in the crowd said, 'Poor sod's in a bad way, even his teeth have been knocked out.'

The ambulance people asked me if I could feel my feet and only then did I look down to see that I still had legs. I'd broken two bones in one leg and one in the other, and was in plaster for three months. My ankles still hurt to this day – but considering what might have happened I'd say it's a small price to pay.

27
Boom

Once Mick's and Keith's feud was resolved, the five of us sat down in the Savoy Hotel on 18 May 1988 – the first time in two years we had all been in the same room. Keith and Mick agreed that it was time to tour again. For Bill, Charlie and me, that was not a moment too soon, but agreeing to get back together again wasn't without its problems. Keith's first solo album, *Talk Is Cheap*, came out, and so did Mick's *She's the Boss*. After that, Keith took off on his tour of the States, first calling his band Organized Crime before changing it to the X-Pensive Winos. It was at the Savoy meeting that I felt the Stones were born again. Our Second Coming.

In January 1989, the Rolling Stones were inducted into the Rock and Roll Hall of Fame and I went to New York with Mick, Keith and Mick Taylor for the ceremony at the Waldorf Astoria. Bill and Charlie remained in England and – as is typically the way whenever some of the Stones show up minus the others – word soon circulated that Bill Wyman was quitting the band and that the Stones were definitely finished.

We were introduced at that ceremony by Pete Townshend, who warned us, 'Whatever you do, don't try to grow old gracefully. It wouldn't suit you.' Mick accepted the honour on our behalf and pointed out how ironic it was, that after so much bad behaviour, here we were on our best. He also mentioned Stu and Brian. We all then took the stage for the usual jam session, along with Tina Turner, who did a duet with Mick on 'Honky Tonk Women', and Little Richard, who sang 'Can't Turn You Loose' and 'Bony Moronie'. This must have been the first time that Mick and Keith had played together, in public, for eight years.

They must have enjoyed it because right after that the two of them got together in Eddie Grant's Barbados studio. That was the first time they had been alone, in the same room, for at least five years. If they still had any differences to settle, whatever they were wound up chucked on the floor because they spent the next two months writing a dozen songs there. The rest of us met up with them, first in Barbados and then in George Martin's studio in Montserrat, recorded those songs and started thinking seriously about the upcoming tour, Steel Wheels.

We then invented our own version of arena dates. None of us thought that we were doing anything out of the ordinary because arenas seemed a natural venue for a rock concert. We went into these venues and around the same time began experimenting with more staging and lighting effects, not to mention explosions, giant inflatable lips and penises, turning our concerts into something more. No other group was doing what we were doing. We redefined the rock concert.

Mick and Charlie design our sets and oversee them being put into practice. So when they discussed the arena concept, they approached designers who knew how to work on a large scale. Arenas meant that the band could now perform in cities that didn't have big stadiums. Designing the 1989 tour, Mick and Charlie went so far beyond anything we'd ever done before that the band was about to rewrite the books all over again. No one had ever seen anything like Steel Wheels before. This tour was going to use the biggest stage we'd ever used, and the plans were to make it the biggest show we'd ever done.

Behind the Rolling Stones was Prince Rupert Loewenstein. He was a banker and personal financial advisor in the City of London back in the 1960s, and he was the man who actually rescued the band in 1970, when the Stones were nearly broke. He realized that Steel Wheels could be a huge commercial opportunity.

Canadian promoter Michael Cohl and his company, Concert Productions International, paid a large amount of money to have the privilege of putting on this spectacle. To help pay for the tour, Michael brought in sponsors. This was also the beginning of pre-show meet-and-greets, which we now regard as limbering up towards stage time. The Faces could really have used a deal like this.

With everything in place, and the tour laid out, we called lour usual press conference to announce Steel Wheels. In July 1989 we had the media meet us at New York's Grand Central Station, on a platform next to a train. Everyone thought we were going to play something live right there, or blow the train up. Instead, Mick just held up an enormous ghetto blaster and played a cassette of our new single, 'Mixed Emotions', which would feature in the tour.

A month later we met in Toronto to rehearse and we were all relieved to be there. There was a meeting in one of the rooms, just the five of us – 'The Board' – which is how we decide a lot of things. I said to them, 'I'm broke and I need money for food to feed my family, do you think you guys could give me a little advance on the tour?' Cash was dispensed and the Woods ate again. Back in the early days, when Stu controlled the money, whenever anyone needed some, he would hand them £20. In a funny way, nothing has changed much except for the amounts.

We put every number under the microscope at rehearsals, because there are songs we choose for clubs, which tend to be more intimate, like 'Fool to Cry' and 'Stray Cat Blues', and there are songs that work better at arenas, like 'Worried 'Bout You' and 'Can't You Hear Me Knockin'?'. Then there are songs we do in stadium shows, which have to be big numbers, like 'Saint of Me' and 'Out of Control'.

We rent entire buildings for rehearsals because we need that much space, and for the past few tours we've taken over schools in Toronto. We fill the places, several floors, with our recording equipment, set up dressing rooms and offices and a canteen and small studios. We also use every inch of the gym as our main rehearsal room, which we build just like a fully equipped recording studio. I love rehearsals, everyone gets hyped up and after not playing for a while it's great to get back to the day job.

We groove on songs we think will work best, say yes to some and no to others as Mick and Chuck run their lists by us, explaining why some should be in and some should be out. If we agree, we rehearse the song. If we can't agree, we don't.

In the corner of the rehearsal room we put a canvas on a stand, and we write down every song we rehearse in magic marker, and put the key that we played it in next to it. Recently I have been painting on these to turn them into little works of art. Then after the rehearsal we hang the frame on the wall of the gym so that we can see what we rehearsed on any given night.

Steel Wheels kicked off and all rumours of a break-up were quashed. We played seventy dates and everyone who saw the show agreed that no band had ever done anything like it.

After breaking for Christmas, we went to Japan for our first ever tour there, selling out ten nights at the 50,000-capacity Tokyo Dome. Then we came to Europe and changed the name of the show to Urban Jungle, because there were few arenas in Europe that were big enough to take the full Steel Wheels experience. When the tour finally ended after 115 shows, someone worked out that we had played live to more than six million people.

Jo brought Leah and Tyrone along with us on Steel Wheels. Having the kids there made the tour much more bearable, because both Jo and I hated to be separated from them. This was Tyrone's first tour – there was no way that we were going to leave him home alone with a nanny. He says that his earliest memories of touring with the Stones are too much noise, too much music, too much shouting and too much sleeping in strange places. He would come to dinner with us and when he was sleepy he'd ask for 'two chairs'. We got two chairs, squashed them together, laid our tired boy on them and covered him in coats and jumpers. He'd fall fast asleep and we'd carry on rocking.

Jamie was attending school back in England, but Leah had a tour tutor. She didn't seem to mind, but later, when Ty was in her position, he couldn't see the difference between a tutor and a babysitter. Leah was a natural to the tour scene. She adored being smothered in love by all the friendly people on tour, watching the shows, helping with the costumes, jumping on planes, helping her mum pack and hanging out with her mentor and 'big sister', Lisa Fisher, our incredible backing vocalist of almost two decades now.

Keith's daughters Angela, Theo and Alex, along with his son Marlon, were also on tour with us, and so were Mick's kids Jade, Jimmy and Lizzie, and later Georgia, Gabriel and Lucas. Charlie's daughter Seraphina was also with us and his granddaughter Charlotte (my dear friend) is the latest welcome addition. The kids hung out together, and grew up touring the world with us.

Jo, Keith, Patti, Mick, Jerry and I thought this was a wonderful experience for them – giving our kids the opportunity to see so much of the world while they were still so young – and having such a great time together. We didn't realize just how great a time they were having until the day Jo got a room-service bill consisting of caviar, foie gras, champagne and chips. Ty and Leah were playing host to their mates and that's what they were eating that night. They were also using the minibar all day like a fridge at home. We were rocking up a storm across the world and so were our kids.

The rumours of Bill leaving the band that had been circulating since 1989 were becoming more and more realistic. Bill Wyman joined the Stones as Bill Perks, his father's name. It was after he did his first gig with them at the Marquee Club, January 1963, that he decided Bill Perks didn't sound raunchy enough and changed it.

When I first met Bill, he was living with the very beautiful and very Swedish Astrid Lundstrom. They were together seventeen years. Bill was the only one of the Stones to be married when they formed the band, and he had a young son named Stephen, making him the first Stone to be a father.

He broke up with Astrid (for the first time) around 1979, and fell in love with a beautiful American model named Suzanne Accosta. It seems they met too early and when they split up Astrid came back on to the scene for a while. Then he and Astrid split up again for good, and Bill's next important relationship made headlines for all the wrong reasons.

Mandy Smith was beautiful, blonde and young. They married when he was fifty-two and she wasn't. Years later he rekindled his love with Suzanne, and a good thing too, as they now have three of the most beautiful kids you could wish for.

For almost his entire career with the Stones, Bill was known as the 'Silent Stone', because when he was onstage he stayed on his spot. He hardly ever moved.

During Steel Wheels, Bill kept telling us that this would be his last tour, that after we got home he was quitting the band. We all knew that he hated flying, but none of us really believed that he hated flying more than he liked being a Rolling Stone.

I got a hint of it, though, on one of of the last flights of that tour. I was sitting near him when he looked out of the window, did a double take and got freaked out. 'Woody, look out there. See that coming off the wing? That's a fuel leak.'

I didn't like the sound of that. 'A fuel leak?'

He insisted. 'We could all go just like that.'

'Could we?' I leant across him to stare out the window, and sure enough, something was coming off the wing. Condensation.

'I hate planes,' he said. 'I'm never getting on another one. This plane should not be allowed to fly.'

'But Bill, we need these things to get to concerts, we're flying to the next one.'

'Not me,' he said, always pointing at the 'fuel leak'. 'This is it. In the future, if I ever get a new band, we're going by car and ferry and train, whatever it takes, but never by plane again.'

He stuck to his word for a long time. I found out later that he did, in fact, fly again but it wasn't until 2001. His brother was working out in the States, so Bill flew to New York to see him. He was due to fly back to England on 11 September. No wonder he's not been on a plane since.

Anyway, the rest of us decided that flying was something we all had to accept and that Bill was simply tired of aeroplanes, but that he'd get over it once we were home. We knew that in eighteen months, when the next tour was announced, he'd be back on the road with us again. None of us believed he was walking away from the Stones. We played a couple of extended dates at Wembley Stadium at the end of the European leg, and that turned out to be Bill's last stage appearance with us.

28
Ireland

At the start of the 1990s we returned from our most lucrative tour to date – Steel Wheels/Urban Jungle had left us flush with money. Consistent with my extravagant nature, it was time to spend.

Jo and I were invited on a trip to Ireland. The idea was to find a place to rent so that we could ease the tax bills. We ended up in County Kildare, just outside a village called Clane, at a house called Sandymount. It belonged to Jonathan Irwin, a tremendously charitable man and father of a large family himself. We hit it off immediately, fell in love with the house and decided to buy it after spending just one night there. Cheers, Steel Wheels!

Sandymount was surrounded by glorious lush land with a canal running alongside, reminding me of my roots. I was home. My only condition was that the house came with its French cart-pulling dog, a Briard called Leroy. We stayed at Moyglare Manor Hotel nearby for a couple of weeks before the deal went through and soon we were making camp at our new house.

Sandymount had outhouses and we got straight to work on them. I turned the old stable into a pub which I named 'Yer Father's Yacht', the cow byre into recording and art studios and another barn into a tape and film archive. We also built a

beautiful indoor pool, a garage for the cars, and stables to indulge in my new hobby – breeding racehorses.

The studio became a focal point. In Sandymount I could make the music I wanted, away from the chains of London and studio bosses. This was a place of my own and today I still look to Ireland as a freeing place, a sanctuary. I buy sculpted or bronzed lions to strengthen the gardens. My first pair of sleeping lions were purchased from a cheerful Dickensian character in Punchestown. He asked me, 'Mr Wood, how do you like the people in Ireland?' My response was 'I haven't met a bad one yet.' He replied, 'Well if you can wait half an hour – my wife will be back.'

Brothers
On 'Yer Father's yacht'

champagne mum

With dad at Wembley, '82

with King Arthur.

Backstage with Reg Squires, ma and pa

with Jo at Drury Lane.

Tea with Auntie Mary at the Lane.

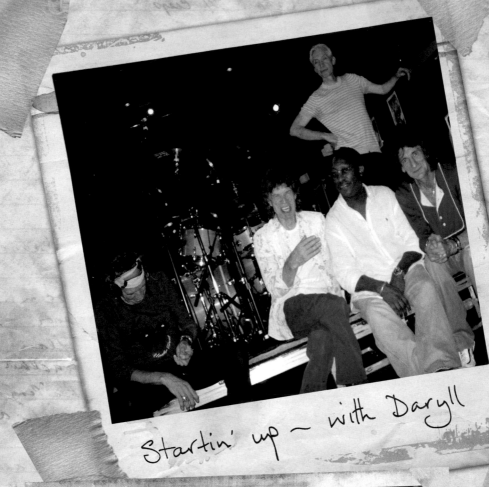

Startin' up ~ with Daryll

Joleah — winning at the Curragh.

Dayjob.

Woodfest Seychelles

Nose-to-nose with Spike

On Manda Island, Kenya

with Jack MacDonald

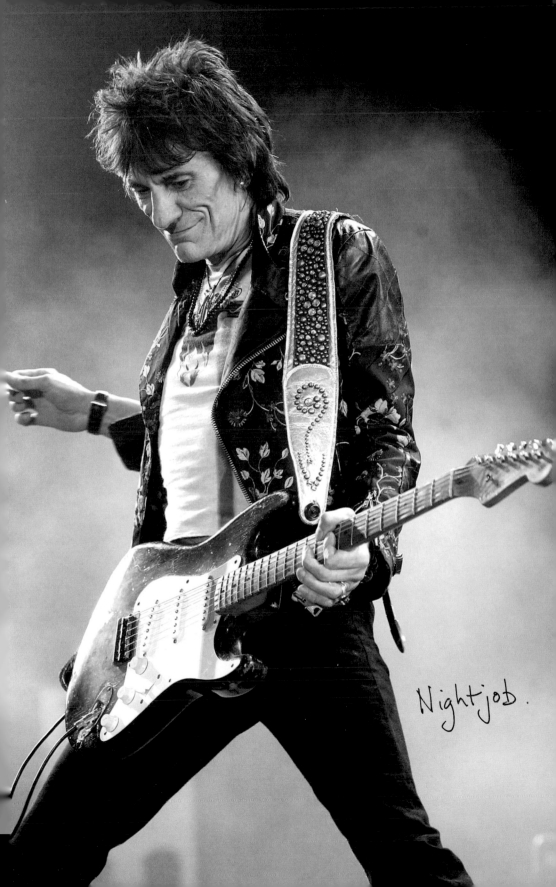

Nightjob.

Sleepin' mountain

Yer Father's Yacht became my creative hub. To christen the studio that had been put in by Eoghan (my brother-in-law) I organized a test session. David Bowie and his Tin Machine came over on the August bank holiday weekend and we recorded 'Stones in My Pathway' for a Robert Johnson tribute album. Bowie gave me a book entitled *Living Sober*, which I immediately put on display behind my bar. The studio is fantastic; I love the freedom of working there and back then I felt the time was right to make another record on my own. I didn't take the plug out for seven months, recording what would become my seventh solo album, *Slide on This*.

We had a lot of fun making *Slide on This*. I decided I wanted the sound of snooker balls being hit to act as a drum lick so we moved to the snooker table, set up the recording equipment and made Jimmy White hit the balls over and over again until we got it just right. The song was called 'You Just Might Get to Like It'.

The gates of the house became revolving doors and in came musicians from all over the globe as we put the album together. Simon Kirke, Doug Wimbish, Wayne P. Sheehy, Def Leppard's Joe Elliot, The Edge (who taught me a thing or two about guitar effects), Chuck Levell (we did fourteen overdubs in one night with two cases of Château Lynch-Bages 1985 for assistance), Charlie Watts, Hothouse Flowers and Bernard Fowler. He's the man who inspires me the best when it comes to my voice on my solo albums.

Ever since I first met him in Japan working with Mick, he's always had the power to blend and adapt. Bernard – he can do it – he can be – he is that voice!

The musical chameleon in me is awakened when I collaborate; recently artists like Stereophonics, the Charlatans, Beverley Knight and Jack White have all taken me in different musical

directions. Blending music comes easily to me, just as it did on past collaborations with people like Bo and Chuck, Freddie Albert, BB King, Albert Collins, Hubert Sumlin, Buddy Guy, Marley, Toots and Dylan. Changing my colour comes naturally – switching style is second nature. I adapt to the challenge of complementing another person's style, hence my bond with the Stones. Earthy guitar pickin' and blues-based melodies are the heart of my influences. From the beginning I learnt the simple power behind this music – finding the basic root, no matter how complicated the structure, and taking it from there. You can apply that to anything. Once you get a feel for it you're halfway there with whoever you may be playing with.

When I bought the house, the local community was less than 400 people and they certainly weren't used to the type of people shacking up at mine to record the album. This was a typical small Irish village and there were twenty pubs (not including mine) within a square mile of my front door. We even had a pub not far from me in the middle of a bog, run by an eccentric old lady who had her chickens running along the bar. Bernard (who calls me Pops), a dreadlocked soulster pal of mine known as 'my mellow' and backing singer to the Stones, would ride to one of the pubs (normally Dillon's) on horseback and the locals would stare on in amazement. 'Holy fuck, it's a black man.' Bernard became a thing of legend round those parts. When we were recording *Slide on This*, he and I and our engineer Eoghan had been in the same room for two months. We were going a little stir crazy, getting cabin fever. We decided to hit the spots like Lilly's Bordello in Dublin to air the cobwebs. After a long boozy night, I went home, leaving the other two in the after-hours bars, like Reynards, which is above what used to be the Pink Elephant. Eoghan was fading too so he put Bernard in a cab and told the driver the directions back to Sandymount. Two weeks later, the three of us hit the bars of Dublin again. This local guy was staring at Bernard and after an hour of this, Bernard approached the man.

'Why do you keep staring at me?'

'Don't you remember me?' replied the local.

'Never seen you in my life,' replied Bernard.

Turns out that night a couple of weeks earlier, Bernard had passed out in the back of the cab, the engine had broken down, another cab was called and the two drivers had to lug the big dreadlock from one cab to another. The driver got lost, drove to the police station and explained his predicament.

The copper knew exactly what was going on.

'That'd be Bernard Fowler; he belongs at Ronnie Wood's house.'

Bernard woke from his slumber just as the cab rolled up to the gates, blissfully unaware.

The Irish community took me to heart, and to this day remains hospitable and welcoming to me and my family. This beautiful country has become a tranquil haven for me. On more than one occasion it has allowed me to escape the madness of life as a Stone and quietly recharge my batteries without being disturbed.

Charlie O'Neill, a charitable local landowning character, still comes to see me on his Harley with his music blaring. He must be seventy – I guess the Irish air makes them live long and happy, an effect which seems to be rubbing off on me.

Snooker follows me everywhere and Ireland is no exception. I garnished Yer Father's Yacht with a beautiful table. Jimmy White found it for me, installed it and he frequently comes over and plays. Over the years various snooker players have come over and left their cues, so I have an awesome collection. Any weight you fancy.

Even jockeys like my good friend Frankie Dettori and Johnny Murtagh, and boxers like Barry 'Danny Boy' McGuigan join me, my two Great Danes and a horse round the table for a few frames on the green baize.

Alex 'Hurricane' Higgins used to play snooker with me there too. He liked to stay with me in Ireland because we could play snooker, drink and go to the races. I honestly think Alex preferred horses to snooker players. He'd come into my room in the morning wearing a pair of women's tights and a little T-shirt, get into my bed with all the papers and the tip sheets, and ask me which horse I liked in the 2:30 at Epsom. All I could do was lie there screaming, 'What are you doing in bed next to me, dressed in my wife's fucking tights?'

We would go to the races together, but it was always difficult being there with him because he had to avoid so many people, especially bookies. He couldn't go near them because he owed this one four grand and that one two grand.

It seems that whenever he was in trouble, which was often, Alex would show up at my place. Once he showed up at Sandy-mount with a small boy and a bicycle; he'd been kicked out of his latest lodgings and had jumped in a cab with his suitcase.

Unsurprisingly, he got kicked out of the cab, too, and was left stranded on the street late at night. He knocked on the nearest door and a boy answered. Being a snooker fan the kid recognized Higgins, which made it easier for Alex to persuade him to cycle his luggage to my house, while Alex walked beside him.

He turned the kid into an Irish version of a Sherpa who carried all Alex's gear over the neighbouring fields. By the time the two of them turned up, they were completely exhausted. But the boy was also a Stones fan and when he saw me, he was completely stunned. I offered him a tea but he scarpered, shouting that he'd better get home before his mum got worried. The poor kid looked like he'd walked out of some very strange dream.

Alex stayed with us for a few days, often sleeping under the snooker table. I know he would have stayed longer but Jo and I had to move him on, so we gave him some fresh clothes and tights, handed him some food and sent him on to whichever friend or acquaintance would offer him his next temporary abode.

Bob Dylan was a guest of a different calibre. We would record there a lot together and he inspired me no end. The thing is that in the middle of these inspirational periods he'd get up, throw on his big coat, flip up the collar and go for long walks. He looked like he was walking down 5th Avenue, avoiding stares, when in fact he was in a muddy field in County Kildare. There really is nowhere better than the Emerald Isle to wander undisturbed and get lost with your thoughts. Unless of course you're recording with Jerry Lee Lewis. A hive of constant activity, recording with Jerry in Ireland felt perilous and mischievous. I was recently listening through the out-takes of a session we had at Sandymount. Keith, Mick, Charlie, Jerry Lee and I were holed up in the studio. The banter drifted over drugs, hair-trigger guns, blues, murder and women. Then Jerry would tickle his ivories and we'd all crack on.

The Stones recorded there a few times. It felt great to be able to offer up my studio and welcome the boys to my retreat. Occasionally we would be interrupted by an unexpected guest. Patti Richards once turned up and Keith, a little shaken by the surprise appearance of his wife, uttered, 'If I'd known you were coming I would have washed my hair.'

At one point we had a dozen horses in training, and we were racing them regularly in England and Ireland. My great friend and the manager of my stables, Patrick Harty, has been with me since I got the house. He oversees everything at Sandymount but the passion we share is horses. From the first horse I got, Alchiea, the stables expanded. The horses like Joleah, Flip the Switch, Zatya and Have Mercy made life in Ireland even more pleasurable. With the help of Jessica Harrington (the renowned trainer of many a winning horse) I got so into racing with the success of Joleah winning a group race at the Curragh that in 1998 the Irish Thoroughbred Breeders' Association named me their 'Small Breeder of the Year'. I was overjoyed, really full of pride. With the help of Julian Lloyd we moved on to further training success, and here's to the continued

The only decent people I ever saw at the racecourse were horses.
James Joyce.

success of Sandymount Earl. Just because we were abroad didn't mean the parties had to stop.

When our pool was finished we decided to throw a party to celebrate. John Hurt loved the new addition to the house and promptly stripped off, showing a hundred or so people his naked swimming technique. On another occasion he rolled up one afternoon in his Sierra and said, 'Hello, dear boy, my wife has just run off with the gardener.' I took him in, and that evening Tyrone (who had just seen the *Alien* film) realized who this man sitting at the table was. We asked him to recreate the scene where he gives birth to an alien. So he did. On the kitchen floor. While we were trying to eat.

He was around a lot, along with my great pals Denny Cordell (whose annual memorial race in Ireland always brings everyone back together for a memorable afternoon/evening/next morning); Julian Lloyd, who archived the whole period with some quite beautiful photographs; the author Mim Scala, who took me fly fishing along the Liffey; and David 'Grumpy' Grenfel, whose quick wit and passion for the English language has mesmerized me for evenings on end. His recommended title for this book was *Diary of a Rock Ape*, which is his nickname for me. That and a 'Hairy Cow Pat'. Where can I start with this man and where could I possibly finish? He brought a new meaning to the art of drinking. 'It's only Ireland,' I would say, as I headed into Dublin again. One time to buy a dodgy B series Mercedes, authentic in every way, another time to pick up my mother on only her second trip out of England (the first time being Paris) to christen the 'Granny Flat', moulded just for her in my Kildare abode. It still stands sparkling in her honour to this day (complete with Marie Antoinette's bed) lodged firmly between the 'musicart' studio, 'Yer Father's Yacht' and the Stables.

She is in heaven.

On her way to the house we stopped by the Guinness Castle, where, being the honoured guest of Desmond and Penny on a wonderfully sunny afternoon, Lizzie was welcomed, in her wheelchair, up the many steps into the twelfth-century master-piece hallway. 'Mrs Wood, you are the first person ever to come in here backwards.'

Desmond extended his charms through a wonderful luncheon accompanied by pipe organ and tourists (who stumbled and lingered in the dining room) as part of their guided tour of the castle. 'Look, ladies and gentlemen, a Rolling Stone,' he would announce.

On New Year's Eve one year we threw a *massive* one. We worked out that we drank fifteen pints of Guinness a minute for over ten hours.

We basically drank County Kildare dry and pissed off a lot of the local pubs. Slash from Guns N' Roses was there trying to control his wife Rene, who was fighting some girl, several people were seen shagging people they shouldn't have, and clothes were found all over the place for days afterwards, even knickers by the roadside.

The house in Ireland was getting worn in nicely.

One night in 1990, Jo and I were out for dinner in Dublin and she got very ill. At first we thought it was some sort of food poisoning but she was in terrible pain and it only got worse so I rushed her to hospital. They did all sorts of tests but couldn't figure out what was wrong, so we went back to London and saw more doctors, who eventually diagnosed her with Crohn's disease.

The doctors confidently prescribed steroids, but she didn't improve. I kept telling myself there must be something else we could do about it, but felt helpless.

We finished the tour and one of the national papers ran an article with the headline 'Stones Wife in Incurable Disease'. Jo's doctors tried to calm us down, telling us they were sensationalizing the situation, but it didn't stop us worrying. Some good came from the piece, though, as she subsequently received many letters from people across the country who also suffered with Crohn's.

Jo read every letter. One in particular caught her eye, it was from a herbalist in Hastings called Gerald Green, who claimed he could put her Crohn's disease into remission for life. Jo jumped into her car and drove straight there, and when the two of them sat down to talk the first thing he wanted to know was, 'What do you eat?'

She spent the entire day with him listening to what manufacturers do to food, how they use pesticides, why she needed to change her diet and how she could live better with organic foods. Gerald Green became her angelic herbalist. She didn't have Crohn's; she had a perforated appendix and was exacerbating her symptoms with steroids.

In those days it wasn't always easy to find organically grown foods, so she decided that if she couldn't buy it she would grow it, and planted a garden to grow our own vegetables. Little by little Jo started feeling good again.

We moved out of our Wimbledon house to start afresh, wanting to put sickness and the death of her dad behind us. We found Richmond irresistible, bought a beautiful town house just on the green and settled in. We all loved this house and it was good to have such great neighbours. Pete Townshend was one and he didn't drink again after our visit to the Cricketers on Richmond Green. He completely bamboozled a fan by crashing backwards, headfirst to the floor instead of answering his question. This was preceded by Pete going to the gents, surfacing wearing the toilet seat around his head, and then sleeping quite contently on a park bench. Pete said, 'I'd be safe if I could live in Ronnie's house' and there he is today, doing the next best thing. Living in the Wick.

We moved between Richmond, Ireland and wherever a world tour would take us. Jo continued on the road to recovery and discovered the benefits of good food and an organic, healthy lifestyle. None of us in the family had a choice about our new diet but the first thing we noticed was that Jo had become a much better cook. She was using better ingredients and food tasted like it did when I was a child.

She loves telling anyone who asks her about how important organic food is and how it saved her life. But she's had a tough time convincing Keith (though he did like the case of organic vodka she sent him recently).

29
Voodoo to Babylon

We were all riding high off the back of Steel Wheels. Rupert negotiated a major deal with Virgin Records for three new albums and the band's back catalogue; I brought out *Slide on This*; Keith brought out his second solo album, *Main Offender*; and Mick brought out his third solo album, *Wandering Spirit*. I played four solo concerts in Japan and Keith went on tour with his X-Pensive Winos, becoming the first of us to play South America. He filled a football stadium in Argentina with 40,000 fans.

In early 1994 the four of us headed to Ireland and assembled at Sandymount, where we put the *Voodoo Lounge* album and tour together. Darryl Jones was recruited as our bass player. He'd worked with Miles Davis, Peter Gabriel, Sting and Madonna. As with me, Mick didn't announce Darryl to the world; there was no talk of a new Rolling Stone.

It was cool with me that Darryl got the gig, because he's perfect. When we were auditioning bassists, I watched each hopeful candidate enter the room before asking, 'Would you like a Guinness, mate?' Darryl got the job because he replied 'Yeah, I'll have a Guinness.'

Charlie immediately clicked with the new boy. It's the jazz connection. Darryl just got onstage where Bill used to stand and made a statement, both musically and visually. The Stones were firing on all cylinders again, and I felt that Keith and I were more inventive than ever. Even Mick's singing seemed stronger. We announced the tour in New York, this time arriving at Pier 60 by boat, and opened in Washington DC. We sold out everywhere, in the States, Canada, Japan, Mexico, Australia and especially South America for the first time.

There was absolute mania. Arriving at the airport was mad enough, with crowds lining the streets as we drove into town. At night there were thousands of people camped out on the grounds below our hotel windows, chanting. They never stopped. It was like having my own private concert. I stood on my balcony and looked down at the crowds who were chanting up at me. 'Olé, olé, olé, olé, oh, ley, oh, ley.' The Stones were bigger than ever.

South Americans have that fever pitch like nowhere else in the world, but then I suppose they were starved of rock groups for so many years. In the 1970s and 1980s no one ever toured South America because you never got your money. It was as simple as that. Many of the promoters were crooks so you never got paid. Now it's opened up and I believe we helped that process, and the audiences are thrilled that they've got rock and roll.

On 10 November 1994, the Stones became the first major rock and roll band to broadcast a concert live on the internet, and by the end of the year we'd sold more than four million copies of the *Voodoo Lounge* album. The North American leg of our tour was proclaimed as the most successful rock tour in history. U2 even sent me a bouquet of flowers with the message: 'Congratulations to the greatest rock 'n' roll band in the world, outside of Ireland.'

The way our tours are organized, there are always breaks worked in throughout them so that we can all recover. During the Christmas break in the middle of Voodoo Lounge, Keith and I hired a boat for three weeks to sail around the Caribbean with both our families. It was Jo and me, Jamie and his girlfriend, Leah and Ty, Keith and Patti and their daughters, Theo and Alex. We had Christmas dinner on the boat and celebrated New Year's Eve on the beach. Like travelling gypsies of the water we island-hopped as one big family.

One night a torrential storm lashed the seas we were on. For twelve hours we clung to anything nailed down, as the ship was hurled over twenty-foot wave after twenty-foot wave. The kids bunked up and we hung on. Patti's queasiness was furthered by Keith's offers of 'Bacon and custard sandwiches, my dear?' The pirate in him seemed to enjoy this adventurous, sickening storm. At one point, this exhausting lashing nearly beat us and we discussed turning back. Instead, we faced it and pushed on through, came out the other side and had a blissful holiday. Our captain had known the storm was coming and two weeks after our adventure he ran the boat into a reef, and it now lies at the bottom of the ocean.

By the time Voodoo Lounge ended, we had played in twenty-six countries, in front of more than 6.5 million people and grossed a lot – I daren't convert it into Yen. I had my slice of the pie and even if it wasn't as big as Mick's and Keith's it was enough to make me believe that I would never be broke again.

We went right into planning our next tour, Bridges to Babylon. In August 1994 we staged the announcement of our tour under the Brooklyn Bridge, on the Brooklyn side, with Manhattan as our backdrop. The press conference was broadcast live on television and online. There was a huge screen set up next to the stage, and the 300 waiting journalists and photographers suddenly saw a helicopter view of a red 1955 Cadillac convertible coming across the bridge, with a police escort. Mick was driving and Keith was sitting next to him. Charlie and I were in the back seat, throwing CDs to the crowds lining the streets.

At the end of the press conference Mick stepped off the stage and walked into the crowd of journalists, saying loud enough for everyone to hear, 'I've always wanted to do this,' then shouted up, 'So Keith, tell us, is this going to be your last tour?'

'Yes,' Keith confirmed, 'this and the next five.'

We played a small club date in Toronto, which has become part of the tradition, then promptly broke with tradition and played a second club date, this one in Chicago, before opening there at Soldiers Field.

From North America we went to Hawaii, Japan, Mexico, Argentina and Brazil, before coming to North America and then going to Europe. Round the world again. We worked it out so that we had free time in Rio, and a bunch of us went to spend the day on Pig Island, just off Copacabana.

We got aboard and pulled away from the shore. The press were following us everywhere in various boats. One of our crew had hot-wired the engine on ours wrongly and suddenly fumes were coming out of the motor. The captain opened a hatch to see what was going on, and that's when black smoke billowed out, showing traces of fire. It was pretty frightening and I gripped my beer a little tighter. The paparazzi were nearby and came over to help us. It felt amusingly ironic having them come to our rescue.

The last person off our boat was the captain, who stayed until the last minute, but wasn't prepared to go down with his ship. There was a picture in the papers of him diving into the sea, as his boat blew up. Over the next few hours we watched it come closer to shore as it eerily sank in front of the island at sunset.

The Bridges to Babylon shows were recorded for a live album, *No Security*, so to support it we decided to just keep on going at the supposed end of the Bridges tour. We went back to the States and Canada for the third time, and then returned to Europe for the second time. The combined tours took in 153 venues in twenty months, making it our longest on-the-road stint ever. It was so long that, during the tour, Mick and Jerry had a baby, then Jerry filed for divorce from Mick after twenty-two years. Oh, and Keith fell off a ladder at home, which meant rescheduling some of the dates.

It was, however, the first time that Rupert cancelled four of our shows in England. He found out that if we played those dates, the Inland Revenue was going to sock us with a bill beyond human comprehension, and we decided that was a pretty good incentive to take a few nights off. We did, however, play an unannounced date at the Shepherd's Bush Empire. Unfortunately it overran, and because we were keeping the neighbours up the local council fined us a much more reasonable sum.

But what really made the Bridges tour unique was that this was the first time we used a B-stage. A catwalk led to a small stage right out in the middle of the audience. It rose out of the floor with only just enough room for Mick, Keith, Charlie and me, plus Darryl and Chuck Leavell. It gave arena and stadium gigs the feel of a small club show. We did three songs from there, like 'Route 66', 'Midnight Rambler', 'Tumbling Dice' and sometimes 'Like a Rolling Stone'. The audience went wild, especially all those people who thought they were in the cheap seats and suddenly found themselves standing right there at our feet. We've used a B-stage ever since.

30

Good and Ugly

My artwork was progressing almost as well as the Stones tours. We figured out that if we put my work into galleries in cities where the Stones were appearing, it would really help sales. I came back from those two years on the road, paid off all my debts and we bought our house in Kingston. A beautiful home appropriately named Holmwood.

I paid a few sacks of gold for the wonderful twenty-room

place built around 1840. It had been given to Prince Albert and Queen Victoria as a wedding present. Albert used it as his lodge whenever he went out hunting for deer in Richmond Park. A legendary regal drinking hole. Perfect!

We've been at Holmwood nearly ten years now. Every corner of the house is filled with artefacts we've collected over the years, and Jo has transformed it into an opulent yet functional family home. She planted a huge organic vegetable patch and fills the rest of the garden with summer parties. Jenny, our fabulous PA and right arm at Holmwood, has been with us for years and makes the running of the house so smooth. I can get down to work any time of the day or night because I had a studio built in the basement and turned the old garage into my art studio. There was a tennis court that I've recently turned into a pool. When the court was there, I had some memorable matches with some of tennis' finest.

I'm both a fan and friend of John McEnroe, and back in 1999 he was supposed to play mixed doubles at Wimbledon with Steffi Graf. At the last minute she decided she was going to save herself for the Wimbledon final, and pulled out of the semi-final with John. They probably would have won the title but Steffi wasn't interested, so just like that the McEngraf steamroller stopped.

John showed up at my house, furious that Steffi had ruined his chances for another Wimbledon title. Still angry, he dragged me on to my tennis court and, in a red-hot mood, fired fast serves down at me. I stood there petrified as they wizzed past me at ferocious speed. Swearing and cursing 'Never play mixed doubles with a potential finalist . . .' Thwack! John continued to pound serves until I got it in my head that I had to protect myself, and started swinging my racket at them. To my own surprise, I actually started returning John's serves, infuriating him further. I was quite pleased with myself and wanted to play on. But John didn't. He spent the rest of the afternoon as it began, cursing Steffi. Pat Cash always looks after me at Wimbledon. This year he introduced me to 'Rafa' Nadal. What a talent and what a gent. He was honoured that I'd placed him in the crowd scene in my painting of the B-stage.

Of course, there was a snooker room at Holmwood when we bought it. But as we were negotiating for the house, the man selling it to us decided that the carpet under the snooker table wasn't included in the price and he wanted it back. I couldn't move the table so I had to pay through the nose for a piece of carpet. The table has had some fabulous matches on it. Jimmy White and Ronnie O'Sullivan come over all the time and have grudge matches on it. I sit there while they're playing and try to explain to them some of the finer points of the game, but somehow I don't think they listen to me.

There are plenty of rooms at Holmwood, which means we usually have a few guests. Most mornings there are people sitting in the kitchen being fed delicious food by Jo. Slash came and stayed with us with his wife Perla. They loved the house so much that they conceived their baby in the Red Room (a sumptuous guest bedroom) and named him London.

We put a gym in and if someone isn't pounding on the running machine there is a yoga session going on with strange smells and 'ooomm' noises materializing from under the door. That's normally when I light a huge fire in the sitting room, step over one of the sleeping dogs and whack on whatever I want to watch on the telly.

Each one of our kids has lived at Holmwood at one stage or another so the place has become a family nest. On Sundays, the family gathers for Jo's famous roast dinners.

Everything was going great. I had a beautiful family, a magnificent band, great art, a bit of cash and a new home. In the words of me and George (Bernard Shaw): 'There are two tragedies in life. One is not getting your heart's desire and the other is getting it.' It's always when everything is going well that I screw things up. While we were still out on the Bridges tour, Nick Cowan met a guy called Andrew Edwards who owned a fabulous building in South Kensington, where the Pineapple Studios had been. Edwards thought it would make a terrific members club, so Nick put a proposal together and started showing it around. He had spent a year or so getting turned down by everybody when he came to us with a beautiful proposition, saying that all he was looking for was a couple of million quid.

The concept that would make the Harrington Club unique was that we were going to create a place where members could hang out all day and all night. Keith kept warning me not to touch it with a barge pole, and I should have listened to him, especially after the Miami-farce of Woody's On The Beach. However, Jo and I both liked the idea so I sold some BSkyB shares I'd bought. They'd done phenomenally well.

We cracked on turning the building into a club. Jo was thrilled to have an opportunity like this and by the time we got back from the tour, Nick had the lease on the building, workmen were in there gutting the place and Jo could start buying furniture and paintings and books, designing the spa and putting in an organic restaurant run by Arthur Jagger, a great chef who now has his own top-notch restaurant in London. No expense was spared.

In the meantime, Nick was struggling to find other investors. Jo was getting involved designing each floor and bills were piling up ominously. So we put in another million, and signed a contract with Edwards.

The Harrington Club was spectacular, opening in September

2000. It featured a spa that had six massage rooms, steam rooms and saunas with huge Hawaiian crystals as centrepieces, and trickling fountains that mellowed the guests as they waited for their treatments. Jo has probably been to more spas around the world than anyone else, and she found inspiration from the best of them. Her organic restaurant opened, serving dishes made up of vegetables grown in our garden. The restaurant was a great success but Nick hadn't secured a late-night booze licence. He told us to hang on; it would be here in a minute.

To get in the door, we set the membership initiation fee at £500, then charged £70 a month. All membership applications had to be approved by the membership committee, which was mainly Jo and me, and we got 300 members straight away. Mick and Jerry joined, and so did Kate Moss, Eric Clapton and Frankie Dettori.

For the first few months, the club was really happening. Jo and I were down there every night, socializing with everybody and keeping things rocking. We even had a Fats Waller-like upright-piano player called Spike, adding a magic atmosphere to the place called Bar Orpen. Then we'd go home, have a rest and go back in the morning for a spa and a big breakfast. The only problem was the booze had to be stopped at midnight. Even so we had some really terrific parties, like the charity event that Mick and Jerry hosted there one night in October 2000. After dinner, Mick and his brother Chris got up on the floor and started to sing. I asked if I could cut in, and started playing with them. Then Bill Wyman got up and played with us, and so did Dave Stewart from the Eurythmics and Michael Kamen, who's composed scores for hundreds of movies, and worked with Clapton, Pink Floyd, the London Philharmonic, Aerosmith and Metallica. As it turned out, that was one of his last onstage appearances because he died a few years later. We shall miss his musical genius.

A year after we opened, Jo and I had put £3 million into the Harrington Club, and the booze licence was still not done. Jo and I decided it was time to get new staff. When Nick told Andrew Edwards that we were looking for new management, Edwards worked out a deal with Nick where we would give him a couple of million quid to run the place. A contract was drawn up and we signed it.

Edwards formed a company called Harrington Club Ltd, which meant that the management contract for the club was now owned by the man who owned the freehold. On top of that, this new contract stipulated that Jo and I owned a 25-year lease on the club, at £550,000 rent a year. So there we were, plodding along, trying to make the Harrington Club work, when, out of the blue, Andrew rang me up to say, 'We need more money.'

I couldn't believe it. I reminded him, 'We've put in more than enough money already.' He told us, 'If you don't put more money in, you have to walk away.'

I said, 'Walk away with nothing?'

And he replied, 'That's right.'

That didn't sound right to me or Jo, and by now Jamie had enough experience in business to know that this needed sorting. Jamie said, 'Lawyers.'

The Stones were just starting to put together our Forty Licks tour, so I went to them to borrow a million dollars just to stay afloat. I needed to pay the rent on the Harrington Club, or it would have gone into liquidation. Mick was growing more and more concerned about my drinking and the coke I was doing and although I didn't know it at the time, I came close to being left out of the Forty Licks tour.

In the middle of all this, my mum died. I knew she was in a

bad way and one day I sent her some flowers but when the delivery guy rang the bell, there was no answer. My lovely mum with bad ankles had got up to answer the door and slipped off her chair, breaking five vertebrae. The bloke ringing the bell had delivered to her before, suspected something was wrong and waited. He was in front of her door for hours until the neighbours spotted him and wondered what was going on.

They broke in and found her on the floor. An ambulance took her to hospital but the accident proved to be the beginning of the end. She had cancer that had been lying dormant for years, and now it just went wild through her body.

I was at the hospital all the time, to be with her and to hold her hand. But seeing the demise of her was awful, especially knowing that there's nothing you can do. They put more and more morphine into her and she just slowly slipped away. At her funeral, relatives I'd never met showed up. There were cousins I never knew I had, and their kids, and their kids' kids. Some lovely people who were there to pay their last respects for a lovely woman.

Once again I found myself unable to grieve.

After going back and forth with Edwards, his lawyers, our lawyers, and even the Stones' lawyers, Jo and I were told we could walk away from the lease on the Harrington Club if we agreed to pay Edwards £350,000. So that's what we did. In the end we lost everything – all the furniture, art and books, and we were even banned from our own club.

I had no cash coming in, and was forced to mortgage both my houses. Jamie and I sat down to discuss the family finances and tried to come to terms with the fact that we were flat broke again. I couldn't understand how we'd got to this, how I'd managed to lose so much money again. Of course, I knew the answer was mainly the Harrington Club, but I was also unhappy with Nick Cowan's management. Jamie said, 'You've got to fire him.'

So that's what I did.

I owed the banks several million quid. I urgently needed someone to sort the mess out but it had to be a person I could actually trust. And I was in no hurry to trust just anyone. That's when I looked around and saw Jamie.

He was a nightmare as a child. The day after Jo's father died, Jamie took his first acid trip. He got thrown out of one school for doing drugs, then started at another and passed his exams just to show that he could. He started to hang out with the wrong crowd, thought he was having a great time but was out of control.

When he was sixteen, he went to Ibiza for a week, stayed four months and met his long-term girlfriend Charlotte. He would stay with her for years and he fathered her son Charlie. He was a loose cannon, undeniably, but we had faith he would come round eventually.

We didn't know what to do with him until our friend Harvey Goldsmith, the concert promoter, offered to hire him. Harvey put him on Madonna and Eric Clapton tours. Our realization that something had to be done was aided by Keith's comment to Jo: 'Put him on a ship and send him out to sea.' So we did the next best thing and convinced Michael Cohl to give him a job on tour. Jamie got straight on that tour, and confessed all his sins to Jo.

He got a loan from me after the tour, bought a load of furniture and set up a furniture-hire business for concerts. That led him into other businesses and eventually he started turning over a lot of money in his own right.

So when the Harrington went tits up and I was in serious

debt, I went to Jamie and asked him to help us. He jumped straight in, pushing his own business to one side, and eventually reached a settlement with Nick.

There were still complications with my artwork though. Nick had a friend who worked for him, running the art business. All my work was kept in an office Nick had in Battersea, but when he fell out with his friend, that friend decided to get all my artwork out of that office and put it somewhere safe, so they could continue selling it. Jamie heard about what was planned and managed to find the Commer van they'd hired to transport the works.

Jamie pulled up alongside the van, jumped out of his own car, opened the door to the Transit and lifted the keys out. The driver didn't know what was going on and the art was returned to my home. God knows how many works had filtered out before that though.

As manager, the first thing Jamie did was put us on a budget. It wasn't easy to accept, but Jo and I both knew it was essential. He cut down on the horses and stopped the flowers we were buying for £1,000 a week. He cut out the car companies we were using (which cost around £170,000 a year), and forced us to cut back on designer clothes.

Gradually, he saved us £2 million a year. He also stopped me lending money to people who came to me when they were desperate. I just couldn't say no to anyone, even the blatant freeloaders. Jamie's solution was: 'I can.'

31

Rehab

'Raise the bar — don't drink it'
Dave Rouze.

We needed to put Nick Cowan, the Harrington Club and all our other financial troubles behind us, and somehow dig ourselves out of the hole that we were in.

My artwork had already helped to pay off a lot of my debts and I intended that it was going to pay off the rest of them now.

But my drinking was getting in the way again. In July 2000 I spent a week at the Priory in Roehampton, not far from home. It had helped a bit, but as soon as I got out I was still convinced that I could have a glass of wine without any problem. Unfortunately, one glass became one bottle which became two bottles. And from wine I slipped back to vodka. I thought I was handling it. But I should have known better because the memory was still fresh in my mind of a drinking bout in the Virgin Islands, a few years before, on holiday there with Keith and our two families. I got heavy into 100% proof Passers Rum and wound up with alcohol poisoning. I spent two weeks in bed. I couldn't even look at a glass of water. I had ruined myself. But even that wasn't enough to scare me away.

Of course, I didn't believe anyone when they tried to convince me that my drinking was getting out of hand. The thing is that some people get nasty when they drink, so that if they wake up the next morning with a hangover and a bloody nose, they start to realize they might have a problem. But it's not like that with me. So I thought, it's broke, how am I gonna fix it?

To change one's life; start immediately.
Do it flamboyantly. No exceptions — no excuses.
William James.

I never thought my drinking had any influence on my guitar playing, that everything was fine. But then I didn't realize just how much my drinking was affecting everything I was doing. Mick and Jo and the rest of my family finally said enough is enough.

Jo called Mick in a panic and he showed up really concerned about me. He was very supportive, came to me as my friend and said, 'I love you. You need to get help.' He and my good friend Richard Lewis (the Prince of Pain), would say, 'Enough, already!'

The question had to be asked and answered by myself. My family agreed to confront my problem, with me listening as they told me how much my drinking had affected them. We've done this on a few occasions over the years and each time I get the message a little clearer. Whether you've been an alcoholic, gambler, over- or under-eater, or a shopaholic; whether it's coffee, the telephone or sex, whatever the nature of the disease, an addict will often leap from one obsession to another. I chose my higher powers to be my talents and seduced them with the same ferocity.

Keep it to a gentle rain, nobody likes
a flood or a drought.
David (Grumpy) (Grenville) Grenfeld

The Stones were putting together the Forty Licks tour, and I was going to have shows at various art galleries along the way. And by now even I knew I had to get clean again, so that's when I went to Cottonwood. I flew to Arizona and went through rehab there. It was tough, maybe the most difficult thing I've ever had to do. It was here that I was asked to draw my life to put it in some sort of perspective. My Cottonwood drawing materialized and I was on the mend. I still have to take each day as it comes, but I'm getting there. Rehab wasn't always the blues, take for example the time when Jo joined me on the path of serenity for a quick shag.

The next thing I knew, I was in Toronto, rehearsing for Forty Licks. I was clean but I was frightened. For the first time ever as a Stone, I was about to go on tour with the band, sober.

The Forty Licks tour was all about celebrating forty years of the Stones. No rock and roll band had ever made it this far. We were in unchartered territory. And I guess Mick's knighthood was about that, too.

His name showed up on the Queen's honours list in December 2003 and some people, Keith included, felt that by accepting the award Mick was turning his back on the Stones' counter-culture, anti-establishment image. But Charlie thought that if Paul McCartney deserved a knighthood, then so did Mick. I was happy for him because a knighthood is Mick's kind of thing.

But we also thought that if Mick got one, then Keith should have been offered one as well. Although, if Buckingham Palace had offered a knighthood to Keith, that would have been something else. They knew he'd never accept it. That those things mean nothing to him.

He told me, 'Being called Sir Keith is not a big enough honour. Fuck knighthood, give me a peerage.' Earl Wood would suit me fine.

In Toronto, we worked on something like 140 songs and wound up using about half of them. I loved that because it meant I was getting to play some favourite songs of mine from the days before I joined. Songs I never got to play before, like 'Street Fighting Man', 'Stray Cat Blues' and 'Can't You Hear

Me Knockin'?' I knew how Brian Jones and Mick Taylor played them, but this meant I could play them my way.

We rehearsed all those songs because Mick decided we would have theme nights on tour. One night we'd feature songs from *Beggars Banquet* and another night we'd do songs from *Exile on Main Street* or *Some Girls*. We also had soul and reggae nights. It was what you might call our first retrospective tour and it was arranged that we would play different-sized venues in each city. We'd do a club, an arena and a stadium. Keith saw it as small, medium and large and dubbed Forty Licks our 'Fruit of the Loom' tour.

But the biggest surprise of the tour was that now, playing sober, I found myself more focused than I'd ever been before. When I was drinking, my playing was good but not concentrated. Suddenly I knew what I was playing. In Keith's mind, he probably thought he'd lost a drinking partner. But in my mind, I was winning the battle and I could hear that in the way I was playing.

On every tour until Forty Licks, I used to put my head down and go for it. I'd feel exhausted. I'd clown around a lot to cover for that. Now I was taking the music seriously. And I wasn't breaking out in an alcohol sweat.

We warmed up for Forty Licks in August 2002 with a surprise club gig at the Palais Royal Ballroom, which couldn't have been much of a surprise because word leaked out and our Toronto fans were queuing up for days. I remember that only a few hundred people got in for ten bucks apiece, that we did a full show for them, running the gamut of our best songs from 'It's Only Rock and Roll' to 'Brown Sugar', and that the place was boiling hot.

Normally we don't get nervous but we were that night. It

THE ROLLING STONES

LICKS WORLD TOUR 2002-2003

SUN, MAR 16, 2003   SHOW #   62   TOKYO DOME 2

#	Song		Stage	Brass/Keys	KEY	TEMPO
1	BROWN SUGAR*	STRAT	BF OFF STAGE	BOBBY	C	126
2	START ME UP*	STRAT (solo)	BF OFF STAGE		F	120
3	IT'S ONLY ROCK AND ROLL*	STRAT	BF & LF OFF STAGE		B	125
4	DON'T STOP*	STRATCHY	BF & LF OFF STAGE		A	124
5	ALL DOWN THE LINE*	STRAT (slide)		BRASS	G	147
6	ANGIE*	J-200		TIM ON KEYS	Am	73
7	MONKEY MAN*	Black Z		2xTENORS	C#	97
8	MIDNIGHT RAMBLER*	DOOZY			B	120
9	TUMBLIN' DICE*	Bender	Band intros after song	BRASS	B	107
10	SLIPPING AWAY* (KR)	STRAT	TIM ON KEYS	BRASS	A	KR
11	HAPPY* (KR)	Lap Steel		BRASS	B	KR
12	SYMPATHY*	STRAT	Walk to B-Stage		E	109
13	WHEN THE WHIP COMES DOWN*	STRAT	B-STAGE		A	126
14	MANNISH BOY*	Dan Armstrong	B-STAGE		A	68
15	YOU GOT ME ROCKING*	Dan Armstrong	B-STAGE	Ramp to A Stage	D	125
16	GIMMIE SHELTER*	STRAT			C#m	116
17	HONKY TONK WOMAN*	Bender		BOBBY	G	107
18	STREET FIGHTING MAN*	SITAR			B	121
19	SATISFACTION*	FIREBIRD		BRASS	E	134
20	J J FLASH*	SITAR	ENCORE		B	135

might have been because we were starting back up again after a long time off, but I think it was really because I'd just come out of rehab and had never done a gig straight. I was nervous and Keith and Charlie were nervous for me. Mick kept telling me, 'You have our support.'

It was very caring. They were all rooting for me. And I made it. For the rest of the eighteen-month tour, I only went to Keith's room a few times. It wasn't always easy and there were times when I was suffering. But Jo was with me and together we saw a lot of movies and got through it.

As the tour wore on it was more and more evident that things were good. I noticed the write-ups and now, instead of calling us 'wrinkly rockers', the reviewers were referring to us as 'These ageless Stones'.

It was a huge boost to my confidence. A real eye-opener. I wasn't burying the butterflies in booze before each show. I was noticing things in the audience for a change, instead of just blindly playing away. Keep it simple. Easy does it. Keep it in the 'now'.

One night in Tennessee Keith phoned me to announce, 'I'm coming up.' He arrived with a bag of goodies and some Fanta, which meant he'd be staying a while. We started jamming together. I was giggling and he kept wondering what was so funny, and eventually I told him that the guitar he was playing 'is Mick's. I borrowed it from him.'

There was something bugging Keith. 'What?' He grabbed the guitar, put it up on the side of the wall, yanked pillows off the bed, put them over the guitar, pulled a gun from his doctor's bag and, right there in our room, shot the guitar. Jo and I couldn't believe it. There were pillow feathers flying every-where. The next day Jo went to our head axe man, Pierre, and

So keep trying to see what
you're capable of

The serves of Nadal
the skills of Ronaldinho,
the wit of Chaplin,
the smoothe of Chevalier.
becoming a great man —
instead of a great drunk

I'm full of inspiration
Yet doused in the demon.

I notice a key change
and a change in me,

Box clever like white
the cheek of Ali
O'Sullivans
the Command of Federa

the speed of Henri
the nut of Rooney
whats wrong with you
you smell like a brewery.

Or watching people
dying by degrees.

the biggest of games
"   "   "   " names
Consistent like Piggott
cheeky Dettori.
the Ruby of Walsh
Fitness is the story.

Federa Henri.
Rooney.
Tracey Gilbert George

Rembradt + Braque

told him, 'I've got really bad news. Keith was in our room last night and shot Mick's guitar.' But Pierre didn't seem to care, 'Don't even worry about it.' Jo asked, 'Why not?' Pierre explained, 'Because it isn't actually Mick's. He borrowed it from Keith.' Neither of them now has this hallowed Gibson acoustic relic. It lies safely in my guitar museum.

While we were playing in San Francisco, Rupert Loewenstein sat down with me in my dressing room and said, 'You're in big trouble.'

I didn't understand. 'What do you mean?'

He said, 'You're not going to make it. You are going to have to sell your houses. The Stones are aware of the debt, they all know how serious it is.'

I knew they knew because they'd helped me by giving me an advance on the tour and the Stones lawyer, Joyce Smythe – who is absolutely wonderful – had helped with some of our negotiations when we were trying to get our money out of the Harrington.

Rupert was now warning me, 'You have to downscale.' It was a stark reminder of just how much trouble I was in. I got down to work. My determination to build my empire again payed off. I dusted myself down and climbed back into the place of guidance and providence. The seat that had been empty for too long.

While we were still on tour, in spring 2003, Toronto was hit with an outbreak of a disease called Severe Acute Respiratory Syndrome (SARS). Hundreds of people got sick and forty-three people died. The World Health Organization slapped a travel warning on Toronto, and the city took an economic nosedive. Tourism ground to a halt.

In July, they lifted the travel warning but the tourists weren't hurrying back, so the city decided to stage a huge concert to announce to the world that Toronto was SARS free. We've spent so much time there that when they called us and asked us to play, we said yes right away. We were very anxious to give something back.

The Molson Canadian Rocks for Toronto concert was held in Downsview Park, about halfway between downtown Toronto and the airport, on Wednesday, 30 July 2003. The park was absolutely teeming with people. A lot of them were wearing T-shirts that read 'I came. I SARS. I conquered.'

No one is sure how many people were crammed into the park that day, but Mick said he thought it was the biggest crowd we'd ever seen up to that time. Some newspapers estimated the crowd at between 450,000 and 500,000. Pope John Paul II did an open Mass in the park and got 800,000. So he probably holds the record. But we've sold more albums than him.

It was a struggle for me round this time. I was battling booze and cash. My playing was the best it had ever been but people were concerned for me. I was concerned for me. But I lifted my confidence, with honesty, gratitude and humility, and made sure that I'd get through it.

32

Drury Lane

*Painting is stronger than me,
it makes me do its bidding.*

Pablo Picasso.

My painting was improving all the time and sales during the Forty Licks tour were in robust health. I had gallery shows in Los Angeles and San Francisco, and in Cleveland I put on a museum show at the Rock and Roll Hall of Fame. Included there, for the first time, were set lists that I'd drawn during rehearsals in Toronto.

During rehearsals, I draw up the set lists on big canvases, putting down the songs and the keys they're in. We hang these set lists on the rehearsal room walls so we know where we'd been and where we're going. I illustrate them, sometimes Keith and Mick add little doodles and they become works of art in their own right.

People were really beginning to notice me as an artist. Early January 2003 I had a gallery show of my paintings in New York to coincide with our concerts at Madison Square Garden. The Americans were so welcoming and appreciative of my work. And although I have no idea where they all came from, 5,000 people showed up at an exhibition of my paintings at a gallery in Osaka, Japan, when we played there.

At that show, a young girl came up to me and started crying. She was so hysterical that Jo thought, 'Oh no, Ronnie must have a kid with her.' She was crying her eyes out, telling me in broken English, 'I've been writing to you every day for ten years and you've never replied.' She said she'd written me hundreds of letters and never got a single answer back. She kept asking why I didn't answer her. She told me that I must hate her. All I could think of doing was giving her a hug, and reassuring her that I never got her letters.

The mystery was solved when she asked, 'You do live at Atlantic Records, don't you?'

I made it through Forty Licks and came out the other end only a million quid in debt, and still sober. And I stayed that way for a few years. Then I had to face tragedy again – I lost my brother Ted. Ted was pivotal in my musical upbringing, a gentleman and a wonderful companion. He was so good to me, inspirational – a kind sweet soul. I think about Ted all the time and have some brilliant photos of us together. He was the one who introduced me to jazz, to Bing Crosby, Paul Whiteman, Leon Bismark Bix Beiderbecke and Louis Armstrong among others. He was the one I followed into art school. When you phone his wife now, she's still got his voice on the answering machine.

'Dont clap too hard, its a very old building'

John Osborne

Going back to the end of Nick Cowan's reign over my career, he had a little gallery under his offices to show my paintings. In 1999 we had an exhibition running and a friend brought the theatre impresario and composer Sir Andrew Lloyd Webber to view it. He was particularly taken with the Jagger painting *Red Mick*.

Andrew and his wife, Madeleine, foremost collectors of Pre-Raphaelite art, were keen to reinvent the established act of capturing social scenes of London, so a few years later he commissioned me to do a group portrait. Andrew's idea was for me to paint people from contemporary British society, and set it in the Ivy, a London restaurant where you often bump into politicians and show-business personalities. He arranged for thirty of the Ivy's regulars to tell him who they'd like to sit next to for lunch, and that formed the basis of the painting.

It stands six foot by eighteen foot, and contains sixty faces in the surroundings of the Ivy. The triptych is composed to show a day at the restaurant. It reads from left to right, from morning to afternoon to evening. The light in the colour of the paint follows this evolution from morning to night. The painting includes everyone from Jo to Elton John, Kate Moss, Naomi Campbell, Stephen Fry, Mick and Jerry, plus notable journalists, television personalities and politicians. I decided to add Jennifer Lopez to the painting because she's got a nice bum. Call it artistic licence.

Jamie had rescued me from Nick Cowan's faltering grasp, and therefore inherited this deal. It ensured a healthy future with the Lloyd Webbers as my new patrons. Contractually Andrew gave me a year to finish *The Ivy*, but the more I got into it, the longer it took. We needed to organize sittings for everyone appearing in the painting, which was a difficult task. Making it even tougher, my work was disrupted by the small matter of a world tour.

With the exception of Elton John, everyone else came to my house in London. Salman Rushdie, still under the death threat

of his fatwa, turned up in a bulletproof car accompanied by Scotland Yard's best. Joan Collins sat for me, thought Jo was a maid and asked her to make some tea. I discovered after Simon Callow's sitting that he was able to tell me the history behind several paintings in my personal collection.

While I was still working on *The Ivy*, Melvyn Bragg brought his camera crew from *The South Bank Show* and did an entire programme on me as a painter. The *Independent* later ran a picture of *The Ivy* on the front page.

The bones of the picture were done before Forty Licks, but it took five months during the tour to complete it. This meant shipping it all over Europe so I could continue painting between shows.

It was finally unveiled at the Royal Academy in September 2003. Unfortunately, the only place that could accommodate it was the café. Still, the buzz was there, and I was back after my previous appearance a few years earlier, when they accepted an oil of a buffalo I did for their Summer Show.

Once the Academy exhibition was over, we needed to decide where the painting should hang. Andrew owns several of the most famous West End theatres and decided to hang it in the Theatre Royal Drury Lane, the oldest working theatre in London. The preliminary sketches I did would also hang there. I didn't know it at this stage, but this historical building would become a significant presence in my life.

Rather appropriately for me, *The Ivy* was hung in the Grand Saloon Bar. Somehow it found itself in a place that encapsulated my interests – wine, women, song and art (not necessarily in that order, of course).

Before I knew it, more and more of my paintings were being shipped to Drury Lane. Apparently the theatre manager, Rupert Bielby, watched in horror as countless paintings, sketches and sculptures moved in – not to mention the art dealers and tourists who followed in their wake. I probably should have wondered what impact this impromptu retrospective would have – instead I was sunning myself with the family in Africa.

The Licks tour was completed and the band had scattered, each doing their own thing for the first time in months. Unfortunately, our break in Africa was not the relaxing time I'd intended – old habits resurfaced and my drinking caused tension. But it did prove to be an inspirational turning point. Jamie was trying his hardest to establish himself as my new manager, a tough job when his only client was pissed. Understandably, he became angry and threatened to quit if I didn't get a grip. But he persevered, working his way through figures, budgets and contracts – it's a good job someone was. He really took the reins of my solo image, which brings me back to Drury Lane.

This place was perfect for my paintings. It dates back to 1662 and King Charles II. Over the years it has burnt down twice, been pulled down and the current building has been standing since 1812; pretty much like me. When I returned to London I was amazed to find the whole bloody building had become a gallery. Everywhere you turned there was a piece of my life – from people to places, my work was everywhere. It was fantastic. I felt fantastic. Time for a party.

I decided to have a private viewing for close friends and family. It was meant to be a small gathering for afternoon tea in the bar, but it quickly ballooned. The Wood family (including my brother Art), Jeff Beck, Mick Jagger, Tracey Emin, Jamie and Jools Oliver, Jerry Hall, Auntie Mary and countless others turned out to see the work. Articles followed in the press and demand grew for a public exhibition.

In between solo gigs at Vicars Street in Dublin and Shepherd's Bush Empire in London, I began to plot a Drury Lane show. With its myriad tiny rooms and secret passages, the Lane reminded me of being backstage at arenas, and was quickly becoming my favourite new hideaway.

One night I turned up, unannounced, in the middle of *My Fair Lady* with the Charlatans. We caused chaos as my guests wanted to see the pictures and also the hidden parts of the building – a bit difficult when a full-scale musical is taking place. We had a go though.

On another occasion I stubbed my fag out on the floor and nearly burnt the place down for the third time. Turns out the floor was the stage.

My love for the theatre grew and I began to see its potential for combining music and art. I hired the theatre for a night and started working on the Ronnie Wood & Fiends Gig and Exhibition, soon to be called Ronnie and the Tu-Tu's. Tickets sold out in minutes and on 13 March 2005 over 2,000 people descended on the Lane.

Art was everywhere, the music was awesome, the atmosphere electric; the theatre rocked. It was one of the proudest moments of my life having Leah and Jesse perform with me, while Jamie and Tyrone were organizing art sales. I was joined onstage by Ray Cooper, Andy Newmark, Darryl Jones (who so kindly stepped in when Willie Weeks couldn't make it), Andrea Corr, Leah Wood and Beverley Knight. Mick Jagger stepped in, as did Bernard Fowler, Kenney Jones and Ian McLagan. As I looked out from the stage I could see the royal box shaking as Kate Moss, Tracey Emin, Jimmy White and of course Jo raucously cheered me on. I hadn't felt this inspired for years.

Backstage was as much of a high as onstage. Running around through corridors and tunnels from under the stage to the top of the fly tower, the Drury Lane is a monumental place in theatre history. King Charles II had a tunnel made leading from backstage to Nell Gwynne's brothel on the Strand – a man after my own heart. Another tunnel led all the way down to the Thames and was used for smuggling, and to get the men from the ships into the theatre in the evenings. That's where the term 'backstage crew' comes from – crew off the ships, backstage in the theatre. The dock doors, the pulley system, the rigging, it all comes from the Lane. I felt like I had found my spiritual home. It makes me laugh to think that King Charles II watched *The Beggars Bush* in 1674, where now our current Queen can walk past my *Beggars Banquet* painting on her way to the Ladies'.

As the night rocked on I felt cleaner than I'd felt in a very long time. I could breathe again. What started as a place to hang one painting had evolved and given me a purpose and a reason to keep pushing myself creatively. I knew that when the next tour was finished I would be going back to Drury Lane again and again.

Around the same time my great friend the artist Tracey Emin decided she needed to show me the ways of the new art world. She calls me and Jo her little wood mice, and she played tour guide for us at the Biennale in Venice. We took in all the art and wound up partying on Microsoft founder Paul Allen's huge yacht in the Lagoon – it had enough room for two helicopters, a mini-submarine and a basketball court.

It also turns out that wherever we go on holiday, Tracey isn't far away. On our last trip to Africa we found her in the small Kenyan town of Lamu. I can only explain that by saying great artistic minds think alike. We spent a glorious day floating off the Kenyan shore on a beautiful dhow, munching on fresh fish, sipping drinks and sharing artistic loves and inspiration whilst bathed in magnificent sun.

Tracey has since introduced us to Gilbert and George. I spent a fabulous night with the two of them when they opened their retrospective – an entire floor of their work spanning four decades – at Tate Modern. I brought the whole family along in February 2007.

Whenever we travel, we make an effort to visit the best museums – on Bigger Bang we did the Prado in Madrid, the Frick in New York, the New Contemporary in Paris and of course the Hermitage in St Petersburg. The Hermitage houses the most outrageous and definitely the most prolific collection of masterpieces and objets d'art in the world. Apparently if you were to give thirty seconds to each one of the objects contained therein it would take you ten years to complete your viewing. Leah's gone off to art school and is doing very well. As manager, Jamie also runs my art business while Tyrone oversees my gallery Scream in the West End. They share my love for artists like William Orpen, who painted in Ireland and England during the first part of the twentieth century, and whose work I both admire and collect. Art has evolved throughout my life from a hobby to an income, and is something other than music which unites the family.

I sometimes get carried away with my passion for art. Jo and I received an invitation from Prince Charles to attend a formal dinner at his house. We dressed up and arrived at Clarence House, where we were cheerfully greeted by the Prince. He had some great art in the house and when I had the chance I wandered round the palace, checking it out. I spotted a beautiful catalogue of all his art, leather-bound with gold leaf, and after the meal Jo and I took it with us.

A week later, I received a letter from HRH saying, 'Dear Ron, thank you for attending the function, etc., etc., we would be grateful if you would return the book that you took from the Palace.' Who'd have thought?

33

Bang

In May 2005 the Stones agreed there were places in the world we still needed to see. We announced the Bigger Bang tour in New York, this time at the Juilliard School of Music. We played a couple of songs, including the appropriate 'Oh No Not You Again', and then made our way to Toronto to put the show together. Rehearsals lasted until we had about seventy songs ready. Forty Licks was all about songs everybody knew but Bigger Bang involved a lot of new stuff, so nailing everything and getting it perfect took time. But that's what rehearsals are about – plus I never get bored playing music for music's sake, especially with Keith. I sometimes wound the boys up with the way I would stop to paint the set lists in between songs, but they acted as an essential reference point for everyone.

We did our customary club show, this time at the Phoenix Concert Theatre, Toronto. Mick's always believed a club show is worth a week of rehearsals and he's right – it gets the juices going more than a rehearsal ever could.

Once we were ready, we hit the road.

I have lived most of my life in a golden prison. That's what it's like to be a Rolling Stone on tour. We have the privileges associated with fame, but from the inside it remains a place with high walls to keep certain people out – and me in.

When we're in England we try to lead lives that are as close to normal as possible. Jo and I are grandparents now, and spend quality time being a family. However, something happens when the four of us get together. The Stones on the road is a travelling circus. Mayhem surrounds us. And that's when we feel like prisoners in a golden jail.

There is tight security all the time. We're forever ducking and diving through kitchen entrances, for example, because people try to follow us everywhere. Thanks to my ever-reliable pal and bodyguard Gardie, I know I'm always protected by the best. There have been times when Mick has gone out of hotels with a sack over his head, lying down in the back of a bread van or an ice-cream van. We go to work with a police escort, complete with sirens – a fabulous way to go to the office.

The demands of touring are incredible and Bigger Bang was the most demanding ever. We have to programme our minds to hotels and the nomadic way of life, leaving our normal selves behind.

We follow an intense schedule, and even when there's a day off there are Stones matters to attend to. A video, a local television interview, whatever. It means getting up much earlier than I would like and going to make-up and wardrobe, but it's gotta be done. We all feel the pressure. If it isn't a meet-and-greet with a label or radio station, it's the mayor or local football team. And it's always someone's birthday. The Stones never miss a birthday on tour – we're always there to sing and help blow out the candles. We never stay anywhere more than two or three days, meaning we're constantly on our way to airports, new hotel rooms, packing and unpacking. There's never a day off, really.

Jo is the only wife on the Stones payroll. Thank God she's with me on tour – and the kids, when they can make it. They just add to the fun. Onstage one night I got a pair of white knickers landing at my feet and I picked them up before Keith could get to them, and after the song I saw there was something written in them. It said 'Dad I love you. Your daughter Leah x.'

Without family I'd go quite mad. Jo adapts to the constant change and makes sure I do too. Her motto is, 'Never show jealousy, don't nag about alcohol and always have sex.'

Believe me, I know how lucky I am.

She and I travel the world together, with anything up to eighteen suitcases and bags. She has a portable cooker so she can whip up the magic; a bathroom flight case – the contents of which could rival a flagship Boots store; plus at least two guitars that we keep for the hotel rooms.

If you think my room sounds organized, Charlie's takes the biscuit. His room is beyond neat. I'm talking immaculate, with everything in its proper place. His packing is the stuff of legend. Savile Row is his haunt. A journalist wrote once that while he was trying to interview him in his room, Charlie was more interested in folding his silk socks and lining them up carefully, one by one, in his dresser drawer. I've seen those drawers and they are a thing of beauty. Charlie is the most organized man you could ever meet. At the end of a show, when we make a mad dash offstage to dive into our limousines with police cars waiting to speed us away from there as fast as possible, there's Charlie looking back at his drum kit, not happy with the way his drumsticks are pointing a few inches to the left.

Having gone to art school, it's not surprising that Charlie sketches brilliantly. When we're on the road he sketches his bedroom, and claims to have drawn every bed he's ever slept in. I think he's also sketched every room-service meal he's ever had. He's very minimalist and his lines are simplistic. He'll look at my drawings and say, 'You've overworked that one,' and I'll look at it again and see that he's right, that I should have kept a drawing the way I did it originally. His advice is always good and I follow it.

He sketches on tour because that's what he does when he gets bored, and he gets bored on tour because he hates touring. He likes keeping his suitcase neat but he hates being away from home. In his mind, every tour is going to be the last one for him, and probably would be, except that he loves to play the drums and you can't be a drummer in a band if you're at home. I'm glad he's there – a constant dinner companion for me and my family and the best face I can imagine to pop into my dressing room pre-gig.

You see Charlie at his best during press conferences. He'll stand there, arms folded, and say nothing. If someone asks him a question his typical answer is, 'I don't know.' Why? Because he doesn't feel like saying anything, and he's happy to let the rest of us do the talking. He's a wonderful man and in many ways a real English eccentric.

Charlie and Bill were always very tight when Bill was in the band. Charlie says he misses hearing Bill saying, 'Cor, I fancy a cuppa tea,' between takes or 'Nice pair of tits over there,' on stage. They're probably closer now than they were then.

A few years ago, right after Forty Licks, Charlie went into hospital. He beat cancer. No fussing, he just beat it.

We have stylists on tour with us but most of the time Jo dresses me. L'Wren dresses Mick and Charlie is easy to style – his only concern is that his T-shirt and socks match the local football strip. Keith only ever wears Keith-clothes. He also cuts his own hair – he'll stand in front of the mirror, take out the scissors and chop away.

We've been through the same borders so many times we've got to know the customs guys and their dogs. I make friends with the sniffer dogs and whenever they came up to me I'll say, 'Sit down,' but when the dog sits down it means he's found something, so then I'll say, 'No, no, don't sit down,' and the customs guys look at me in a strange way.

The four of us have dressing rooms that have to be set up the same way every time, which makes arriving at all those different venues much easier. Mine is called Recovery; next door is Keith (Camp X-Ray); Charlie calls his Cotton Club; Mick's is Work Out. Recovery is all about comfort – made warm and welcoming with candles, stereo and a ready-to-go espresso machine. That's where I generally prefer to be. I'll tune guitars with my roadies Dave Rouze and Pierre de Beauporte, do a sketch or two and have a fag.

Keith decorates Camp X-Ray with a life-size cardboard cut-out of Elvis in the gold suit. He drills through Elvis' teeth and sticks a joint in there. In Memphis, when Scotty Moore (Elvis' guitar player) showed up and saw the cardboard cut-out, I asked him, 'What do you think, seeing Elvis like that?'

He answered, 'I should have strangled him when I had the chance.'

Another room where we spend time backstage is the Rattlesnake lounge, a hang-out for all. A den of debauchery, conversation, song and fine food, where everyone gets a chance to rev up before the gig.

The organizer is also obliged to set up a snooker table for Keith and me. It is a non-negotiable requirement and the contract rider even says 'Snooker table, not pool table'. So with time to kill, Keith and I have a game before a show, a very necessary requirement. But our games never last very long because we're forever getting dragged away for obligations. Lovely to see you. No, I'm Ron, he's Keith. The four of us file past limitless people, smiling and shaking hands, waiting while sponsors and their clients snap photos. We understand why it has to be done, and now we've got to the point where we do it efficiently, taking no prisoners, before rushing back to the safety of our dressing rooms. We ask each other if that was the fastest ever greet. No sooner are we done with that, it's into make-up and wardrobe.

There's always loads of family around. Wherever we are, no matter what. Mick has 119 relatives. And we have girls claiming to be Keith's ex-girlfriend in every city too.

I try to have a lie down before every concert but I never get very far because people are always coming out of the woodwork. Ronnie, come meet the mayor, come meet Sam's nephew. Who?

When times get heavy Keith and I say, 'I can't wait to go onstage so I can get some peace and quiet.'

Eventually the four of us agreed that we were making life too difficult for ourselves. It's difficult being held prisoner backstage for so long before every gig, so Keith came up with the idea that we'd cut out the soundchecks onstage. It meant that when we brought Bigger Bang to Europe, instead of getting to the venue at three for a nine o'clock show, we didn't have to turn up until six. Then we'd meet in the snooker room where the crew had arranged our gear in a tiny set-up so that we could routine a few songs. That would be me, Keith, Charlie, our keyboard man, Chuck Leavell, bass player Darryl Jones and singers Bernard Fowler, Lisa Fisher and Blondie Chaplin, with Mick saving his voice for the show.

The roadies take care of our guitars, and I always travel with around forty or more. I have to because I change guitars for just about every song – and I always want to have a spare for a spare.

I use a Fender Telecaster B bender, a strap-worn guitar which gives the effect of a pedal steel on numbers like 'Honky Tonk Women' and 'Dead Flowers'; a black Zemaitis on 'Let It Bleed',

'You Got Me Rockin'' and 'Rough Justice'; a Duesenberg or my Slash Les Paul on 'Midnight Rambler'. I also have a sitar for 'Paint It Black'; a pedal steel for 'Far Away Eyes' and 'Bob Wills Is Still the King'; a lap steel for 'Happy' and a Weisenborn for songs like 'No Expectations'. I'll put on a Fender Stratocaster for 'Brown Sugar' and most of the rest, unless it's acoustic, in which case Keith and I use Gibsons.

I keep a full set of guitars in the States for touring there, and another full set in Europe. And people are always giving us guitars on tour. Some of them are really fantastic, like the one that Billy Gibbons from ZZ Top gave me, a beautiful silver guitar that I use on 'Satisfaction'.

Whenever someone gives me a guitar, I take it to my room and check it out and then put it with the others. After all these years, for instance, I've got a family of Taylor guitars, baby, medium and pops.

For some reason, when people ask me about guitars they always want to know about the 'bog seat' guitar that someone made for me in 1970. They remember it because it looked like a toilet seat and turns up in photos from the Faces days. There's also a clip of me playing it on *Top of the Pops*. But to set the record straight, it didn't work then and I've never played it since.

After the show, we'll be rushed straight offstage and taken home with our police escort. Then, back at the hotel, there'll be more trouble because it takes a couple of hours to come down. My room is no longer 'Party Central'. I'll turn on the telly and watch *CSI* or *Law and Order SVU*, do a painting and relax with Jo and the kids. Bernard Fowler will come and check on me. Mick will sometimes stop by. And Keith will say, 'Come on down to my room.'

One of the few good things about living in hotels while touring is that I can catch up on *CSI*. I'm a massive fan, and there was a time during Bigger Bang when there was nothing else on my DVD player. So you can imagine how I loved it when, after one of our gigs in L.A., I got to meet the cast of *CSI Miami*, *Vegas* and *New York*. They rented a bus and thirty-one of them showed up for the gig. I kept telling them how much I love the show and they invited Jo and me to visit the set of *CSI Miami*. After a day hanging out with them in the lab, morgue and armoury, they introduced me to the writers. I told them the kinds of plots I loved and suggested some storylines. That's when one of the producers came over and invited me to guest-star in one of the episodes. The writers decided I could play 'Uncle Ron', a safe-cracker, and right there and then we started brainstorming a story.

A month or so later, I was watching a brand-new episode and worked out the crime before the characters had. It was a story that hung on a guy who has too much THC in his blood-stream. I realized the solution to the crime was down to these traces of marijuana, so I rang up one of the actors – who shall remain nameless – to brag about my detective skills. 'Hi, it's Ronnie. I've figured it out. It's the THC in the system.'

He didn't understand what I was talking about.

I repeated, 'The THC, man. The marijuana.'

Now he panicked. 'Where are you? How do you know?'

He was freaking out. I explained I was talking about the pro-gramme and the 'copper' on the other end of the line admitted he thought I knew he was at a party where some people were smoking joints.

Ha! I busted a *CSI* cop.

Our first stop on Bigger Bang was Boston, where we played on the hallowed baseball field of the Red Sox, Fenway Park. It turned out to be an odd place and I can understand why it doesn't often get used for concerts. They put our huge stage in the outfield, several hundred feet from the stands, and allowed some fans to be directly in front of the stage, on the field, but wouldn't allow any fans to stand in the infield. There were fans in front of us and a gap behind them leading to the stands, which made it feel like we were playing a half-empty stadium. We didn't know at the time, but once we left Fenway the Red Sox complained that the weight of our stage had depressed the entire outfield. Forty thousand square feet of outfield had to be replaced.

During rehearsals they had to keep our new stage in an aircraft hangar because it was too big to be assembled anywhere else – Boston was the first time we had a chance to work on it. There was plenty of room for all of us to move around but for the first time, actually on the stage with us, were boxes for 250 fans. They needed to have a head for heights because the stage went exceptionally high, and it gave them a chance to share the experience of being onstage, letting them see what it looks like for us, with the masses out front. Bigger Bang was off and running.

Now on the road, we changed set lists for every show. A lot of people think we've always done that, but the first time was Forty Licks. Before then, it was a cut-and-dried set every night with the occasional small change. For Bigger Bang, we were moving four, five and six new songs a night.

Chuck Leavell had the records of what we'd sung in what city, so he knew the exact date of every concert and every song we played there. He conferred with Mick before every show and would remind him, we can't do this song because we did it in this very city twice before. Once they'd made up their minds, they'd come to us with a set list to throw around. Mick would use a teleprompter to keep on top of things. In the Faces, when Rod Stewart and I had the words written down we'd put them

THE ROLLING STONES
A BIGGER BANG WORLD TOUR EURO7

SAT, 18, AUG, 2007		SHOW # 144	DUBLIN SLANE CASTLE SHOW	

#	Song		Notes		KEY	TEMPO
1	START ME UP	*Blond*	BV+BC GTR	Off stage	F	120
2	YOU GOT ME ROCKING	*Z*	BV		D	125
3	ROUGH JUSTICE	*Z*	BF	On stage	D	138
4	ALL DOWN THE LINE	R *N.O.*	BRASS+BV		G	147
5	DEAD FLOWERS	R *Red B Bender*	BV		D	130
6	CAN'T ALWAYS GET	*Custom Z*	MD+BV+TR B3		C	85
7	MIDNIGHT RAMBLER	*Slash*			B	77
8	I'LL GO CRAZY	*Blue lite*	BRASS + BV		E	???
9	TUMBLIN' DICE *BBB*	Band intros after song	BRASS+BV		B	107
10	YOU GOT THE SILVER (KR)	*12-string slide aceoustic.*			E	KR
11	I WANNA HOLD YOU (KR)	*Jesse Ed*	BRASS+BV		G	140
12	MISS YOU	*JJ strat* B-STAGE	BV	Off Stage	Am	108
13	IT'S ONLY ROCK AND ROLL	B-STAGE *D'ARM*	BV		B	125
14	SATISFACTION	B-STAGE *D'ARM*	BV+BC GTR		E	134
15	HONKY TONK WOMAN	B-STAGE *BBB*	BRASS+BV	On at end	G	107
16	SYMPATHY	*ARThuR .*	BF		E	109
17	PAINT IT BLACK	*SITAR*	TR Keys+ BF		Em	132
18	J J FLASH	*SIMPLADIOUS* All off stage	BV		B	135
19	BROWN SUGAR	*Custom Z*	BRASS+BV		C	126

on music stands and never tape them down, so as soon as there was a little breeze, the words would go flying off the stage and we'd wind up inventing very interesting lyrics.

Right from Fenway Park I could tell that I was playing better – we all were. It worked well, and this was evident to anyone who saw us. A top band on the top of their game.

I wasn't with the band forty years ago when the Americans had their first Superbowl, but that night the Stones had been booked for the *Ed Sullivan Show*. The audience of millions were so delighted about this that the timing of the Superbowl was moved, allowing everyone to see both. Nowadays, the Super-bowl pulls in a billion viewers, so for Superbowl XLT we decided to share the limelight in Detroit.

Our tongue-shaped stage that was due to lick the pitch at half-time had to be specially designed. It weighed eighteen tons and had to be moved on to the pitch in pieces. The 350 volunteers (who'd been rehearsing for weeks) only had five minutes and thirty seconds to do it. Our dressing room was actually inside the stage, and we were hidden in this black box which they rolled on to the field as part of the stage. We were trapped in there, the four of us plus guitars, looking at each other and hoping that everything was going to happen on time. And it worked. We were shitting ourselves, but in a memorable way.

Two years before we played the Superbowl, Janet Jackson did the show – her costume slipped and a billion people got a view of one of her tits. The following year they brought in Paul McCartney because nobody cared about his tits. The National Football League and the US network didn't care about any of our body parts, just about our language.

We said we would do our thing and they were welcome to do theirs, so they worked out a way to mute certain words. The sponsors held their breath, praying none of us would slip an extra 'fuck' into a song to outwit the bloke with the mute button.

The stage got hooked together, we popped out, the place went wild, and twelve minutes later we left.

Then there was Rio. A free concert on the beach at Copaca-bana, which meant 50,000 to 100,000 people could actually see us onstage. The beach was long and the rest of the people – somewhere between 1 and 2 million – were either stretched down the beach for a mile and a half or hanging off balconies to our left along the street. Or they were in boats to our right. Or they were simply in the water.

The stage also had to be redesigned for this show, because it was too heavy for the beach, and we had to set up massive screens the whole length of the beach so that everybody could see something. We also had to set up a mile and a half's worth of speakers, down the beach, which created real problems for the soundmen because of the delay at that distance.

This show was historic. No one had ever done anything this big. Rod Stewart holds the all-time record for a concert crowd on Copacabana Beach, but he played there on a New Year's Eve and it's tradition that everybody in Rio celebrates New Year's Eve on the beach, so – no disrespect to Rod – people would have been there anyway. We claim the record for the most people ever on the beach who came to see a concert.

From the minute we arrived in Rio there was pandemonium. We sat locked down inside the hotel for three days before the show. Our chief security guards, Eric and Guardi, have never worked so hard. Documentary and press helicopters relentlessly hovered above. From our balconies at the Copacabana Palace we saw thousands of fans watch the soundcheck, the stage being built, and numerous transvestites strutting up and down the parade. Fans would spot us when we came out on that high balcony and a roar would engulf us. The true frenzy is indescribable.

No one had a clue about exactly how many people would show up, and the beach in front of the stage stayed pretty empty until a few hours before the concert – but the beach behind was heaving. The hotel was just across the street from the beach and they had to build a walkway over the road to get us there. Trying to cross the street that night, we wouldn't have got there till the following Wednesday.

By eight o'clock it was really filling up and when we crossed the walkway there were a million or more people screaming, shouting and singing at the four of us. Flashbulbs were going off everywhere. By the time we'd walked across, it felt like everybody in South America had turned up to watch.

It was only when we got on to the B-stage that we realized the full extent of the crowd. In Rio, when the B-stage moved us into the audience the noise was deafening, nothing like we'd ever heard before, and that's when the four of us suddenly under-stood that we were completely surrounded by almost two million people. When you think about the sheer volume of people, and that no one tried to spoil the party – it can only be described as mass happiness.

My family and I watched the beach get cleaned the next day – it must have been hard to find a lime in Rio for days after the millions of Caipirinhas that were drunk that night.

Buenos Aires was another kind of joyous mayhem. During the trip from hotel to stadium we were surrounded again, this time by hundreds of people on motorcycles – not holding on, but sitting sidesaddle so they could take pictures. We were watching them from the bus, shouting, 'Be careful, get away from the bus!' It's a wonder no one was killed.

The fans were everywhere in Argentina, as they always are, even chanting under our balconies. They stand there all day, singing out our names until three in the afternoon, before breaking for lunch and coming back at five to chant the whole night long. This is a new type of mania.

During our second show in Buenos Aires, at the massive River Plate soccer stadium, it poured with rain, bucketing down for the entire set. In the old days, playing in the rain was a problem. Nowadays everything is waterproofed so we don't get electrocuted, but we still get soaked.

All we could see from the main stage was steam clouds rising from the waves of throbbing wet people. And on the B-stage, wet T-shirts flew at us. We had hats on to try and keep dry, but they didn't work – and anyway, the wet T-shirts came at us so fast and furious that we ended up splattered by them and as soaked as everybody else. Mick started the whole thing by waving a T-shirt above his head, and then everybody in the audience started waving theirs until all you could see was this field of spinning shirts. But then they were coming at us from every direction, non-stop, while we played – which meant a lot of girls flashing their tits in the rain.

That was fine – until some of the T-shirts landed under the B-stage and jammed the gears. We couldn't get off. There we were in the middle of the audience, with no way to escape. In the middle of a sweaty, topless Argentinian crowd, until the crew eventually freed us and we were on our way back to the lesser danger of the A-stage.

I had invited Maradona to come back and see me after the show. I kept calling him Ronnie and he called me Diego as we joked around for a few hours swapping tales. With all the football fans back home in England I persuaded Leah to call and let everyone know who we were with. Not being the biggest football fan herself, she rang home and relayed the news, 'I'm with Madonna, apparently he's quite good at football.'

And let's not forget China, which was both an historic and bizarre experience. We'd been scheduled to perform there in 2003 and had planned concerts in both Beijing and Shanghai, but were forced to cancel due to the SARS crisis. So we were determined to make it this time. Keith even decided that it made him feel like Marco Polo.

We were criticized for performing in an 8,000-seat theatre instead of a stadium. The reason we played the smaller venue was because we were breaking new ground and didn't know what to expect. Anyway, we televized it so the whole country could make up their minds about this rock and roll.

Mick decided we should have a special guest to duet on 'Wild Horses' with him, so he invited Cui Jian – the godfather of Chinese rock – to join us. This is a guy who's had his songs censored by the government all his life. We felt for him and he felt for us.

The Chinese censors originally decided that four songs would be banned: 'Honky Tonk Women', 'Let's Spend the Night Together', 'Brown Sugar' and 'Beast of Burden'. And when we arrived they came to us and said that we couldn't sing 'Rough Justice' either.

The gig was historically important and groundbreaking on a personal level. Putting my feet on Chinese soil was a previously uncharted buzz. I'm pretty sure everyone got into this strange foreign foursome as even the armed soldiers were tapping their feet.

We had played China, finally. Now it was time to put my art to the test. I had an exhibition organized in a beautiful house in Shanghai. The paintings were hung outdoors and the whole evening had an amazing oriental charm to it. Outside, the rushing claustrophobia of the city sped by. Shanghai is *Blade Runner* meets a 1960s Kung Fu movie. Though the city is crowded and lacks decent air, inside was calm. Vasco Vasilev played gypsy violin, and China seemed to like my art. It was fantastic. I was having a party. Again.

From China we went to Australia, and from Australia to New Zealand. By then we'd been on the road for eight months and were exhausted. We all needed a break so Jo, me, Patti and Keith headed off to Fiji.

It's a serene and lush place, with the mellowest of locals. Deer and wild horses wander about and beautiful rare birds (including Jo and Patti) colour the island. We all settled in and

Keith and I kayaked over endless coral that stretched out in front of us like an artist's palette. The four of us were loving the little break – until Keith hurt his head. For a couple of days after falling he just had a nagging headache but then things got real ugly and we all knew it was far more serious.

He was taken from the island, embroiled in a media circus and fixed up. I was worried and scared for my mate and his family. Jo and I missed the frenzy as we stayed in Fiji to pack up Keith's and Patti's stuff. When we got the all-clear there was a true sense of relief for me and all my family. It took something like this to help illuminate how close the Richards and the Woods are. Mick, Charlie and I needed our band back, I needed my friend back and the world needed Keef. It looks like we're stuck with him now.

Mick announced that we would cancel some shows to give Keith time to recover. We'd cancelled a few shows in the past for Keith, like when he fell off a ladder at home in 1998, and when one of his fingers got infected after he punctured it on a blade just before Knebworth, but this was six weeks in the middle of a world tour. There was even some speculation in the press that Keith would not be back at all and we'd have to ditch the rest of Bigger Bang. But anyone suggesting it was over didn't know the skull on this man. Ahar, Jim lad.

It was July before we hit the road again and this time we headed for Europe. Mick had to postpone Porto and the Spanish shows. He's got a tough throat, but there were forest fires in Portugal; when we got to Porto there was so much smoke in the air even breathing was difficult. Because of this unexpected break, I got to rediscover the Prado museum and introduce my family to Picasso's *Guernica,* plus the firing squads of Degas and Goya.

In Italy, we played San Siro stadium right after the Italians won the World Cup. Mick sang in Italian, and during the encore we brought the players Alessandro Del Piero and Marco Materazzi on to the stage – the latter had been headbutted by the French player Zidane in his moment of madness. I headbutted him again, much to the delight of the French in the audience.

In England we played the Twickenham rugby stadium, and Jo and I hosted our usual 'Woodfest'. Whenever the Stones play London we throw a party for everybody, as a way of saying thanks. The whole band and crew comes back to celebrate and have a good knees-up. They take about three days to set up and our whole garden is transformed into a themed, tented city. These legendary parties started for my fiftieth birthday which had a Cowboy and Indian theme. Since then we've had Chinese parties, underwater parties . . . you think of it, we've done it.

Jo, Miss Organic that she is, loves to include a healthy element so we have a juice bar. The guest list is our nearest and dearest. All our kids, all the Stones' kids, my best mate Jimmy White, Kelly Jones, Pat Cash, Cilla Black, Tracey Emin, Ronnie O'Sullivan, Tom Stoppard, Owen Wilson, Michael Owen and Kate Moss, to name just a few.

Keith's son Marlon introduced me to Kate at Noel Gallagher's Supernova Heights home, and we've been attached ever since. She and Johnny Depp used to come over. The first time, Johnny brought a beautiful lap steel guitar for me as a gift, and I showed him my collection as we smoked his blend of tobacco in liquorice Rizlas. Those two were a mysterious couple and were impossibly good-looking. Jo still raves about the day Johnny gave her his shirt! My son Jesse had a brief encounter with Kate over a long exciting summer. They came to Ireland, Kate filmed and overdubbed incredible music on her Super 8. We'd sit and have wonderful sunny days on my tennis court at Holmwood. Kate became part of our gang. Then one day, Jesse came to me and said, 'Dad I've got to get off this roller coaster.'

She's still a welcome, friendly face and brings over her daughter Lila to play, while we exchange adventures.

Our Woodfests work because there is such a diverse group of people mixed together. The outcome is always delicious. They get a little noisy but after all these years, our neighbours are getting used to them. And they get a free firework show. The most recent being my gypsy sixtieth-birthday bash – the most outrageous, exotic and enjoyable yet.

From Europe, we went back to the States. On our second swing through New York we were joined by Bill and Hillary Clinton. He was celebrating his sixtieth birthday at the Beacon Theater and scheduled the event to double as a fundraiser for his charitable foundation, and as the central piece in a film Martin Scorsese was making about the Stones. Marty at work is incredible to watch, a man really immersed in his craft. We spent a week filming with him and an amazing host of Hollywood's top cinematographers.

It felt like there were more cameramen than audience and hanging with the Clintons turned into the biggest meet-and-greet of them all. Bill, Hillary and the Stones shook hands with innumerable high-paying guests, some of whom had coughed up $500,000 for the privilege.

I'd met Bill before, but didn't have much of a chance to speak to him that night because there were just so many people. He was his usual charming self, and showed great interest in everyone he met. Jo had recently launched her organic beauty range and gave some products to Hillary. She took especially well to the body oil and asked Jo how to use it. Jo mentioned pouring some into a warm bath, putting some on her skin before bed, or even rubbing it all over Bill, which resulted in a democratic smile.

Coinciding with our NYC shows, I had an exhibition at the Pop Gallery in Greenwich Village. It went well and I was knocked out that the Big Apple loved my art. It wasn't just New York either. After meeting Muhammad Ali's agent, I was introduced to Daniel Crosby who has a serious amount of experience in the art business in the States. This man has represented the work of Warhol and Haring so I'm in good company.

Daniel and I coordinated an art tour through the US with the intention of introducing my work to fine-art collectors. Hosting shows in major cities like NYC, San Francisco, L.A. and Vegas enabled us to reach collectors that had never seen it before.

POP International in NY, San Francisco Art Exchange in San Fran, Gallery 319 in L.A. and Jack Gallery in Las Vegas all hosted successful shows for me. What I didn't know was that Bill and Hillary liked it too. The night after Bill's party the phone rang in my hotel suite and, sure enough, a no-nonsense woman at the other end said, 'Sir, I have the President of the United states on the line.'

Me: 'Oh wow!'

Her: 'You will accept the call.'

Excited by this great beginning to a phone call, I was suddenly confronted by a now familiar Southern drawl. Bill said, 'Your art show that we talked about yesterday, what's the address of the gallery? I'd love to come down and see some of your work while it's in town.'

The show was being packed up to move on to the next stop – but this was Bill, so I grabbed the phone and set the wheels in motion to rehang the exhibition. I went down ahead of Bill. In typical Bill fashion he was a little late as he had been busy soaking up the Village atmosphere, greeting people and making time to have a chat with my driver. He and I wandered round and talked about our favourite artists. When he went home, he had two of my paintings under his arm. One was a portrait of

Billie Holiday and Bessie Smith, which he had fallen in love with. The other was a scene of the Stones on the B-stage. I wrote on that one, 'Happy Birthday to you, Mr President.' And I really meant it. Since then he has rung me up in England and told me that Billie graces a wall in his office while the other overlooks a river near his Little Rock home.

The following morning the phone rang again, and this time it was Hillary. She was phoning on her own – no secretary, no formal introduction, just her familiar voice saying, 'My husband came home last night with two beautiful pictures.' She was totally charming and I thought to myself, maybe they'll hang in the Oval Office one day. We chatted for a few minutes, and then she thanked me in her official capacity as the US Senator for New York for everything the Stones have done for New York City.

Considering that the whole tour environment is soaked in booze, staying sober is a real challenge. My workplace is generally rife with heavy drinkers. I'm doing well and have attained a new form of clarity. One of the benefits of sobriety is how it illuminates the qualities of the incredible people around me. Look at Keith. For the first time in a long time, I really take in what Keith's got to say. Although there are a few pins in his head, there's also a great brain, filled with history and humour. And now I don't forget what he tells me.

In November 2006, in the middle of Bigger Bang, just as we were getting ready to wind down for Christmas, my brother Art died. I'd flown back between shows to be with him and was there when he closed his eyes. A few weeks later, I wrote this to read at his funeral:

We have a special guest with us today: King Arthur.
Now I am head of the family, much sooner than I

expected to be and I would like to thank you all for coming to see my brother Arthur off today. Without him and his teachings I would definitely not be where I am today. Not only as a musician and an artist but as a person who deep inside had the pleasure and satisfaction of knowing him as a friend and an inspiration. He was like a brother to me. In fact, he was.

We all remember Uncle Art with affection. There was nothing that he would not do for you. I am so proud of Angie (his wife) and I am proud of Simon (his son) and his family.

When I was young Mum and Dad helped us three boys by having broad minds and not restricting us in any way. From the back-room rehearsals, the art-school mob, the beatniks and the girls, his early musical pioneering which crossed over from the jazz of Louis Armstrong and Sidney Bechet, Big Bill Broonzy and the Chris Barber Jazz Band through Cyril Davis and Alexis Korner and the first Art Wood Combo which evolved into the Art Woods. We have Jon (Lord), Derek (Griffiths) and Malcolm (Pool) here with us today. They all embarked on cutting new musical ground with people like Charlie (Watts), encouraged by Rod (Stewart) and Long John Baldry. Art welcomed to England such blues greats as Howlin' Wolf and Little Walter at such historic venues as Eel Pie Island, the Marquee, the 100 Club and Ken Colyers.

He taught me my first guitar chords on Daisy's guitar, songs like 'Hard Travelling', 'Midnight Special', 'Froggy Went a Courtin'', 'Smokestack Lightning' and my first Spanish guitar lick, helped by Jim Willis and Lawrence Sheaff.

I wrote him many letters throughout his national service days with the Royal Army Pay Corps and with the help of Mick Barrett, his army sergeant, they are famous for keeping the Japs out of Devizes.

I do not feel like I have lost everyone from my direct family because Jo and I have all of you who loved Art so dearly. My grandson, Little Arthur, in his own words says, 'I'm the only Arthur now.' I'd like to thank all his friends from the Tide End pub who were always a strong support system for him and Angie. And the band, Pete and Mick and all the boys.

He did ask me to tell you this joke. There were two snakes going through the jungle and one snake said to the other, 'Are we venomous or constrictors?' The second snake said, 'That's a strange question between snakes, why are you asking?' And the first one answered, 'Because I've just bit my lip.'

If anybody needs help grieving, I do . . . except that how special it was for me when I got the chance to say goodbye to him personally and I said, 'Your spirit and your love will last forever.'

We are saying farewell to a special man today . . . King Arthur.

Until I read the obituaries that were written about him, I'd forgotten how Art and Ted had both gone down with whooping cough during World War II – this was before I was born – and that my dad brought our Anderson shelter inside from the garden, and bought them crayons and colouring books, so that his boys could draw and not worry about the bombs falling on London. Because they could draw, they both wound up in art school. And because they did, so did I.

Ted played jazz, while Art moved into blues and rock, playing with everybody over the years all over England and France. When he could no longer earn a living with music, he started doing commercial art – designing brochures and leaflets – and continued to play, just for himself. There wasn't a single jealous bone in his body – or Ted's – and Art would always say, 'I'm glad Ronnie made it big enough for all three of us.'

We gave him a proper send-off, and a few months later put together a bunch of his old mates for one last Art Wood All-Stars concert in his honour. It was held on the seventh day of the seventh month in 2007, the day he would have turned seventy. He would have liked that, a lot.

I miss Art and Ted because family is so important to me. Ted's send off was an untouchable collection of British jazz greats called 'Ted Wood: A Celebration of his Life'. Jo and I have always put our family first, the kids and our grandchildren, because family matters. Actually, we're all pretty much that way. Mick's dad Joe died while we were on tour, and after Jo and I made that one-day trip back to England to say goodbye to Art, Mick did the same thing for his dad. If the Rolling Stones are a travelling circus, at least we're a family circus.

Exhausted from Bigger Bang, and before going out again for a mini-tour in spring 2007 (to make good on the dates we had to cancel) we took a family holiday in the Seychelles: me, Jo and Tyrone; Jesse and his wife, Tilly, with their kids, Arthur and Lola; Jamie and his wife, Jodie, plus sons Charlie and Leo; and finally Leah and her fiancé, Jack. But it rained for several days and Jo decided that instead of sitting in the rain (we could have stayed at home and done that) we should find sun. We headed for Kenya.

Every time we visit Africa, what strikes me is how beautiful the planet is and how close we're coming to ruining it. As a carbon offender with the amount of flying I do, I decided I needed to do something about it. I began by doing a number of paintings of endangered species to raise money for various projects. One of those paintings, of an elephant and a rhino, wound up on 40,000 T-shirts that were sold by the charity TUSK to raise money to help protect endangered species.

More recently, I created the Ronnie Wood Wood, a forest in Mozambique. I teamed up with the CarbonNeutral Company to plant trees in the Gorongosa National Park, an area under serious threat. The trees we planted help to soak up carbon dioxide, and in turn protect our climate. Obviously, I can't do it alone, so I started offering fans a chance to help me. Thousands stepped up to the plate, joining the crusade and filling the Ronnie Wood Wood with trees.

At last it was the final leg of Bigger Bang. I had my real sixtieth birthday in Belgium (and a celebration gypsy bash back home a few months later) because the band were rehearsing there.

I had a fabulous eighteen-course meal that took six hours to prepare and six seconds to eat. I feel much younger than a man who is entitled to a free government-issued bus pass. Again I was surrounded by family and friends and showered in gifts. Frankie Dettori (my jockey friend) won the Derby in both England and France. Then on 10 June 2007, we played our first festival in the UK for over thirty years. Closing the Isle of Wight festival took us all back years and I loved being surrounded by the acts of today. On that gorgeous sunny day we rocked the festival into the night and were joined on stage by the likes of Amy Winehouse for 'Ain't Too Proud To Beg'. The four of us treasured being back after our break. The crowd were euphoric, even berserk.

My time off tour had been spent most fruitfully, hard at work with brush and pen. I was working with the Royal Ballet painting their rehearsals and shows, hanging with my family and writing this book. I was in a good space and ready to hit the road again.

The floodgates then opened as we rolled through Europe at a blurring pace. Changing territories every two days, with Jo's packing skills being put to the test, we marched through France, Spain, Portugal and Italy. Rick Barnes was drafted in to support me and keep the monster at bay. We rolled through the B's (Belgrade, Brno, Budvar, Bucharest and Budapest). Fleeting visits to the wonders of these cities were squeezed in, and I've promised myself to get back to a few of these places for a proper look around.

As the tour progressed the architecture got more and more gypsy, which suited me just fine. It only emphasized that I was on the final heave home.

It was on to St Petersburg, where I found myself happily faced with the Hermitage museum and the Winter Palace as we played to thousands on the historic grounds of the October revolution in Palace Square. The following day (as the stage was being dismantled in the square) we walked round the museum to gorge on a visual feast of Rembrandts and El Grecos. Like the rest of the tour, our stroll round Catherine's corridors happened too fast, so trying to grasp it all became a sensory, visual overload.

While in Russia, we celebrated Mick's birthday at the palace where Rasputin was finally assassinated after eight or so attempts. Mick was asked to dance by a gaggle of Russian beauties, who had performed for us all. My hand was grabbed by one of them and I spun around the room in a native dance.

At Keith's youngest daughter Alexandra's birthday the night before, the caviar was overflowing. It was the night before the export laws for Beluga changed due to a global shortage, so we made the most of it. Apologies to all sturgeon farmers.

The pace was slowed as the B's (Bobby Keys, Bernard, Blondie) Jo and I took the train out of Russia and headed to Helsinki. Russia is a tough, harsh place steeped in sombre history and Finland was certainly welcome, as a warmer type of cold, with brighter faces. Then from Finland to Denmark, where Toots and the Maytals were supporting us.

I wanted to find Toots before he went on. In the bowels of the stadium I found a ghostly ice rink, where the ice melted into a marijuana mist. We followed the trail to his welcoming conveyor belt of spliff rolling. Then to Germany, where the crowds outside the hotels got more and more intense as if they, like us, sensed the imminent end of the tour.

The final lap was approaching and the bell sounded as our private plane landed at 2 a.m. in Dublin, at the new terminal, which had been built at huge expense and I reckon in the wrong place. It was great to be among people with a real sense of humour.

I had an art show in Dublin, which was successfully received with open arms, and the warmth of the people was magnified

as we peered down from a helicopter at the throbbing enthusiasm of Slane castle.

It was just right being able to leave for work from my own
front door, rather than a hotel lobby. In retrospect, a resound-
ing realization of a right-regal moment.

Twenty-five years after we first played these historical grounds,
we were back. Most of the faces around were the same, with just
a few more smile lines. This was like a home gig to me due to my
special relationship with the emerald isle. Mick introduced me as
the boy from Naas, which lit up a certain sort of pride in me. I
added it to my collection of introductions – Ronnie Rembrandt,
the Renoir of Rock or the Goya of the Guitar.

And then to London. Home to home. Sandymount to
Holmwood. A Holmwood that had taken on a new intensity as it
had been decorated while we'd been away. Home at last. My gypsy
party was being set up in the garden as we did our final three gigs
at the Millennium Dome. I kept my feet firmly in the water and
soaked up the historic sights of London as we motored to the dome
– the arena with the best sound in Europe and half of America
(according to our sound guy Dave Natale). This extra-terrestrial
monstrosity holding inside acoustically able bowels.

My concentration was kept at full tilt by the support of
Rick, who programmed me to live, act and focus for myself.
Gently coaxing me (in an environment he could connect with)
to enjoy the madness and appreciate the peace of mind I could
find. This peace brought with it a new dexterity and enjoyment
on the guitar and the brush. My two great passions.

The last show ended on a high – I relished playing my
twelve string on 'You Got the Silver' and got off on seeing my
family and friends rocking. Concert number 147 – the highest
and most perfect break in the game – turned out to be the best
show of the lot.

34

Where is this boy now?

It's strange to finally reach a point where I can say, 'And that's the story so far, folks . . .' Months ago I sat down with this new kind of blank canvas and no idea how the picture should look. But here it is. How did that happen?

Trying to remember everything with clarity has not been the easiest process, especially given my drunken behaviour over the years. But – as with many things in my life – I somehow appear to have got through it. In fact, if asked to summarize my life I would happily say, 'I've had to go through it, to get to it.'

Not that it's been a painless ride. Raking over memories and seeing how the sledgehammer blow of Stephanie's car crash affected me from the age of seventeen. How a dramatic feeling of emptiness was soothed by alcohol. How this screwed-up attitude towards a substance is something I never addressed.

I've also seen that I grew up quickly – maybe too quickly. Maybe that's why nowadays I sometimes feel like a big kid.

Having said that, writing this has also given me the kick up the arse I never knew I needed. It's made me realize that I'm solid now, and, more importantly, how much I want to hold on to that. I've messed things up before and landed in hot water, and I hope these mistakes stay firmly in the past. I've faced some demons and experienced that clichéd whirlwind of emotions and memories, thoughts and realizations. Perhaps this is the catharsis I've heard so much about.

Don't get me wrong – I'm aware that my life has been blessed. From an early age I've been a lucky boy. Musically I've found it easy to change styles and adapt to the opportunities coming my way. And that skill has taken me all over the world. I've done the best I could with what I was given, but I also think fate has helped shape my journey. I seem to have a knack of being in the right place at the right time. Some say the angel Gabriel protects me – it certainly feels that way sometimes. I might have misplaced him at times, but generally I'd say angel G's done good.

I'll always battle the demons but right now I seem to be winning. My head is finally in a good place. I don't feel my age – thank God. Instead I feel alive, free, and at times like the naughty boy I was growing up.

I'm proud of my achievements, but I'm not ready to rest on my laurels just yet. I tell myself every day that there's always more to accomplish. More to do, see, feel and experience. Whatever the future holds, I intend to grab it and run with it.

I feel blessed to have the support of my family and friends in everything I do – there have always been people to pick me up, carry me further and help me though. I've driven them crazy, no doubt about it, but for some reason they stand by me. Must be my good looks.

Whilst this chapter is the end of my book, it also signifies the next phase in my life. The band is going back on the road and I'm enjoying the music more than ever. Before, I was always too stoned to realize that what I was playing was any good, but now I understand and have the drive to keep playing and improving. I love being with the band and I feel that we've got even more

Tamara Rojo
Tu-Tu Diaries

to offer (CDs, T-shirts, mugs, key rings . . .) and don't see us throwing in the towel while we're still performing noble, wonderful shows.

Aside from the music I've got my art to keep me busy. If Drury Lane doesn't kick me out, with a bit of luck I can keep the current exhibition running and get a few more gigs done before it disappears again. If Andrew sells it then who knows, maybe I'll find another theatre, or maybe I'll buy it myself and change the name to the Theatre Royal Drury Wood Lane.

It's not just Drury Lane that I'll be re-exploring when I'm back off the road. Definitely more Sunday-night 'Fiends' shows. I've got my wonderful adventures ahead of me at the Royal Opera House – I'm starting a new collection of paintings, some based on sketches taken as the dancers rehearsed, people like my good friends Tamara Rojo, Jonathon Cope, Carlos Acosta and Darcey Bussell, with the help of Janine Limberg and Monica Mason, who I like to call Eminem. A sweet wrapper. I hope the project will be a combination of pastel drawings and full-scale oil paintings, building towards another exhibition. Maybe another book?

I'd like to explore sculpting in different media: driftwood sculptures, more bronzes, alabasters, wood and clay to marble (I can hear the groan from Bernard as I speak). Perhaps I'll consult with Tyrone, whose future looks rosie (*sic*) right now. Or maybe I'll get myself to Italy, where Michelangelo dug his marble.

I'm in the process of compiling short films to accompany my art exhibitions around the world, especially themes on the ballet, landscapes, portraits, horses and abstracts. I'd also like to throw in a tiny ticking time bomb nestling in my head and that is my desire to write a novel, it's all books from here on. Something dark and intricate, with twists aplenty. Who knows, maybe a Faces reunion tour in the new year – all the lads seem to be keen.

In sobriety I've learnt to quash my wayward tendencies with music and art. I've been privileged enough to watch my kids grow and wave them off on their travels, just like their dad once did. I've felt almost euphoric though sobriety and how it's allowed me to truly appreciate life, family, the band, art and all our achievements. Even if 'Yer Father's Yacht' turns out to be a canal barge, you can still really go places in it and have a ball doing it.

Like saying goodbye to a painting when it's sold, this book leaves me with the feeling of waving an old friend off on his travels. I'll see him weathered and improved one day, ready to pick up and work again, refreshed and new.

I can't say what the future holds for me, but I can tell you, I'm not finished yet.

this will suffice for now.

R.W.